Medical & Other Scientific Librarian Use of Google & its Features and Apps

ISBN 978-1-57440-429-6

Table of Contents

THE QUESTIONNAIRE

1. Please provide the following contact information

   A. Name:
   B. Organization:
   C. Email Address:
   D. Work Title:
   E. Country

2. Type of institution

   A. Academic Medical Library
   B. Academic Scientific Library
   C. Government or Non-Profit Scientific or Medical Library (Non- Higher ed)
   D. Private company medical or scientific library
   E. Other (please specify)

3. Age range of the survey participant

   A. Under 30
   B. 30-39
   C. 40-49
   D. 50-59
   E. 60-69
   F. 70 or Over

4. Your library's annual budget for all purposes, including salaries, materials, building maintenance, etc. is approximately:

(Please specify the currency if not in US dollars)

5. Work specialization or title of the survey participant

   A. reference or information literacy
   B. research or subject specialist
   C. administration
   D. technical services or cataloging
   E. special collections
   F. acquisitions or collection development
   G. Other (please specify)

6. Compensation range of the survey participant

   A. Less than $40,000
   B. $40,000 to $55,000
   C. $55,000+ to $70,000
   D. $70,000+ to $90,000
   E. $90,000+ to $110,000
   F. More than $110,000

7. Gender of the survey participant

   A. Male
   B. Female

8. Your main subject focus is:

   A. Medical, Biological or Pharmaceutical
   B. Engineering
   C. Physics or Astronomy
   D. Chemistry or Materials
   E. Other (please specify)

9. What percentage of your total use of search engines would you estimate is accounted for by your use of the Google search engine?

10. How often do you use the following features of Google?

	Never really use it	Seldom use it	Sometimes use it	Often Use it	Very often use it
Google Maps					
Google Advanced Search					
Google Alerts					
Google Notifications					
Google Images					
Google Photos					

Google Calendar					
Chrome					
Google Books					
Google Scholar					
Google Scholar My Citations					
Google Translate					
Google Public Data Explorer					
Google Drive					
Gmail					
Google Earth					
Google Sky					
Google+					
Google Hangouts					
Google Bookmarks					
Google Patent Search					
Google Forms					
Google Slides					
Google Groups					
Google Analytics					
AdWords					
AdSense					
Blogger					
YouTube					

11. When you do use the following features of Google how useful are they to you?

	Don't use this at all	Not very useful	Somewhat useful	Useful	Quite useful	Essential
Google Maps						
Google Advanced Search						
Google Alerts						
Google Notifications						
Google Images						
Google Photos						
Google Calendar						
Chrome						
Google Books						
Google Scholar						
Google Scholar My Citations						
Google Translate						
Google Public Data Explorer						
Google Drive						
Google Earth						
Google Sky						
Google+						
Google Hangouts						
Gmail						

Google Bookmarks						
Google Patent Search						
Google Forms						
Google Slides						
Google Groups						
Google Analytics						
Blogger						
YouTube						

12. For those Google features that you labeled "Quite Useful" or "Essential" what were these features and what do you use them for?

13. Approximately how much time in the past month have you personally spent (in hours or fractions thereof) using the following Google features in connection with your work? If you have not used the feature in the past month put in a zero.

A. Google Maps
B. Google Advanced Search
C. Google Alerts
D. Google Notifications
E. Google Images
F. Google Calendar
G. Chrome
H. Google Books
I. Google Scholar
J. Google Translate
K. Google Public Data Explorer
L. Google Drive
M. Google Earth
N. Google Sky
O. Google+
P. Google Hangouts
Q. Gmail
R. Google Bookmarks
S. Google Patent Search

T. Google Forms
U. Google Slides
V. Google Groups
W. Google Analytics
X. Blogger
Y. YouTube

14. What other apps or features offered by Google but not listed above have you found useful and why?

15. Which single Google app or feature has saved you the most time or made you much more productive?

16. About what percentage of the time that you spend on medical or scientific research is done through Google Scholar or Google Books?

17. If there was one app or feature in Google that you would like to let your peers know about which one would that be.

INSTITUTIONAL AFFILIATIONS OF THE SURVEY PARTICIPANTS

ACS
Ascension Wisconsin
California Health Sciences University
City University of New York
Colorado School of Mines
Coventry University
Drew University
Duquesne University
Ecole Polytechnique Federale de Lausanne
Georgetown University
Gorgas Memorial Library
Harvard Medical School
Hennepin County Medical Center Medical Library
Icahn School of Medicine at Mt Sinai
Johns Hopkins University, William H. Welch Medical Library
Kaiser Permanente
NHS Education for Scotland
Ohio University
Ohio Valley Medical Center
Saint Agnes Medical Center
Santa Clara Valley Medical Center
Southern California University of Health Science
St. Vincent Hospital
Thunder Bay District Health Unit
UNC Health Sciences Library
University of Illinois at Chicago
University of Kentucky
University of Leeds
University of Lethbridge
University of London, St George's
Vanderbilt University

Characteristics of the Sample

Type of institution

	#
Academic Medical Library	12
Academic Scientific Library	10
Non-Educational Medical/Scientific Library	9
Total	31

Age range of the survey participant

	#
Under 40	9
40-59	15
60 or Over	7
Total	31

Work specialization or title of the survey participant

	#
reference or information literacy	10
research or subject specialist	14
other	7
Total	31

Compensation range of the survey participant

	#
Less than $55,000	10
$55,000+ to $70,000	14
More than $70,000	7
Total	31

Gender of the survey participant

	#
Male	7
Female	24
Total	31

Your main subject focus is:

	#
Medical, Biological or Pharmaceutical	22
Other Scientific	9
Total	31

SUMMARY OF MAIN FINDINGS

Characteristics of the Sample

The sample had 31 survey participants including 12 from academic medical libraries, 10 from academic scientific libraries, and 9 from non-educational medical/scientific libraries. 10 survey participants specialized in reference or information literacy, 14 worked in research or a specialized subject, and 7 worked in another area. 22 survey participants focused mainly on medical, biological or pharmaceutical science, while 9 focused on other scientific subject matter. Nearly half of the survey participants were between forty and fifty-nine years old and 24 of the 31 participants were female. 10 survey participants earned less than $55,000 per year, 14 earned $55,000+ to $70,000, and 7 earned more than $70,000 a year.

Annual Budget for the Libraries Sampled

On average, libraries in the sample had an overall annual budget of $3,648,595, including salaries, materials, building maintenance, and all other expenses. Academic medical libraries had a mean budget of $5,321,369, some ranging as high as $15,200,000 and others as low as $267,192. Academic scientific libraries had a mean budget of $3,944,198, while non-educational libraries had a mean budget of $342,000. Survey participants earning more than $70,000 a year tended to work in libraries with a larger annual budget, a mean of $6,261,209, while those earning $55,000+ to $70,000 had a mean annual budget under $1,400,000.

Use of Google Search Engine

Survey participants used the Google search engine for roughly 55% of their online searches, though this percentage is somewhat higher among participants in academic medical libraries and those focused primarily on medicine, biology or pharmacology. Survey participants under sixty used the Google search engine for the majority of their searches, whereas participants that were sixty or older used Google for only 32% of searches. Male participants used Google for 63.8% of searches, whereas female participants used it for only 52.35% of searches.

Use of Google Maps

38.71% of survey participants use Google Maps very often and 29.03% use it often, whereas 16.13% report seldom or no use at all. 12.9% of survey participants sometimes use Google Maps, including 30% of participants in academic scientific libraries and 11.11% of those in non-educational libraries. 50% of participants specializing in reference or information literacy use Google Maps often or very often, compared with 71.42% of participants working in research or a specialized subject, and 85.71% of participants in other fields.

Use of Google Advanced Search

Google Advanced Search is sometimes used by 41.94% of survey participants and used often by 32.26%. It is used least in academic scientific libraries and by survey participants under forty, a third of which report seldom use. 9.68% of survey participants use Google Advanced Search very often, all of these women between the ages of forty and fifty-nine. In general, Google Advanced Search is used more by female survey participants than by male participants, 28.57% of which report seldom use and 57.14% of which use it sometimes.

Use of Google Alerts

61.29% of survey participants don't use Google Alerts, whereas 12.9% report seldom use, 19.35% use it sometimes, and just 3.32% use it often. 57.14% of male survey participants sometimes use Google Alerts, while 70.83% of female participants don't use it at all. 11.11% of survey participants in non-educational libraries use Google Alerts to some extent, compared with 40% of participants in academic scientific libraries and half of those in academic medical libraries.

Use of Google Notifications

77.42% of survey participants do not use Google Notifications at all, while 19.36% report seldom or sometime use. Use is limited to survey participants in academic libraries, most of whom are men aged sixty or older.

Use of Google Images

In contrast, 19.35% of survey participants use Google Images very often, 29.03% use it often, and 35.48% use it sometimes. Just 3.23% of participants never use Google Images, all working in academic scientific libraries in research or a specialized subject. 66.67% of survey participants in academic medical libraries use Google Images often or very often, whereas 30% of those in academic scientific libraries and 44.44% of those in non-educational libraries do so. 54.54% of survey participants focused on medical, biological or pharmaceutical science use Google Images often or very often, while a third of those focused on other areas of study do so.

Use of Google Photos

Less than half of participants in the sample use Google Photos, with 19.35% using it sometimes and 12.91% using it often or very often. 70% of survey participants in academic scientific libraries use Google Photos to some extent, as do 41.67% of participants in academic medical libraries and 22.2% of participants in non-educational libraries.

Use of Google Calendar

Google Calendar is used very often by 19.35% of survey participants and often by another 9.68%, while 22.58% report seldom or sometime use and 48.39% don't use it all. 50% of survey participants in academic scientific libraries use Google Calendar very often, most working in reference or information literacy and focused on subjects other than medicine, biology or pharmaceutical science. Google Calendar is used least by survey participants between forty and fifty-nine years old, 13.33% of which use it sometimes and another 13.33% of which use it very often.

Use of Chrome

Chrome is used by every survey participant and used often or very often by 80.64% of participants, making it one of the most popular Google features. 51.61% of survey participants use Chrome very often, including 88.89% of participants under forty and 70% of those specializing in reference or information literacy. Chrome is used somewhat less by survey participants aged sixty or older, 28.57% of which use it sometimes, and by male participants, 14.29% of which report seldom use.

Use of Google Books

Google Books is used sometimes by 35.48% of participants and often or very often by 19.36%. Survey participants in non-educational libraries tend to use Google Books more than do participants in academic libraries, with 22.22% of this group using it often and 11.11% using it very often. 57.11% of survey participants sixty or older make seldom use of Google Books, compared with 11.11% of participants under forty and 26.67% of those between forty and fifty-nine. 45.45% of participants earning more than $70,000 a year use Google Books sometimes, whereas 30.77% of participants earning between $55,000 and $70,000 and 28.57% of those earning under $55,000 use it sometimes.

Use of Google Scholar

Google Scholar is used very often by 55.84% of survey participants, including 62.5% of female survey participants and 73.33% of participants between the age of forty and fifty-nine. Another 25.81% of survey participants use Google Scholar often and 19.36% report sometime or seldom use. Google Scholar My Citations, on the other hand, is used often or very often by less than a quarter of survey participants and not used at all by 35.48%. 30% of participants in academic scientific libraries use My Citations very often, whereas 0% of those in academic medical libraries or non-educational libraries do so. Nearly 70% of survey participants earning between $55,000 and $70,000 a year don't use My Citations, while 85.72% of those earning less than $55,000 use it to some extent.

Use of Google Translate

Google Translate is used sometimes by 41.94% of the sample and used in seldom instances by 22.58%. 6.45% of survey participants use Google Translate very often, all women under sixty. 40% of participants working in reference or information literacy do not use Google Translate, though another 40% use it sometimes and 10% use it often. Google Translate is used less by survey participants focused on medicine, biology or pharmaceutical science, 31.82% of which report seldom use, than by participants focused on other scientific fields of study, 33.33% of which use it often or very often.

Use of Google Public Data Explorer

12.9% of survey participants use Google Public Data Explorer to some extent, though none use it often. Most participants that use this feature are under forty, specialize in research or a subject speciality, and work in an academic scientific library.

Use of Google Drive

Google Drive is used very often by 29.03% of survey participants, but used not at all by 25.81%. 50% of participants in academic scientific libraries and 66.67% of participants under forty use Google Drive very often, whereas two-thirds of those in non-educational libraries and 42.86% of those aged sixty or over never use it. Google Drive is used most by survey participants with a salary under $55,000 a year, 57.14% of which use it very often and 14.29% of which use it sometimes, and least by participants earning over $70,000, 36.36% of which don't use the feature.

Use of Gmail

Gmail is used sometimes by 16.13% of survey participants, used often by 9.68%, and used very often by 38.71%. 77.78% of participants under forty use Gmail often or very often, whereas just 14.29% of participants sixty or older do so. 45.83% of female survey participants use Gmail very often, more than three times the percentage of male participants that use it very often. 100% of survey participants in academic scientific libraries use Gmail, 30% using it sometimes and 60% using it very often. In contrast, 11.11% of survey participants in non-educational libraries use Gmail sometimes and a third do not use it at all.

Use of Google Earth

41.94% of survey participants make seldom use of Google Earth, 19.35% use it sometimes, and 12.91% use it often or very often. 22.58% of survey participants do not use Google Earth, including 16.67% of participants in academic medical libraries, 10% of those in academic scientific libraries, and 44.44% of those in non-educational libraries. Google Sky is used often or very often by just 6.46% of survey participants and used sometimes by 9.68%. 61.29% of survey participants never really use Google Sky, 77.27% of participants focused on medical, biological or pharmaceutical science, and 22.22% of those focused on other scientific subject matter.

Use of Google+

Google+ is also used by relatively few survey participants, with 6.45% of participants using it very often, 3.23% using it often, and the majority of participants not using it all. Google+ is used exclusively by female survey participants, many of which work in academic medical or academic scientific libraries. Use of Google Hangouts is also limited to female survey participants, with 33.34% having used it to some extent. 67.74% of survey participants never use Google Hangouts, while 6.45% use it sometimes and 9.69% use it often or very often.

Use of Google Bookmarks

25.8% of survey participants use Google Bookmarks to some extent, though just 3.23% use it very often and none use it often. Google Bookmarks is used most by survey participants in non-educational libraries, a third of which use it sometimes or very often, and by participants whose subject focus is medical, biological or pharmaceutical science, 31.83% of which use it to some extent.

Use of Google Patent Search

Google Patent Search is used by 32.26% of the sample, but only used often or very often by 9.68%. 20% of survey participants specializing in reference or information use the Patent Search feature often or very often, compared with 7.14% of participants working in research or a specialized subject, and 0% of those working in other capacities. Patent Search is used more by participants earning less than $55,000 a year, 28.57% of which use it sometimes, than by those earning upwards of $55,000, most of whom do not use it at all.

Use of Google Forms

58.06% of survey participants do not use Google Forms and 12.9% make seldom use of it. 16.13% of participants use Google Forms often or very often, 13.64% of survey participants focused on medical, biological or pharmaceutical science and 22.22% of those focused on other fields of inquiry. No participants aged sixty or over use Google Forms, while 55.55% of participants under forty use it to some extent. Google Slides, meanwhile, is used by 29.03% of survey participants, 16.67% of participants in academic medical libraries, 50% of participants in academic scientific libraries, and 22.22% of participants in non-educational libraries.

Use of Google Groups

Google Groups is used in seldom instances by 19.35% of survey participants, used sometimes by 12.9% of participants, and used often or very often by 6.46% of participants. Among those that use Google Groups most often are survey participants in academic scientific libraries, 20% of which use it often or very often, and participants working in research or a specialized subject.

Use of Google Analytics

More than a quarter of survey participants use Google Analytics sometimes, though only 3.23% use it very often and none use it often. Participants in non-educational libraries are least likely to use Google Analytics, two-thirds saying that they never use it. As with most other Google features, survey participants under forty tend to use Google Analytics more than older participants do, though most report seldom use and none use it often.

Use of Other Google Features

No survey participants have used AdWords or AdSense, and just 6.46% have used Blogger, all participants in academic medical libraries. YouTube, on the other hand, is used by all participants in the survey, including 25.81% that use it often and an additional 19.35% that use it very often. 35.48% of survey participants sometimes use YouTube, including 25% of participants in academic medical libraries and a plurality of those in academic scientific libraries and non-educational libraries. 36.36% of survey participants earning more than $70,000 a year report seldom use of YouTube, compared with 0% of participants earning less than $55,000 and 7.69% of those earning between $55,000 and $70,000.

Utility of Google Features

Utility of Google Maps

48.39% of survey participants consider Google Maps quite useful and 29.03% consider it essential, the latter figure including 41.67% of participants in academic medical libraries and 40% of participants that work in reference or a specialized subject. 81.82% of survey participants earning more than $70,000 a year consider Google Maps quite useful and the remaining 18.18% deem it essential, whereas the feature is somewhat less useful to participant earning less than $55,000, 14.29% of which don't use it all.

Utility of Google Advanced Search

Google Advance Search is considered useful by 29.03% of survey participants, quite useful by 35.48% of participants, and essential by 16.13%. It is especially popular among participants in academic medical libraries, 58.34% of which find it quite useful or essential, and participants working in reference or information literacy, 70% of which feel the same way.

Utility of Google Alerts and Google Notifications

Google Alerts, in contrast, are not used by most survey participants and are considered quite useful by just 3.23%, all working in research or a specialized subject. Male survey participants had a higher opinion of Google Alerts than did female participants, with 42.86% calling them somewhat or quite useful. Even fewer survey participants use Google Notifications or consider them useful; 9.68% of participants describe Google Notifications as somewhat useful, 6.45% say that they are useful, and none call them quite useful or essential.

Utility of Google Images

29.03% of survey participants consider Google Images useful, including 44.44% of participants in non-educational libraries and 42.86% of participants over the age of sixty. 9.68% of participants consider Google Images essential and 35.48% say it is quite useful, many of these participants in academic medical libraries, 50% of which feel this way.

Utility of Google Photos

Google Photos, meanwhile, is considered useful by 12.9% of survey participants and quite useful or essential by 16.13%. Less than a quarter of survey participants earning between $55,000 and $70,000 a year use Google Photos, though most of those that do use it deem it essential.

Utility of Google Calendar

Google Calendar is thought useful or quite useful by 22.58% of survey participants and essential by 12.9% of participants. 6.45% of participants consider Google Calendar not very useful, all men between the ages of forty and fifty-nine and working in an academic library of some kind. Of those that consider the app essential, most work in reference or information literacy and earn less than $55,000 in annual compensation.

Utility of Chrome

Chrome is dubbed essential by 41.94% of survey participants and quite useful by 32.36%. All participants feel that it is at least somewhat useful, with female survey participants and participants in academic medical libraries among its most enthusiastic proponents. Participants earning more than $70,000 a year also consider it highly useful, with 54.55% of this group calling it essential.

Utility of Google Books and Google Scholar

22.58% of survey participants find Google Books useful and the same number find it somewhat useful. 19.35% of participants feel that Google Books is quite useful and 9.68% say that it's essential. Survey participants aged sixty or over find Google Books less useful than do younger participants, 42.86% calling it somewhat useful and 14.29% saying it is not very useful. Google Scholar is also considered less useful by older survey participants, though most think it quite useful or essential. Overall, 29.03% of survey participants find Google Scholar quite useful and 54.84% find essential, with just 3.23% saying that it is not very useful. Google Scholar My Citations is used by considerably fewer participants and is considered quite useful or essential by 22.58%. These include 40% of survey participants in academic scientific libraries and 36.36% of participants earning more than $70,000 a year.

Utility of Google Translate and Google Public Data Explorer

29.04% of survey participants consider Google Translate quite useful, including 41.67% of survey participants in academic medical libraries and 33.33% of those in non-educational libraries. While a third of survey participants under forty consider Google Translate useful and another third say it is quite useful or essential, 11.11% do not use it and the same percentage say it is not very useful. Google Public Data Explorer does not have nearly the same utility; just 12.9% of survey participants find it at all useful, many specializing in reference or information literacy.

Utility of Google Drive

Though 32.36% of survey participants do not use Google Drive, 25.81% deem it useful or useful and 29.03% deem it essential. The latter includes 50% of survey participants in academic scientific libraries, as well as 35% of those in academic medical libraries and 11.11% of those in non-educational libraries. While the majority of survey participants older than sixty do not use Google Drive, most of those that do find it essential. The same is true of 55.56% of participants under forty, but just 13.33% of those between forty and fifty-nine.

Utility of Google Earth and Google Sky

While no survey participants consider Google Earth essential, 22.58% consider it useful and 12.9% say it is quite useful. Google Earth is least useful to survey participants specializing in reference or information literacy, most of which do not use it or say it is not very useful. That opinion is not shared by the majority of participants working in research or a specialized subject, 21.43% of which consider it quite useful. Google Sky is used by less than 30% of survey participants and of those none consider it quite useful or essential. 16.13% of participants consider Google Sky somewhat useful, including 26.67% of participants between forty and fifty-nine years old.

Utility of Google+ and Google Hangouts

Google+ is considered quite useful by 6.45% of survey participants and essential by 3.23%. Just below 10% of participants find Google+ useful or somewhat useful, most working in academic scientific libraries. Survey participants in academic medical libraries find it moderately more useful, 25% calling the app quite useful or essential, while just a few participants in non-educational libraries find it all useful. Google Hangouts is used by more survey participants, but only slightly more. 9.68% of participants consider Google Hangouts useful and 12.91% consider it quite useful or essential, all female participants working in libraries that focus mainly on medical, biological or pharmaceutical science.

Utility of Gmail

Gmail is considered useful by 6.45% of survey participants, quite useful by 16.13% of participants, and essential by 45.16%. Even so, 44.44% of survey participants in non-educational libraries do not use Gmail, nor do 16.67% of participants in academic medical libraries. Survey participants aged sixty or over are the most divided on Gmail, with 57.14% considering it essential, 28.58% considering it somewhat or not very useful, and 14.29% saying they do not use it at all. In contrast, 88.89% of survey participants under forty consider Gmail useful, quite useful, or essential.

Utility of Google Bookmarks

12.9% of survey participants feel that Google Bookmarks is useful, while 6.46% consider it quite useful or essential. Nearly two-thirds of survey participants do not use Google Bookmarks, including 75% of participants in academic medical libraries and 85.71% of participants earning less than $55,000 a year.

Utility of Google Patent Search & Google Slides

Google Patent Search is considered quite useful by 19.35% of survey participants, though most don't use it at all. 42.86% of survey participants working in research or specialized subjects find Google Patent Search useful or quite useful, but only 10% of those in reference or information literacy feel the same way. Similarly, Google Forms is considered useful by 9.68% of survey participants, quite useful by 3.23%, and essential by 12.9%, but the majority of participants in the sample don't use this feature either. Google Slides is useful to 6.45% of survey participants and very useful or essential to 9.68%, whereas Google Groups is considered useful, quite useful, or essential to 22.58% of survey participants. Most of these participants focus on medical, biological or pharmaceutical science, and earn less than $55,000 in annual compensation.

Utility of Google Analytics

Google Analytics is considered quite useful or essential by 12.91% of survey participants and useful or somewhat useful by 19.35% of participants. Among those that consider Google Analytics useful are 28.57% of survey participants focused on research or a specialized subject and 22.22% of participants under the age of forty.

Utility of Blogger and YouTube

Just 6.45% of survey participants find Blogger to be at all useful, all between the ages of forty and fifty-nine, and none earning less than $55,000 a year. YouTube is dramatically more popular, with 22.58% of survey participants calling it quite useful and 29.03% calling it essential. More than 80% of survey participants in academic libraries consider YouTube useful, quite useful or essential, whereas 22.22% of participants in non-educational libraries consider it somewhat useful and 11.11% say that it is not very useful. 20% of survey participants working in reference or information literacy consider YouTube essential, as opposed to 21.43% of participants working in research or a specialized subject area, and 57.14% of those working in another facet of the library.

Time Spent Using Google Features

Time Spent Using Google Maps

Over the past month, survey participants have spent a mean of 1.94 hours and a maximum of 30 hours using Google Maps. Survey participants under forty have spent 4.86 hours using Google Maps, compared with 0.96 hours spent by those between forty and fifty-nine and 0.5 hours spent by those sixty or over.

Time Spent Using Google Advanced Search, Google Notifications and Google Calendar

During this same period, survey participants spent a mean of 1.85 hours using Google Advanced Search, but just 0.12 hours using Google Alerts and even less time using Google Notifications. Participants specializing in reference or information literacy spent 3.25 hours using Google Advanced Search over the past month, while those working in research or a specialized subject area spent 1.39 hours. Survey participants spent a mean of 2.39 hours using Google Calendar over the past month, though those in libraries focused on medical, biological or pharmaceutical science spent just 0.38 hours using it.

Time Spent Using Google Images

Use of Google Images accounted for a mean of 5.82 work hours over the past month, with participants in academic medical libraries spending more than 15 hours this way. Survey participants under forty years old spent 18.08 hours using Google Images, whereas those over sixty dedicated just 1 hour a month to this end.

Time Spent Using Chrome

Over the past month, survey participants have spent a mean of 38.83 hours using Chrome in connection with work. While participants under age forty spent the most time using Chrome, participants aged sixty or over actually spent considerably more time using Chrome than did those between forty and fifty-nine. The former spent a mean of 48.33 hours using Chrome, whereas the latter spent a mean of 17.09 hours. Female survey participants spent a mean of 43.65 hours using Chrome, more than three times the amount of time male participants spent.

Time Spend Using Google Books, Google Scholar and Google Translate

Survey participants spent a mean of only 1.37 hours over the past month using Google Books and a mean of 11.19 hours using Google Scholar. In both cases, female survey participants spent considerably more hours using the apps than did male participants. Participants in academic scientific libraries spent approximately 7 hours using Google Scholar, whereas those in non-educational libraries spent 18.22 hours to this effect. Google Translate was used for a mean of 1.25 hours over the past month, though survey participants earning less than $55,000 a year spent a mean of 2.25 hours using it.

Time Spent using Google Drive, Gmail and YouTube

Google Drive was used by survey participants for a mean of 8.56 hours over the past month, with some participants under forty years old spending up to 80 hours using Drive. Use was much higher by survey participants under 40 years of age. Survey participants spent a mean of 13.4 hours using Gmail, 16 hours among female survey participants but just 0.63 hours for male participants. Google Forms was used for a mean of 2.41 hours, 6.67

hours among participants in academic medical libraries and 1.86 hours among those in academic scientific libraries. On average, survey participants spent 3.68 hours using YouTube over the past month; use was disproportionately by female participants, participants under forty, and those in academic medical libraries.

Time Spent Using Google Earth, Google Sky, Google Public Data Explorer, Google Bookmarks, Google Slides and Google Patent Search

In comparison, survey participants spent just 0.18 hours using Google Earth, 0.01 hours using Google Sky, 0.05 hours using Google Public Data Explorer, 0.09 hours using Google+, 0.06 hours using Google Bookmarks, 0.07 hours using Google Slides, and 0.1 hours using Google Analytics. Participants spent slightly more time using Google Groups and Google Hangouts, 0.40 hours each, and 0.24 hours using Google Patent Search.

Use of Other Google Features and Apps

Other features that survey participants found useful, but which were not included in the survey, were Google Voice, Google Talk, Google Docs, and Google News. Of the latter, one participant wrote: "(I) used to use the google news feature that indexed newspapers, but it disappeared a long time ago. This was extremely valuable for academic searching in political studies, sociology, current events, and other disciplines."

Google Features and Apps that Save the Most Time

When asked which single Google app or feature has saved them the most time, 9 survey participants listed Google Scholar and 3 listed Google Drive. Other features that were mentioned include: Chrome, Gmail, Advanced Search, Google Forms, Google Maps, Google Images, and Google Docs. Similarly, when asked which app or feature they would recommend most highly to their peers, 8 survey participants cited Google Scholar, with several emphasizing the Citations feature. Other features that were listed include: Advanced Search, Chrome, Google Alerts, Google Earth, Google Patent Search, and Google Public Data Explorer.

Scientific Research Time Accounted for by Use of Google Scholar or Google Books

Of the time survey participants spend performing medical or scientific secondary research, 20.56% is spent using Google Scholar or Google Books. Survey participants in non-educational libraries spend 35.75% of research time using Google Scholar or Google Books, whereas those in academic medical libraries spent 7.31% of research time using these apps. Survey participants under forty spend 33.83% of research time using Google Scholar or Google Books, compared with 20.5% of research time among those between forty and fifty-nine, and 7.42% of research time among those that are sixty or older.

Table 1.1 Your library's annual budget for all purposes, including salaries, materials, building maintenance, etc. is approximately? ($)

	Mean	Median	Minimum	Maximum
Entire sample	3648595.23	1400000.00	10000.00	15200000.00

Table 1.2 Your library's annual budget for all purposes, including salaries, materials, building maintenance, etc. is approximately? ($) Broken out by Type of institution

Type of institution	Mean	Median	Minimum	Maximum
Academic Medical Library	5321369.07	5058463.00	267192.00	15200000.00
Academic Scientific Library	3944197.53	5000000.00	320987.65	7000000.00
Non-Educational Medical/Scientific Library	342000.00	220000.00	10000.00	750000.00

Table 1.3 Your library's annual budget for all purposes, including salaries, materials, building maintenance, etc. is approximately? ($) Broken out by Age range of the survey participant

Age range of the survey participant	Mean	Median	Minimum	Maximum
Under 40	3355555.56	1666666.67	1400000.00	7000000.00
40-59	4038827.85	750000.00	10000.00	15200000.00
60 or Over	3272456.00	350000.00	70000.00	10000000.00

Table 1.4 Your library's annual budget for all purposes, including salaries, materials, building maintenance, etc. is approximately? ($) Broken out by Work specialization or title of the survey participant

Work specialization or title of the survey participant	Mean	Median	Minimum	Maximum
reference or information literacy	2167865.33	463596.00	10000.00	7000000.00
research or subject specialist	4930764.67	5529231.50	320987.65	10000000.00
other	3374000.00	350000.00	220000.00	15200000.00

Table 1.5 Your library's annual budget for all purposes, including salaries, materials, building maintenance, etc. is approximately? ($) (please specify the currency if not in US dollars) Broken out by Compensation range of the survey participant

Compensation range of the survey participant	Mean	Median	Minimum	Maximum
Less than $55,000	4356666.67	6000000.00	70000.00	7000000.00
$55,000+ to $70,000	1380538.48	660000.00	10000.00	7000000.00
More than $70,000	6261209.00	5058463.00	220000.00	15200000.00

Table 1.6 Your library's annual budget for all purposes, including salaries, materials, building maintenance, etc. is approximately? ($) Broken out by Gender of the survey participant

Gender of the survey participant	Mean	Median	Minimum	Maximum
Male	4854188.28	5029231.50	1400000.00	10000000.00
Female	3092167.67	350000.00	10000.00	15200000.00

Table 1.7 Your library's annual budget for all purposes, including salaries, materials, building maintenance, etc. is approximately? ($) Broken out for medical and other scientific libraries

Your main subject focus is:	Mean	Median	Minimum	Maximum
Medical, Biological or Pharmaceutical	3557706.83	705000.00	10000.00	15200000.00
Other Scientific	4133333.33	5000000.00	1400000.00	6000000.00

Table 2.1 What percentage of your total use of search engines would you estimate is accounted for by your use of the Google search engine?

	Mean	Median	Minimum	Maximum
Entire sample	54.95	50.00	10.00	100.00

Table 2.2 What percentage of your total use of search engines would you estimate is accounted for by your use of the Google search engine? Broken out by Type of institution

Type of institution	Mean	Median	Minimum	Maximum
Academic Medical Library	65.44	90.00	10.00	100.00
Academic Scientific Library	50.00	40.00	10.00	100.00
Non-Educational Medical/Scientific Library	45.00	40.00	20.00	95.00

Table 2.3 What percentage of your total use of search engines would you estimate is accounted for by your use of the Google search engine? Broken out by Age range of the survey participant

Age range of the survey participant	Mean	Median	Minimum	Maximum
Under 40	59.29	40.00	20.00	100.00
40-59	63.40	62.50	10.00	99.00
60 or Over	32.00	20.00	10.00	90.00

Table 2.4 What percentage of your total use of search engines would you estimate is accounted for by your use of the Google search engine? Broken out by Work specialization or title of the survey participant

Work specialization or title of the survey participant	Mean	Median	Minimum	Maximum
reference or information literacy	45.56	40.00	10.00	90.00
research or subject specialist	69.25	95.00	15.00	100.00
other	49.00	50.00	10.00	100.00

Table 2.5 What percentage of your total use of search engines would you estimate is accounted for by your use of the Google search engine? Broken out by Compensation range of the survey participant

Compensation range of the survey participant	Mean	Median	Minimum	Maximum
Less than $55,000	55.00	40.00	20.00	100.00
$55,000+ to $70,000	59.38	57.50	20.00	100.00
More than $70,000	51.00	50.00	10.00	100.00

Table 2.6 What percentage of your total use of search engines would you estimate is accounted for by your use of the Google search engine? Broken out by Gender of the survey participant

Gender of the survey participant	Mean	Median	Minimum	Maximum
Male	63.80	95.00	10.00	100.00
Female	52.35	50.00	10.00	100.00

Table 2.7 What percentage of your total use of search engines would you estimate is accounted for by your use of the Google search engine? Broken out for medical and other scientific libraries

Your main subject focus is:	Mean	Median	Minimum	Maximum
Medical, Biological or Pharmaceutical	56.60	50.00	10.00	100.00
Other Scientific	51.43	50.00	10.00	100.00

Table 3 How often do you use the following features of Google?

Table 3.1.1 How often do you use Google Maps?

	No Answer	Never really use it	Seldom use it	Sometimes use it	Often Use it	Very often use it
Entire sample	3.23%	9.68%	6.45%	12.90%	29.03%	38.71%

Table 3.1.2 How often do you use Google Maps? Broken out by Type of institution

Type of institution	No Answer	Never really use it	Seldom use it	Sometimes use it	Often Use it	Very often use it
Academic Medical Library	0.00%	8.33%	8.33%	0.00%	50.00%	33.33%
Academic Scientific Library	10.00%	0.00%	0.00%	30.00%	10.00%	50.00%
Non-Educational Medical/Scientific Library	0.00%	22.22%	11.11%	11.11%	22.22%	33.33%

Table 3.1.3 How often do you use Google Maps? Broken out by Age range of the survey participant

Age range of the survey participant	No Answer	Never really use it	Seldom use it	Sometimes use it	Often Use it	Very often use it
Under 40	0.00%	11.11%	0.00%	11.11%	22.22%	55.56%
40-59	6.67%	13.33%	0.00%	13.33%	26.67%	40.00%
60 or Over	0.00%	0.00%	28.57%	14.29%	42.86%	14.29%

Table 3.1.4 How often do you use Google Maps? Broken out by Work specialization or title of the survey participant

Work specialization or title of the survey participant	No Answer	Never really use it	Seldom use it	Sometimes use it	Often Use it	Very often use it
reference or information literacy	10.00%	20.00%	0.00%	20.00%	20.00%	30.00%
research or subject specialist	0.00%	7.14%	7.14%	14.29%	35.71%	35.71%
Other	0.00%	0.00%	14.29%	0.00%	28.57%	57.14%

Table 3.1.5 How often do you use Google Maps? Broken out by Compensation range of the survey participant

Compensation range of the survey participant	No Answer	Never really use it	Seldom use it	Sometimes use it	Often Use it	Very often use it
Less than $55,000	14.29%	14.29%	0.00%	14.29%	28.57%	28.57%
$55,000+ to $70,000	0.00%	15.38%	0.00%	7.69%	23.08%	53.85%
More than $70,000	0.00%	0.00%	18.18%	18.18%	36.36%	27.27%

Table 3.1.6 How often do you use Google Maps? Broken out by Gender of the survey participant

Gender of the survey participant	No Answer	Never really use it	Seldom use it	Sometimes use it	Often Use it	Very often use it
Male	0.00%	0.00%	14.29%	28.57%	28.57%	28.57%
Female	4.17%	12.50%	4.17%	8.33%	29.17%	41.67%

Table 3.1.7 How often do you use Google Maps? Broken out for medical and other scientific libraries

Your main subject focus is:	No Answer	Never really use it	Seldom use it	Sometimes use it	Often Use it	Very often use it
Medical, Biological or Pharmaceutical	0.00%	13.64%	9.09%	4.55%	36.36%	36.36%
Other Scientific	11.11%	0.00%	0.00%	33.33%	11.11%	44.44%

Table 3.2.1 How often do you use Google Advanced Search?

	Never really use it	Seldom use it	Sometimes use it	Often Use it	Very often use it
Entire sample	3.23%	12.90%	41.94%	32.26%	9.68%

Table 3.2.2 How often do you use Google Advanced Search? Broken out by Type of institution

Type of institution	Never really use it	Seldom use it	Sometimes use it	Often Use it	Very often use it
Academic Medical Library	0.00%	16.67%	25.00%	50.00%	8.33%
Academic Scientific Library	0.00%	20.00%	50.00%	30.00%	0.00%
Non-Educational Medical/Scientific Library	11.11%	0.00%	55.56%	11.11%	22.22%

Table 3.2.3 How often do you use Google Advanced Search? Broken out by Age range of the survey participant

Age range of the survey participant	Never really use it	Seldom use it	Sometimes use it	Often Use it	Very often use it
Under 40	0.00%	33.33%	55.56%	11.11%	0.00%
40-59	0.00%	0.00%	33.33%	46.67%	20.00%
60 or Over	14.29%	14.29%	42.86%	28.57%	0.00%

Table 3.2.4 How often do you use Google Advanced Search? Broken out by Work specialization or title of the survey participant

Work specialization or title of the survey participant	Never really use it	Seldom use it	Sometimes use it	Often Use it	Very often use it
reference or information literacy	0.00%	0.00%	50.00%	40.00%	10.00%
research or subject specialist	0.00%	21.43%	50.00%	28.57%	0.00%
other	14.29%	14.29%	14.29%	28.57%	28.57%

Table 3.2.5 How often do you use Google Advanced Search? Broken out by Compensation range of the survey participant

Compensation range of the survey participant	Never really use it	Seldom use it	Sometimes use it	Often Use it	Very often use it
Less than $55,000	0.00%	14.29%	28.57%	57.14%	0.00%
$55,000+ to $70,000	0.00%	7.69%	69.23%	7.69%	15.38%
More than $70,000	9.09%	18.18%	18.18%	45.45%	9.09%

Table 3.2.6 How often do you use Google Advanced Search? Broken out by Gender of the survey participant

Gender of the survey participant	Never really use it	Seldom use it	Sometimes use it	Often Use it	Very often use it
Male	0.00%	28.57%	57.14%	14.29%	0.00%
Female	4.17%	8.33%	37.50%	37.50%	12.50%

Table 3.2.7 How often do you use Google Advanced Search? Broken out for medical and other scientific libraries

Your main subject focus is:	Never really use it	Seldom use it	Sometimes use it	Often Use it	Very often use it
Medical, Biological or Pharmaceutical	4.55%	9.09%	40.91%	36.36%	9.09%
Other Scientific	0.00%	22.22%	44.44%	22.22%	11.11%

Table 3.3.1 How often do you use Google Alerts?

	No Answer	Never really use it	Seldom use it	Sometimes use it	Often Use it	Very often use it
Entire sample	3.23%	61.29%	12.90%	19.35%	3.23%	0.00%

Table 3.3.2 How often do you use Google Alerts? Broken out by Type of institution

Type of institution	No Answer	Never really use it	Seldom use it	Sometimes use it	Often Use it	Very often use it
Academic Medical Library	0.00%	50.00%	16.67%	25.00%	8.33%	0.00%
Academic Scientific Library	10.00%	50.00%	20.00%	20.00%	0.00%	0.00%
Non-Educational Medical/Scientific Library	0.00%	88.89%	0.00%	11.11%	0.00%	0.00%

Table 3.3.3 How often do you use Google Alerts? Broken out by Age range of the survey participant

Age range of the survey participant	No Answer	Never really use it	Seldom use it	Sometimes use it	Often Use it	Very often use it
Under 40	0.00%	66.67%	11.11%	22.22%	0.00%	0.00%
40-59	6.67%	60.00%	6.67%	20.00%	6.67%	0.00%
60 or Over	0.00%	57.14%	28.57%	14.29%	0.00%	0.00%

Table 3.3.4 How often do you use Google Alerts? Broken out by Work specialization or title of the survey participant

Work specialization or title of the survey participant	No Answer	Never really use it	Seldom use it	Sometimes use it	Often Use it	Very often use it
reference or information literacy	10.00%	70.00%	10.00%	10.00%	0.00%	0.00%
research or subject specialist	0.00%	57.14%	14.29%	28.57%	0.00%	0.00%
other	0.00%	57.14%	14.29%	14.29%	14.29%	0.00%

Table 3.3.5 How often do you use Google Alerts? Broken out by Compensation range of the survey participant

Compensation range of the survey participant	No Answer	Never really use it	Seldom use it	Sometimes use it	Often Use it	Very often use it
Less than $55,000	14.29%	71.43%	0.00%	14.29%	0.00%	0.00%
$55,000+ to $70,000	0.00%	61.54%	7.69%	23.08%	7.69%	0.00%
More than $70,000	0.00%	54.55%	27.27%	18.18%	0.00%	0.00%

Table 3.3.6 How often do you use Google Alerts? Broken out by Gender of the survey participant

Gender of the survey participant	No Answer	Never really use it	Seldom use it	Sometimes use it	Often Use it	Very often use it
Male	0.00%	28.57%	14.29%	57.14%	0.00%	0.00%
Female	4.17%	70.83%	12.50%	8.33%	4.17%	0.00%

Table 3.3.7 How often do you use Google Alerts? Broken out for medical and other scientific libraries

Your main subject focus is:	No Answer	Never really use it	Seldom use it	Sometimes use it	Often Use it	Very often use it
Medical, Biological or Pharmaceutical	0.00%	68.18%	9.09%	18.18%	4.55%	0.00%
Other Scientific	11.11%	44.44%	22.22%	22.22%	0.00%	0.00%

Table 3.4.1 How often do you use Google Notifications?

	No Answer	Never really use it	Seldom use it	Sometimes use it	Often Use it	Very often use it
Entire sample	3.23%	77.42%	16.13%	3.23%	0.00%	0.00%

Table 3.4.2 How often do you use Google Notifications? Broken out by Type of institution

Type of institution	No Answer	Never really use it	Seldom use it	Sometimes use it	Often Use it	Very often use it
Academic Medical Library	0.00%	75.00%	16.67%	8.33%	0.00%	0.00%
Academic Scientific Library	10.00%	60.00%	30.00%	0.00%	0.00%	0.00%
Non-Educational Medical/Scientific Library	0.00%	100.00%	0.00%	0.00%	0.00%	0.00%

Table 3.4.3 How often do you use Google Notifications? Broken out by Age range of the survey participant

Age range of the survey participant	No Answer	Never really use it	Seldom use it	Sometimes use it	Often Use it	Very often use it
Under 40	0.00%	88.89%	11.11%	0.00%	0.00%	0.00%
40-59	6.67%	80.00%	6.67%	6.67%	0.00%	0.00%
60 or Over	0.00%	57.14%	42.86%	0.00%	0.00%	0.00%

Table 3.4.4 How often do you use Google Notifications? Broken out by Work specialization or title of the survey participant

Work specialization or title of the survey participant	No Answer	Never really use it	Seldom use it	Sometimes use it	Often Use it	Very often use it
reference or information literacy	10.00%	80.00%	10.00%	0.00%	0.00%	0.00%
research or subject specialist	0.00%	71.43%	21.43%	7.14%	0.00%	0.00%
other	0.00%	85.71%	14.29%	0.00%	0.00%	0.00%

Table 3.4.5 How often do you use Google Notifications? Broken out by Compensation range of the survey participant

Compensation range of the survey participant	No Answer	Never really use it	Seldom use it	Sometimes use it	Often Use it	Very often use it
Less than $55,000	14.29%	71.43%	14.29%	0.00%	0.00%	0.00%
$55,000+ to $70,000	0.00%	84.62%	15.38%	0.00%	0.00%	0.00%
More than $70,000	0.00%	72.73%	18.18%	9.09%	0.00%	0.00%

Table 3.4.6 How often do you use Google Notifications? Broken out by Gender of the survey participant

Gender of the survey participant	No Answer	Never really use it	Seldom use it	Sometimes use it	Often Use it	Very often use it
Male	0.00%	42.86%	42.86%	14.29%	0.00%	0.00%
Female	4.17%	87.50%	8.33%	0.00%	0.00%	0.00%

Table 3.4.7 How often do you use Google Notifications? Broken out for medical and other scientific libraries

Your main subject focus is:	No Answer	Never really use it	Seldom use it	Sometimes use it	Often Use it	Very often use it
Medical, Biological or Pharmaceutical	0.00%	86.36%	9.09%	4.55%	0.00%	0.00%
Other Scientific	11.11%	55.56%	33.33%	0.00%	0.00%	0.00%

Table 3.5.1 How often do you use Google Images?

	No Answer	Never really use it	Seldom use it	Sometimes use it	Often Use it	Very often use it
Entire sample	3.23%	3.23%	9.68%	35.48%	29.03%	19.35%

Table 3.5.2 How often do you use Google Images? Broken out by Type of institution

Type of institution	No Answer	Never really use it	Seldom use it	Sometimes use it	Often Use it	Very often use it
Academic Medical Library	0.00%	0.00%	0.00%	33.33%	50.00%	16.67%
Academic Scientific Library	10.00%	10.00%	10.00%	40.00%	20.00%	10.00%
Non-Educational Medical/Scientific Library	0.00%	0.00%	22.22%	33.33%	11.11%	33.33%

Table 3.5.3 How often do you use Google Images? Broken out by Age range of the survey participant

Age range of the survey participant	No Answer	Never really use it	Seldom use it	Sometimes use it	Often Use it	Very often use it
Under 40	0.00%	11.11%	11.11%	33.33%	22.22%	22.22%
40-59	6.67%	0.00%	6.67%	26.67%	46.67%	13.33%
60 or Over	0.00%	0.00%	14.29%	57.14%	0.00%	28.57%

Table 3.5.4 How often do you use Google Images? Broken out by Work specialization or title of the survey participant

Work specialization or title of the survey participant	No Answer	Never really use it	Seldom use it	Sometimes use it	Often Use it	Very often use it
reference or information literacy	10.00%	0.00%	10.00%	40.00%	20.00%	20.00%
research or subject specialist	0.00%	7.14%	7.14%	42.86%	35.71%	7.14%
other	0.00%	0.00%	14.29%	14.29%	28.57%	42.86%

Table 3.5.5 How often do you use Google Images? Broken out by Compensation range of the survey participant

Compensation range of the survey participant	No Answer	Never really use it	Seldom use it	Sometimes use it	Often Use it	Very often use it
Less than $55,000	14.29%	0.00%	0.00%	28.57%	28.57%	28.57%
$55,000+ to $70,000	0.00%	7.69%	15.38%	30.77%	38.46%	7.69%
More than $70,000	0.00%	0.00%	9.09%	45.45%	18.18%	27.27%

Table 3.5.6 How often do you use Google Images? Broken out by Gender of the survey participant

Gender of the survey participant	No Answer	Never really use it	Seldom use it	Sometimes use it	Often Use it	Very often use it
Male	0.00%	0.00%	14.29%	28.57%	57.14%	0.00%
Female	4.17%	4.17%	8.33%	37.50%	20.83%	25.00%

Table 3.5.7 How often do you use Google Images? Broken out for medical and other scientific libraries

Your main subject focus is:	No Answer	Never really use it	Seldom use it	Sometimes use it	Often Use it	Very often use it
Medical, Biological or Pharmaceutical	0.00%	0.00%	9.09%	36.36%	36.36%	18.18%
Other Scientific	11.11%	11.11%	11.11%	33.33%	11.11%	22.22%

Table 3.6.1 How often do you use Google Photos?

	No Answer	Never really use it	Seldom use it	Sometimes use it	Often Use it	Very often use it
Entire sample	3.23%	51.61%	12.90%	19.35%	9.68%	3.23%

Table 3.6.2 How often do you use Google Photos? Broken out by Type of institution

Type of institution	No Answer	Never really use it	Seldom use it	Sometimes use it	Often Use it	Very often use it
Academic Medical Library	0.00%	58.33%	8.33%	25.00%	8.33%	0.00%
Academic Scientific Library	10.00%	20.00%	30.00%	20.00%	20.00%	0.00%
Non-Educational Medical/Scientific Library	0.00%	77.78%	0.00%	11.11%	0.00%	11.11%

Table 3.6.3 How often do you use Google Photos? Broken out by Age range of the survey participant

Age range of the survey participant	No Answer	Never really use it	Seldom use it	Sometimes use it	Often Use it	Very often use it
Under 40	0.00%	66.67%	11.11%	0.00%	22.22%	0.00%
40-59	6.67%	40.00%	20.00%	26.67%	0.00%	6.67%
60 or Over	0.00%	57.14%	0.00%	28.57%	14.29%	0.00%

Table 3.6.4 How often do you use Google Photos? Broken out by Work specialization or title of the survey participant

Work specialization or title of the survey participant	No Answer	Never really use it	Seldom use it	Sometimes use it	Often Use it	Very often use it
reference or information literacy	10.00%	40.00%	10.00%	20.00%	10.00%	10.00%
research or subject specialist	0.00%	57.14%	21.43%	14.29%	7.14%	0.00%
other	0.00%	57.14%	0.00%	28.57%	14.29%	0.00%

Table 3.6.5 How often do you use Google Photos? Broken out by Compensation range of the survey participant

Compensation range of the survey participant	No Answer	Never really use it	Seldom use it	Sometimes use it	Often Use it	Very often use it
Less than $55,000	14.29%	42.86%	0.00%	28.57%	14.29%	0.00%
$55,000+ to $70,000	0.00%	53.85%	15.38%	15.38%	7.69%	7.69%
More than $70,000	0.00%	54.55%	18.18%	18.18%	9.09%	0.00%

Table 3.6.6 How often do you use Google Photos? Broken out by Gender of the survey participant

Gender of the survey participant	No Answer	Never really use it	Seldom use it	Sometimes use it	Often Use it	Very often use it
Male	0.00%	57.14%	14.29%	28.57%	0.00%	0.00%
Female	4.17%	50.00%	12.50%	16.67%	12.50%	4.17%

Table 3.6.7 How often do you use Google Photos? Broken out for medical and other scientific libraries

Your main subject focus is:	No Answer	Never really use it	Seldom use it	Sometimes use it	Often Use it	Very often use it
Medical, Biological or Pharmaceutical	0.00%	59.09%	9.09%	18.18%	9.09%	4.55%
Other Scientific	11.11%	33.33%	22.22%	22.22%	11.11%	0.00%

Table 3.7.1 How often do you use Google Calendar?

	Never really use it	Seldom use it	Sometimes use it	Often Use it	Very often use it
Entire sample	48.39%	9.68%	12.90%	9.68%	19.35%

Table 3.7.2 How often do you use Google Calendar? Broken out by Type of institution

Type of institution	Never really use it	Seldom use it	Sometimes use it	Often Use it	Very often use it
Academic Medical Library	50.00%	8.33%	25.00%	16.67%	0.00%
Academic Scientific Library	20.00%	10.00%	10.00%	10.00%	50.00%
Non-Educational Medical/Scientific Library	77.78%	11.11%	0.00%	0.00%	11.11%

Table 3.7.3 How often do you use Google Calendar? Broken out by Age range of the survey participant

Age range of the survey participant	Never really use it	Seldom use it	Sometimes use it	Often Use it	Very often use it
Under 40	33.33%	0.00%	11.11%	22.22%	33.33%
40-59	66.67%	6.67%	13.33%	0.00%	13.33%
60 or Over	28.57%	28.57%	14.29%	14.29%	14.29%

Table 3.7.4 How often do you use Google Calendar? Broken out by Work specialization or title of the survey participant

Work specialization or title of the survey participant	Never really use it	Seldom use it	Sometimes use it	Often Use it	Very often use it
reference or information literacy	30.00%	10.00%	10.00%	10.00%	40.00%
research or subject specialist	50.00%	14.29%	14.29%	7.14%	14.29%
other	71.43%	0.00%	14.29%	14.29%	0.00%

Table 3.7.5 How often do you use Google Calendar? Broken out by Compensation range of the survey participant

Compensation range of the survey participant	Never really use it	Seldom use it	Sometimes use it	Often Use it	Very often use it
Less than $55,000	57.14%	14.29%	0.00%	0.00%	28.57%
$55,000+ to $70,000	38.46%	15.38%	15.38%	15.38%	15.38%
More than $70,000	54.55%	0.00%	18.18%	9.09%	18.18%

Table 3.7.6 How often do you use Google Calendar? Broken out by Gender of the survey participant

Gender of the survey participant	Never really use it	Seldom use it	Sometimes use it	Often Use it	Very often use it
Male	71.43%	0.00%	0.00%	14.29%	14.29%
Female	41.67%	12.50%	16.67%	8.33%	20.83%

Table 3.7.7 How often do you use Google Calendar? Broken out for medical and other scientific libraries

Your main subject focus is:	Never really use it	Seldom use it	Sometimes use it	Often Use it	Very often use it
Medical, Biological or Pharmaceutical	54.55%	13.64%	13.64%	9.09%	9.09%
Other Scientific	33.33%	0.00%	11.11%	11.11%	44.44%

Table 3.8.1 How often do you use Chrome?

	Never really use it	Seldom use it	Sometimes use it	Often Use it	Very often use it
Entire sample	0.00%	3.23%	16.13%	29.03%	51.61%

Table 3.8.2 How often do you use Chrome? Broken out by Type of institution

Type of institution	Never really use it	Seldom use it	Sometimes use it	Often Use it	Very often use it
Academic Medical Library	0.00%	0.00%	25.00%	25.00%	50.00%
Academic Scientific Library	0.00%	10.00%	10.00%	20.00%	60.00%
Non-Educational Medical/Scientific Library	0.00%	0.00%	11.11%	44.44%	44.44%

Table 3.8.3 How often do you use Chrome? Broken out by Age range of the survey participant

Age range of the survey participant	Never really use it	Seldom use it	Sometimes use it	Often Use it	Very often use it
Under 40	0.00%	0.00%	11.11%	0.00%	88.89%
40-59	0.00%	6.67%	13.33%	46.67%	33.33%
60 or Over	0.00%	0.00%	28.57%	28.57%	42.86%

Table 3.8.4 How often do you use Chrome? Broken out by Work specialization or title of the survey participant

Work specialization or title of the survey participant	Never really use it	Seldom use it	Sometimes use it	Often Use it	Very often use it
reference or information literacy	0.00%	0.00%	20.00%	10.00%	70.00%
research or subject specialist	0.00%	7.14%	7.14%	35.71%	50.00%
other	0.00%	0.00%	28.57%	42.86%	28.57%

Table 3.8.5 How often do you use Chrome? Broken out by Compensation range of the survey participant

Compensation range of the survey participant	Never really use it	Seldom use it	Sometimes use it	Often Use it	Very often use it
Less than $55,000	0.00%	14.29%	14.29%	14.29%	57.14%
$55,000+ to $70,000	0.00%	0.00%	15.38%	30.77%	53.85%
More than $70,000	0.00%	0.00%	18.18%	36.36%	45.45%

Table 3.8.6 How often do you use Chrome? Broken out by Gender of the survey participant

Gender of the survey participant	Never really use it	Seldom use it	Sometimes use it	Often Use it	Very often use it
Male	0.00%	14.29%	14.29%	28.57%	42.86%
Female	0.00%	0.00%	16.67%	29.17%	54.17%

Table 3.8.7 How often do you use Chrome? Broken out for medical and other scientific libraries

Your main subject focus is:	Never really use it	Seldom use it	Sometimes use it	Often Use it	Very often use it
Medical, Biological or Pharmaceutical	0.00%	0.00%	22.73%	31.82%	45.45%
Other Scientific	0.00%	11.11%	0.00%	22.22%	66.67%

Table 3.9.1 How often do you use Google Books?

	No Answer	Never really use it	Seldom use it	Sometimes use it	Often Use it	Very often use it
Entire sample	3.23%	12.90%	29.03%	35.48%	16.13%	3.23%

Table 3.9.2 How often do you use Google Books? Broken out by Type of institution

Type of institution	No Answer	Never really use it	Seldom use it	Sometimes use it	Often Use it	Very often use it
Academic Medical Library	0.00%	16.67%	25.00%	50.00%	8.33%	0.00%
Academic Scientific Library	10.00%	20.00%	20.00%	30.00%	20.00%	0.00%
Non-Educational Medical/Scientific Library	0.00%	0.00%	44.44%	22.22%	22.22%	11.11%

Table 3.9.3 How often do you use Google Books? Broken out by Age range of the survey participant

Age range of the survey participant	No Answer	Never really use it	Seldom use it	Sometimes use it	Often Use it	Very often use it
Under 40	0.00%	22.22%	11.11%	44.44%	22.22%	0.00%
40-59	6.67%	6.67%	26.67%	40.00%	13.33%	6.67%
60 or Over	0.00%	14.29%	57.14%	14.29%	14.29%	0.00%

Table 3.9.4 How often do you use Google Books? Broken out by Work specialization or title of the survey participant

Work specialization or title of the survey participant	No Answer	Never really use it	Seldom use it	Sometimes use it	Often Use it	Very often use it
reference or information literacy	10.00%	30.00%	30.00%	10.00%	10.00%	10.00%
research or subject specialist	0.00%	0.00%	28.57%	57.14%	14.29%	0.00%
other	0.00%	14.29%	28.57%	28.57%	28.57%	0.00%

Table 3.9.5 How often do you use Google Books? Broken out by Compensation range of the survey participant

Compensation range of the survey participant	No Answer	Never really use it	Seldom use it	Sometimes use it	Often Use it	Very often use it
Less than $55,000	14.29%	14.29%	14.29%	28.57%	28.57%	0.00%
$55,000+ to $70,000	0.00%	7.69%	46.15%	30.77%	7.69%	7.69%
More than $70,000	0.00%	18.18%	18.18%	45.45%	18.18%	0.00%

Table 3.9.6 How often do you use Google Books? Broken out by Gender of the survey participant

Gender of the survey participant	No Answer	Never really use it	Seldom use it	Sometimes use it	Often Use it	Very often use it
Male	0.00%	14.29%	28.57%	57.14%	0.00%	0.00%
Female	4.17%	12.50%	29.17%	29.17%	20.83%	4.17%

Table 3.9.7 How often do you use Google Books? Broken out for medical and other scientific libraries

Your main subject focus is:	No Answer	Never really use it	Seldom use it	Sometimes use it	Often Use it	Very often use it
Medical, Biological or Pharmaceutical	0.00%	9.09%	36.36%	36.36%	13.64%	4.55%
Other Scientific	11.11%	22.22%	11.11%	33.33%	22.22%	0.00%

Table 3.10.1 How often do you use Google Scholar?

	Never really use it	Seldom use it	Sometimes use it	Often Use it	Very often use it
Entire sample	0.00%	9.68%	9.68%	25.81%	54.84%

Table 3.10.2 How often do you use Google Scholar? Broken out by Type of institution

Type of institution	Never really use it	Seldom use it	Sometimes use it	Often Use it	Very often use it
Academic Medical Library	0.00%	8.33%	8.33%	33.33%	50.00%
Academic Scientific Library	0.00%	10.00%	10.00%	30.00%	50.00%
Non-Educational Medical/Scientific Library	0.00%	11.11%	11.11%	11.11%	66.67%

Table 3.10.3 How often do you use Google Scholar? Broken out by Age range of the survey participant

Age range of the survey participant	Never really use it	Seldom use it	Sometimes use it	Often Use it	Very often use it
Under 40	0.00%	11.11%	11.11%	33.33%	44.44%
40-59	0.00%	0.00%	13.33%	13.33%	73.33%
60 or Over	0.00%	28.57%	0.00%	42.86%	28.57%

Table 3.10.4 How often do you use Google Scholar? Broken out by Work specialization or title of the survey participant

Work specialization or title of the survey participant	Never really use it	Seldom use it	Sometimes use it	Often Use it	Very often use it
reference or information literacy	0.00%	20.00%	0.00%	20.00%	60.00%
research or subject specialist	0.00%	7.14%	14.29%	35.71%	42.86%
other	0.00%	0.00%	14.29%	14.29%	71.43%

Table 3.10.5 How often do you use Google Scholar? Broken out by Compensation range of the survey participant

Compensation range of the survey participant	Never really use it	Seldom use it	Sometimes use it	Often Use it	Very often use it
Less than $55,000	0.00%	14.29%	0.00%	28.57%	57.14%
$55,000+ to $70,000	0.00%	7.69%	7.69%	23.08%	61.54%
More than $70,000	0.00%	9.09%	18.18%	27.27%	45.45%

Table 3.10.6 How often do you use Google Scholar? Broken out by Gender of the survey participant

Gender of the survey participant	Never really use it	Seldom use it	Sometimes use it	Often Use it	Very often use it
Male	0.00%	28.57%	0.00%	42.86%	28.57%
Female	0.00%	4.17%	12.50%	20.83%	62.50%

Table 3.10.7 How often do you use Google Scholar? Broken out for medical and other scientific libraries

Your main subject focus is:	Never really use it	Seldom use it	Sometimes use it	Often Use it	Very often use it
Medical, Biological or Pharmaceutical	0.00%	9.09%	9.09%	22.73%	59.09%
Other Scientific	0.00%	11.11%	11.11%	33.33%	44.44%

Table 3.11.1 How often do you use Google Scholar My Citations?

	No Answer	Never really use it	Seldom use it	Sometimes use it	Often Use it	Very often use it
Entire sample	3.23%	35.48%	29.03%	9.68%	12.90%	9.68%

Table 3.11.2 How often do you use Google Scholar My Citations? Broken out by Type of institution

Type of institution	No Answer	Never really use it	Seldom use it	Sometimes use it	Often Use it	Very often use it
Academic Medical Library	0.00%	41.67%	33.33%	16.67%	8.33%	0.00%
Academic Scientific Library	0.00%	10.00%	40.00%	10.00%	10.00%	30.00%
Non-Educational Medical/Scientific Library	11.11%	55.56%	11.11%	0.00%	22.22%	0.00%

Table 3.11.3 How often do you use Google Scholar My Citations? Broken out by Age range of the survey participant

Age range of the survey participant	No Answer	Never really use it	Seldom use it	Sometimes use it	Often Use it	Very often use it
Under 40	0.00%	44.44%	22.22%	11.11%	11.11%	11.11%
40-59	6.67%	33.33%	26.67%	0.00%	20.00%	13.33%
60 or Over	0.00%	28.57%	42.86%	28.57%	0.00%	0.00%

Table 3.11.4 How often do you use Google Scholar My Citations? Broken out by Work specialization or title of the survey participant

Work specialization or title of the survey participant	No Answer	Never really use it	Seldom use it	Sometimes use it	Often Use it	Very often use it
reference or information literacy	0.00%	30.00%	40.00%	0.00%	10.00%	20.00%
research or subject specialist	7.14%	28.57%	21.43%	21.43%	14.29%	7.14%
other	0.00%	57.14%	28.57%	0.00%	14.29%	0.00%

Table 3.11.5 How often do you use Google Scholar My Citations? Broken out by Compensation range of the survey participant

Compensation range of the survey participant	No Answer	Never really use it	Seldom use it	Sometimes use it	Often Use it	Very often use it
Less than $55,000	14.29%	0.00%	71.43%	0.00%	0.00%	14.29%
$55,000+ to $70,000	0.00%	69.23%	7.69%	7.69%	7.69%	7.69%
More than $70,000	0.00%	18.18%	27.27%	18.18%	27.27%	9.09%

Table 3.11.6 How often do you use Google Scholar My Citations? Broken out by Gender of the survey participant

Gender of the survey participant	No Answer	Never really use it	Seldom use it	Sometimes use it	Often Use it	Very often use it
Male	0.00%	42.86%	28.57%	14.29%	14.29%	0.00%
Female	4.17%	33.33%	29.17%	8.33%	12.50%	12.50%

Table 3.11.7 How often do you use Google Scholar My Citations? Broken out for medical and other scientific libraries

Your main subject focus is:	No Answer	Never really use it	Seldom use it	Sometimes use it	Often Use it	Very often use it
Medical, Biological or Pharmaceutical	4.55%	45.45%	31.82%	9.09%	9.09%	0.00%
Other Scientific	0.00%	11.11%	22.22%	11.11%	22.22%	33.33%

Table 3.12.1 How often do you use Google Translate?

	Never really use it	Seldom use it	Sometimes use it	Often Use it	Very often use it
Entire sample	22.58%	22.58%	41.94%	6.45%	6.45%

Table 3.12.2 How often do you use Google Translate? Broken out by Type of institution

Type of institution	Never really use it	Seldom use it	Sometimes use it	Often Use it	Very often use it
Academic Medical Library	8.33%	33.33%	50.00%	0.00%	8.33%
Academic Scientific Library	30.00%	10.00%	40.00%	20.00%	0.00%
Non-Educational Medical/Scientific Library	33.33%	22.22%	33.33%	0.00%	11.11%

Table 3.12.3 How often do you use Google Translate? Broken out by Age range of the survey participant

Age range of the survey participant	Never really use it	Seldom use it	Sometimes use it	Often Use it	Very often use it
Under 40	22.22%	33.33%	22.22%	11.11%	11.11%
40-59	20.00%	20.00%	46.67%	6.67%	6.67%
60 or Over	28.57%	14.29%	57.14%	0.00%	0.00%

Table 3.12.4 How often do you use Google Translate? Broken out by Work specialization or title of the survey participant

Work specialization or title of the survey participant	Never really use it	Seldom use it	Sometimes use it	Often Use it	Very often use it
reference or information literacy	40.00%	10.00%	40.00%	10.00%	0.00%
research or subject specialist	14.29%	28.57%	50.00%	7.14%	0.00%
other	14.29%	28.57%	28.57%	0.00%	28.57%

Table 3.12.5 How often do you use Google Translate? Broken out by Compensation range of the survey participant

Compensation range of the survey participant	Never really use it	Seldom use it	Sometimes use it	Often Use it	Very often use it
Less than $55,000	14.29%	14.29%	42.86%	14.29%	14.29%
$55,000+ to $70,000	30.77%	30.77%	30.77%	7.69%	0.00%
More than $70,000	18.18%	18.18%	54.55%	0.00%	9.09%

Table 3.12.6 How often do you use Google Translate? Broken out by Gender of the survey participant

Gender of the survey participant	Never really use it	Seldom use it	Sometimes use it	Often Use it	Very often use it
Male	14.29%	42.86%	42.86%	0.00%	0.00%
Female	25.00%	16.67%	41.67%	8.33%	8.33%

Table 3.12.7 How often do you use Google Translate? Broken out for medical and other scientific libraries

Your main subject focus is:	Never really use it	Seldom use it	Sometimes use it	Often Use it	Very often use it
Medical, Biological or Pharmaceutical	22.73%	31.82%	40.91%	0.00%	4.55%
Other Scientific	22.22%	0.00%	44.44%	22.22%	11.11%

Table 3.14.1 How often do you use Google Public Data Explorer?

	No Answer	Never really use it	Seldom use it	Sometimes use it	Often Use it	Very often use it
Entire sample	3.23%	83.87%	6.45%	6.45%	0.00%	0.00%

Table 3.14.2 How often do you use Google Public Data Explorer? Broken out by Type of institution

Type of institution	No Answer	Never really use it	Seldom use it	Sometimes use it	Often Use it	Very often use it
Academic Medical Library	0.00%	91.67%	0.00%	8.33%	0.00%	0.00%
Academic Scientific Library	10.00%	60.00%	20.00%	10.00%	0.00%	0.00%
Non-Educational Medical/Scientific Library	0.00%	100.00%	0.00%	0.00%	0.00%	0.00%

Table 3.14.3 How often do you use Google Public Data Explorer? Broken out by Age range of the survey participant

Age range of the survey participant	No Answer	Never really use it	Seldom use it	Sometimes use it	Often Use it	Very often use it
Under 40	0.00%	66.67%	22.22%	11.11%	0.00%	0.00%
40-59	6.67%	86.67%	0.00%	6.67%	0.00%	0.00%
60 or Over	0.00%	100.00%	0.00%	0.00%	0.00%	0.00%

Table 3.14.4 How often do you use Google Public Data Explorer? Broken out by Work specialization or title of the survey participant

Work specialization or title of the survey participant	No Answer	Never really use it	Seldom use it	Sometimes use it	Often Use it	Very often use it
reference or information literacy	10.00%	80.00%	0.00%	10.00%	0.00%	0.00%
research or subject specialist	0.00%	78.57%	14.29%	7.14%	0.00%	0.00%
other	0.00%	100.00%	0.00%	0.00%	0.00%	0.00%

Table 3.14.5 How often do you use Google Public Data Explorer? Broken out by Compensation range of the survey participant

Compensation range of the survey participant	No Answer	Never really use it	Seldom use it	Sometimes use it	Often Use it	Very often use it
Less than $55,000	14.29%	71.43%	0.00%	14.29%	0.00%	0.00%
$55,000+ to $70,000	0.00%	92.31%	7.69%	0.00%	0.00%	0.00%
More than $70,000	0.00%	81.82%	9.09%	9.09%	0.00%	0.00%

Table 3.14.6 How often do you use Google Public Data Explorer? Broken out by Gender of the survey participant

Gender of the survey participant	No Answer	Never really use it	Seldom use it	Sometimes use it	Often Use it	Very often use it
Male	0.00%	85.71%	0.00%	14.29%	0.00%	0.00%
Female	4.17%	83.33%	8.33%	4.17%	0.00%	0.00%

Table 3.14.7 How often do you use Google Public Data Explorer? Broken out for medical and other scientific libraries

Your main subject focus is:	No Answer	Never really use it	Seldom use it	Sometimes use it	Often Use it	Very often use it
Medical, Biological or Pharmaceutical	0.00%	90.91%	0.00%	9.09%	0.00%	0.00%
Other Scientific	11.11%	66.67%	22.22%	0.00%	0.00%	0.00%

Table 3.15.1 How often do you use Google Drive?

	Never really use it	Seldom use it	Sometimes use it	Often Use it	Very often use it
Entire sample	25.81%	19.35%	19.35%	6.45%	29.03%

Table 3.15.2 How often do you use Google Drive? Broken out by Type of institution

Type of institution	Never really use it	Seldom use it	Sometimes use it	Often Use it	Very often use it
Academic Medical Library	8.33%	25.00%	50.00%	0.00%	16.67%
Academic Scientific Library	10.00%	20.00%	0.00%	20.00%	50.00%
Non-Educational Medical/Scientific Library	66.67%	11.11%	0.00%	0.00%	22.22%

Table 3.15.3 How often do you use Google Drive? Broken out by Age range of the survey participant

Age range of the survey participant	Never really use it	Seldom use it	Sometimes use it	Often Use it	Very often use it
Under 40	0.00%	22.22%	0.00%	11.11%	66.67%
40-59	33.33%	20.00%	26.67%	6.67%	13.33%
60 or Over	42.86%	14.29%	28.57%	0.00%	14.29%

Table 3.15.4 How often do you use Google Drive? Broken out by Work specialization or title of the survey participant

Work specialization or title of the survey participant	Never really use it	Seldom use it	Sometimes use it	Often Use it	Very often use it
reference or information literacy	20.00%	0.00%	20.00%	10.00%	50.00%
research or subject specialist	14.29%	42.86%	14.29%	7.14%	21.43%
other	57.14%	0.00%	28.57%	0.00%	14.29%

Table 3.15.5 How often do you use Google Drive? Broken out by Compensation range of the survey participant

Compensation range of the survey participant	Never really use it	Seldom use it	Sometimes use it	Often Use it	Very often use it
Less than $55,000	14.29%	14.29%	14.29%	0.00%	57.14%
$55,000+ to $70,000	23.08%	23.08%	23.08%	7.69%	23.08%
More than $70,000	36.36%	18.18%	18.18%	9.09%	18.18%

Table 3.15.6 How often do you use Google Drive? Broken out by Gender of the survey participant

Gender of the survey participant	Never really use it	Seldom use it	Sometimes use it	Often Use it	Very often use it
Male	28.57%	42.86%	14.29%	14.29%	0.00%
Female	25.00%	12.50%	20.83%	4.17%	37.50%

Table 3.15.7 How often do you use Google Drive? Broken out for medical and other scientific libraries

Your main subject focus is:	Never really use it	Seldom use it	Sometimes use it	Often Use it	Very often use it
Medical, Biological or Pharmaceutical	27.27%	22.73%	27.27%	0.00%	22.73%
Other Scientific	22.22%	11.11%	0.00%	22.22%	44.44%

Table 3.16.1 How often do you use Gmail?

	No Answer	Never really use it	Seldom use it	Sometimes use it	Often Use it	Very often use it
Entire sample	6.45%	12.90%	16.13%	16.13%	9.68%	38.71%

Table 3.16.2 How often do you use Gmail? Broken out by Type of institution

Type of institution	No Answer	Never really use it	Seldom use it	Sometimes use it	Often Use it	Very often use it
Academic Medical Library	8.33%	8.33%	33.33%	8.33%	16.67%	25.00%
Academic Scientific Library	0.00%	0.00%	10.00%	30.00%	0.00%	60.00%
Non-Educational Medical/Scientific Library	11.11%	33.33%	0.00%	11.11%	11.11%	33.33%

Table 3.16.3 How often do you use Gmail? Broken out by Age range of the survey participant

Age range of the survey participant	No Answer	Never really use it	Seldom use it	Sometimes use it	Often Use it	Very often use it
Under 40	11.11%	0.00%	11.11%	0.00%	11.11%	66.67%
40-59	0.00%	20.00%	20.00%	13.33%	13.33%	33.33%
60 or Over	14.29%	14.29%	14.29%	42.86%	0.00%	14.29%

Table 3.16.4 How often do you use Gmail? Broken out by Work specialization or title of the survey participant

Work specialization or title of the survey participant	No Answer	Never really use it	Seldom use it	Sometimes use it	Often Use it	Very often use it
reference or information literacy	20.00%	0.00%	20.00%	20.00%	0.00%	40.00%
research or subject specialist	0.00%	21.43%	14.29%	14.29%	14.29%	35.71%
other	0.00%	14.29%	14.29%	14.29%	14.29%	42.86%

Table 3.16.5 How often do you use Gmail? Broken out by Compensation range of the survey participant

Compensation range of the survey participant	No Answer	Never really use it	Seldom use it	Sometimes use it	Often Use it	Very often use it
Less than $55,000	14.29%	14.29%	14.29%	14.29%	0.00%	42.86%
$55,000+ to $70,000	7.69%	7.69%	23.08%	7.69%	15.38%	38.46%
More than $70,000	0.00%	18.18%	9.09%	27.27%	9.09%	36.36%

Table 3.16.6 How often do you use Gmail? Broken out by Gender of the survey participant

Gender of the survey participant	No Answer	Never really use it	Seldom use it	Sometimes use it	Often Use it	Very often use it
Male	0.00%	28.57%	14.29%	28.57%	14.29%	14.29%
Female	8.33%	8.33%	16.67%	12.50%	8.33%	45.83%

Table 3.16.7 How often do you use Gmail? Broken out for medical and other scientific libraries

Your main subject focus is:	No Answer	Never really use it	Seldom use it	Sometimes use it	Often Use it	Very often use it
Medical, Biological or Pharmaceutical	9.09%	13.64%	22.73%	9.09%	13.64%	31.82%
Other Scientific	0.00%	11.11%	0.00%	33.33%	0.00%	55.56%

Table 3.17.1 How often do you use Google Earth?

	No Answer	Never really use it	Seldom use it	Sometimes use it	Often Use it	Very often use it
Entire sample	3.23%	22.58%	41.94%	19.35%	9.68%	3.23%

Table 3.17.2 How often do you use Google Earth? Broken out by Type of institution

Type of institution	No Answer	Never really use it	Seldom use it	Sometimes use it	Often Use it	Very often use it
Academic Medical Library	0.00%	16.67%	41.67%	25.00%	16.67%	0.00%
Academic Scientific Library	10.00%	10.00%	60.00%	20.00%	0.00%	0.00%
Non-Educational Medical/Scientific Library	0.00%	44.44%	22.22%	11.11%	11.11%	11.11%

Table 3.17.3 How often do you use Google Earth? Broken out by Age range of the survey participant

Age range of the survey participant	No Answer	Never really use it	Seldom use it	Sometimes use it	Often Use it	Very often use it
Under 40	0.00%	22.22%	66.67%	11.11%	0.00%	0.00%
40-59	6.67%	26.67%	20.00%	33.33%	6.67%	6.67%
60 or Over	0.00%	14.29%	57.14%	0.00%	28.57%	0.00%

Table 3.17.4 How often do you use Google Earth? Broken out by Work specialization or title of the survey participant

Work specialization or title of the survey participant	No Answer	Never really use it	Seldom use it	Sometimes use it	Often Use it	Very often use it
reference or information literacy	10.00%	30.00%	30.00%	10.00%	10.00%	10.00%
research or subject specialist	0.00%	21.43%	50.00%	21.43%	7.14%	0.00%
other	0.00%	14.29%	42.86%	28.57%	14.29%	0.00%

Table 3.17.5 How often do you use Google Earth? Broken out by Compensation range of the survey participant

Compensation range of the survey participant	No Answer	Never really use it	Seldom use it	Sometimes use it	Often Use it	Very often use it
Less than $55,000	14.29%	28.57%	42.86%	14.29%	0.00%	0.00%
$55,000+ to $70,000	0.00%	30.77%	23.08%	23.08%	15.38%	7.69%
More than $70,000	0.00%	9.09%	63.64%	18.18%	9.09%	0.00%

Table 3.17.6 How often do you use Google Earth? Broken out by Gender of the survey participant

Gender of the survey participant	No Answer	Never really use it	Seldom use it	Sometimes use it	Often Use it	Very often use it
Male	0.00%	0.00%	71.43%	28.57%	0.00%	0.00%
Female	4.17%	29.17%	33.33%	16.67%	12.50%	4.17%

Table 3.17.7 How often do you use Google Earth? Broken out for medical and other scientific libraries

Your main subject focus is:	No Answer	Never really use it	Seldom use it	Sometimes use it	Often Use it	Very often use it
Medical, Biological or Pharmaceutical	0.00%	31.82%	36.36%	18.18%	9.09%	4.55%
Other Scientific	11.11%	0.00%	55.56%	22.22%	11.11%	0.00%

Table 3.18.1 How often do you use Google Sky?

	No Answer	Never really use it	Seldom use it	Sometimes use it	Often Use it	Very often use it
Entire sample	3.23%	61.29%	19.35%	9.68%	3.23%	3.23%

Table 3.18.2 How often do you use Google Sky? Broken out by Type of institution

Type of institution	No Answer	Never really use it	Seldom use it	Sometimes use it	Often Use it	Very often use it
Academic Medical Library	0.00%	66.67%	16.67%	16.67%	0.00%	0.00%
Academic Scientific Library	10.00%	40.00%	40.00%	10.00%	0.00%	0.00%
Non-Educational Medical/Scientific Library	0.00%	77.78%	0.00%	0.00%	11.11%	11.11%

Table 3.18.3 How often do you use Google Sky? Broken out by Age range of the survey participant

Age range of the survey participant	No Answer	Never really use it	Seldom use it	Sometimes use it	Often Use it	Very often use it
Under 40	0.00%	55.56%	44.44%	0.00%	0.00%	0.00%
40-59	6.67%	53.33%	6.67%	20.00%	6.67%	6.67%
60 or Over	0.00%	85.71%	14.29%	0.00%	0.00%	0.00%

Table 3.18.4 How often do you use Google Sky? Broken out by Work specialization or title of the survey participant

Work specialization or title of the survey participant	No Answer	Never really use it	Seldom use it	Sometimes use it	Often Use it	Very often use it
reference or information literacy	10.00%	70.00%	10.00%	0.00%	0.00%	10.00%
research or subject specialist	0.00%	64.29%	21.43%	14.29%	0.00%	0.00%
other	0.00%	42.86%	28.57%	14.29%	14.29%	0.00%

Table 3.18.5 How often do you use Google Sky? Broken out by Compensation range of the survey participant

Compensation range of the survey participant	No Answer	Never really use it	Seldom use it	Sometimes use it	Often Use it	Very often use it
Less than $55,000	14.29%	57.14%	14.29%	14.29%	0.00%	0.00%
$55,000+ to $70,000	0.00%	69.23%	15.38%	7.69%	0.00%	7.69%
More than $70,000	0.00%	54.55%	27.27%	9.09%	9.09%	0.00%

Table 3.18.6 How often do you use Google Sky? Broken out by Gender of the survey participant

Gender of the survey participant	No Answer	Never really use it	Seldom use it	Sometimes use it	Often Use it	Very often use it
Male	0.00%	71.43%	14.29%	14.29%	0.00%	0.00%
Female	4.17%	58.33%	20.83%	8.33%	4.17%	4.17%

Table 3.18.7 How often do you use Google Sky? Broken out for medical and other scientific libraries

Your main subject focus is:	No Answer	Never really use it	Seldom use it	Sometimes use it	Often Use it	Very often use it
Medical, Biological or Pharmaceutical	0.00%	77.27%	9.09%	9.09%	0.00%	4.55%
Other Scientific	11.11%	22.22%	44.44%	11.11%	11.11%	0.00%

Table 3.19.1 How often do you use Google+?

	No Answer	Never really use it	Seldom use it	Sometimes use it	Often Use it	Very often use it
Entire sample	3.23%	61.29%	22.58%	3.23%	3.23%	6.45%

Table 3.19.2 How often do you use Google+? Broken out by Type of institution

Type of institution	No Answer	Never really use it	Seldom use it	Sometimes use it	Often Use it	Very often use it
Academic Medical Library	0.00%	50.00%	25.00%	8.33%	8.33%	8.33%
Academic Scientific Library	10.00%	50.00%	40.00%	0.00%	0.00%	0.00%
Non-Educational Medical/Scientific Library	0.00%	88.89%	0.00%	0.00%	0.00%	11.11%

Table 3.19.3 How often do you use Google+? Broken out by Age range of the survey participant

Age range of the survey participant	No Answer	Never really use it	Seldom use it	Sometimes use it	Often Use it	Very often use it
Under 40	0.00%	55.56%	33.33%	0.00%	11.11%	0.00%
40-59	6.67%	66.67%	13.33%	0.00%	0.00%	13.33%
60 or Over	0.00%	57.14%	28.57%	14.29%	0.00%	0.00%

Table 3.19.4 How often do you use Google+? Broken out by Work specialization or title of the survey participant

Work specialization or title of the survey participant	No Answer	Never really use it	Seldom use it	Sometimes use it	Often Use it	Very often use it
reference or information literacy	10.00%	50.00%	20.00%	10.00%	0.00%	10.00%
research or subject specialist	0.00%	71.43%	28.57%	0.00%	0.00%	0.00%
other	0.00%	57.14%	14.29%	0.00%	14.29%	14.29%

Table 3.19.5 How often do you use Google+? Broken out by Compensation range of the survey participant

Compensation range of the survey participant	No Answer	Never really use it	Seldom use it	Sometimes use it	Often Use it	Very often use it
Less than $55,000	14.29%	57.14%	14.29%	0.00%	14.29%	0.00%
$55,000+ to $70,000	0.00%	61.54%	15.38%	7.69%	0.00%	15.38%
More than $70,000	0.00%	63.64%	36.36%	0.00%	0.00%	0.00%

Table 3.19.6 How often do you use Google+? Broken out by Gender of the survey participant

Gender of the survey participant	No Answer	Never really use it	Seldom use it	Sometimes use it	Often Use it	Very often use it
Male	0.00%	100.00%	0.00%	0.00%	0.00%	0.00%
Female	4.17%	50.00%	29.17%	4.17%	4.17%	8.33%

Table 3.19.7 How often do you use Google+? Broken out for medical and other scientific libraries

Your main subject focus is:	No Answer	Never really use it	Seldom use it	Sometimes use it	Often Use it	Very often use it
Medical, Biological or Pharmaceutical	0.00%	63.64%	18.18%	4.55%	4.55%	9.09%
Other Scientific	11.11%	55.56%	33.33%	0.00%	0.00%	0.00%

Table 3.20.1 How often do you use Google Hangouts?

	No Answer	Never really use it	Seldom use it	Sometimes use it	Often Use it	Very often use it
Entire sample	6.45%	67.74%	9.68%	6.45%	6.45%	3.23%

Table 3.20.2 How often do you use Google Hangouts? Broken out by Type of institution

Type of institution	No Answer	Never really use it	Seldom use it	Sometimes use it	Often Use it	Very often use it
Academic Medical Library	8.33%	75.00%	8.33%	0.00%	0.00%	8.33%
Academic Scientific Library	10.00%	50.00%	10.00%	10.00%	20.00%	0.00%
Non-Educational Medical/Scientific Library	0.00%	77.78%	11.11%	11.11%	0.00%	0.00%

Table 3.20.3 How often do you use Google Hangouts? Broken out by Age range of the survey participant

Age range of the survey participant	No Answer	Never really use it	Seldom use it	Sometimes use it	Often Use it	Very often use it
Under 40	0.00%	66.67%	0.00%	11.11%	22.22%	0.00%
40-59	6.67%	66.67%	13.33%	6.67%	0.00%	6.67%
60 or Over	14.29%	71.43%	14.29%	0.00%	0.00%	0.00%

Table 3.20.4 How often do you use Google Hangouts? Broken out by Work specialization or title of the survey participant

Work specialization or title of the survey participant	No Answer	Never really use it	Seldom use it	Sometimes use it	Often Use it	Very often use it
reference or information literacy	20.00%	50.00%	20.00%	0.00%	10.00%	0.00%
research or subject specialist	0.00%	78.57%	7.14%	7.14%	7.14%	0.00%
other	0.00%	71.43%	0.00%	14.29%	0.00%	14.29%

Table 3.20.5 How often do you use Google Hangouts? Broken out by Compensation range of the survey participant

Compensation range of the survey participant	No Answer	Never really use it	Seldom use it	Sometimes use it	Often Use it	Very often use it
Less than $55,000	14.29%	71.43%	0.00%	0.00%	14.29%	0.00%
$55,000+ to $70,000	7.69%	61.54%	15.38%	0.00%	7.69%	7.69%
More than $70,000	0.00%	72.73%	9.09%	18.18%	0.00%	0.00%

Table 3.20.6 How often do you use Google Hangouts? Broken out by Gender of the survey participant

Gender of the survey participant	No Answer	Never really use it	Seldom use it	Sometimes use it	Often Use it	Very often use it
Male	0.00%	100.00%	0.00%	0.00%	0.00%	0.00%
Female	8.33%	58.33%	12.50%	8.33%	8.33%	4.17%

Table 3.20.7 How often do you use Google Hangouts? Broken out for medical and other scientific libraries

Your main subject focus is:	No Answer	Never really use it	Seldom use it	Sometimes use it	Often Use it	Very often use it
Medical, Biological or Pharmaceutical	4.55%	77.27%	9.09%	0.00%	4.55%	4.55%
Other Scientific	11.11%	44.44%	11.11%	22.22%	11.11%	0.00%

Table 3.21.1 How often do you use Google Bookmarks?

	No Answer	Never really use it	Seldom use it	Sometimes use it	Often Use it	Very often use it
Entire sample	3.23%	70.97%	9.68%	12.90%	0.00%	3.23%

Table 3.21.2 How often do you use Google Bookmarks? Broken out by Type of institution

Type of institution	No Answer	Never really use it	Seldom use it	Sometimes use it	Often Use it	Very often use it
Academic Medical Library	0.00%	66.67%	16.67%	16.67%	0.00%	0.00%
Academic Scientific Library	10.00%	80.00%	10.00%	0.00%	0.00%	0.00%
Non-Educational Medical/Scientific Library	0.00%	66.67%	0.00%	22.22%	0.00%	11.11%

Table 3.21.3 How often do you use Google Bookmarks? Broken out by Age range of the survey participant

Age range of the survey participant	No Answer	Never really use it	Seldom use it	Sometimes use it	Often Use it	Very often use it
Under 40	0.00%	88.89%	11.11%	0.00%	0.00%	0.00%
40-59	6.67%	60.00%	6.67%	20.00%	0.00%	6.67%
60 or Over	0.00%	71.43%	14.29%	14.29%	0.00%	0.00%

Table 3.21.4 How often do you use Google Bookmarks? Broken out by Work specialization or title of the survey participant

Work specialization or title of the survey participant	No Answer	Never really use it	Seldom use it	Sometimes use it	Often Use it	Very often use it
reference or information literacy	10.00%	60.00%	20.00%	0.00%	0.00%	10.00%
research or subject specialist	0.00%	92.86%	0.00%	7.14%	0.00%	0.00%
other	0.00%	42.86%	14.29%	42.86%	0.00%	0.00%

Table 3.21.5 How often do you use Google Bookmarks? Broken out by Compensation range of the survey participant

Compensation range of the survey participant	No Answer	Never really use it	Seldom use it	Sometimes use it	Often Use it	Very often use it
Less than $55,000	14.29%	71.43%	14.29%	0.00%	0.00%	0.00%
$55,000+ to $70,000	0.00%	69.23%	15.38%	7.69%	0.00%	7.69%
More than $70,000	0.00%	72.73%	0.00%	27.27%	0.00%	0.00%

Table 3.21.6 How often do you use Google Bookmarks? Broken out by Gender of the survey participant

Gender of the survey participant	No Answer	Never really use it	Seldom use it	Sometimes use it	Often Use it	Very often use it
Male	0.00%	100.00%	0.00%	0.00%	0.00%	0.00%
Female	4.17%	62.50%	12.50%	16.67%	0.00%	4.17%

Table 3.21.7 How often do you use Google Bookmarks? Broken out for medical and other scientific libraries

Your main subject focus is:	No Answer	Never really use it	Seldom use it	Sometimes use it	Often Use it	Very often use it
Medical, Biological or Pharmaceutical	0.00%	68.18%	13.64%	13.64%	0.00%	4.55%
Other Scientific	11.11%	77.78%	0.00%	11.11%	0.00%	0.00%

Table 3.22.1 How often do you use Google Patent Search?

	Never really use it	Seldom use it	Sometimes use it	Often Use it	Very often use it
Entire sample	67.74%	6.45%	16.13%	6.45%	3.23%

Table 3.22.2 How often do you use Google Patent Search? Broken out by Type of institution

Type of institution	Never really use it	Seldom use it	Sometimes use it	Often Use it	Very often use it
Academic Medical Library	83.33%	8.33%	8.33%	0.00%	0.00%
Academic Scientific Library	60.00%	0.00%	20.00%	10.00%	10.00%
Non-Educational Medical/Scientific Library	55.56%	11.11%	22.22%	11.11%	0.00%

Table 3.22.3 How often do you use Google Patent Search? Broken out by Age range of the survey participant

Age range of the survey participant	Never really use it	Seldom use it	Sometimes use it	Often Use it	Very often use it
Under 40	77.78%	0.00%	11.11%	0.00%	11.11%
40-59	60.00%	6.67%	20.00%	13.33%	0.00%
60 or Over	71.43%	14.29%	14.29%	0.00%	0.00%

Table 3.22.4 How often do you use Google Patent Search? Broken out by Work specialization or title of the survey participant

Work specialization or title of the survey participant	Never really use it	Seldom use it	Sometimes use it	Often Use it	Very often use it
reference or information literacy	70.00%	0.00%	10.00%	20.00%	0.00%
research or subject specialist	57.14%	14.29%	21.43%	0.00%	7.14%
other	85.71%	0.00%	14.29%	0.00%	0.00%

Table 3.22.5 How often do you use Google Patent Search? Broken out by Compensation range of the survey participant

Compensation range of the survey participant	Never really use it	Seldom use it	Sometimes use it	Often Use it	Very often use it
Less than $55,000	42.86%	14.29%	28.57%	14.29%	0.00%
$55,000+ to $70,000	69.23%	7.69%	7.69%	7.69%	7.69%
More than $70,000	81.82%	0.00%	18.18%	0.00%	0.00%

Table 3.22.6 How often do you use Google Patent Search? Broken out by Gender of the survey participant

Gender of the survey participant	Never really use it	Seldom use it	Sometimes use it	Often Use it	Very often use it
Male	71.43%	0.00%	28.57%	0.00%	0.00%
Female	66.67%	8.33%	12.50%	8.33%	4.17%

Table 3.22.7 How often do you use Google Patent Search? Broken out for medical and other scientific libraries

Your main subject focus is:	Never really use it	Seldom use it	Sometimes use it	Often Use it	Very often use it
Medical, Biological or Pharmaceutical	72.73%	9.09%	13.64%	4.55%	0.00%
Other Scientific	55.56%	0.00%	22.22%	11.11%	11.11%

Table 3.23.1 How often do you use Google Forms?

	No Answer	Never really use it	Seldom use it	Sometimes use it	Often Use it	Very often use it
Entire sample	6.45%	58.06%	12.90%	6.45%	6.45%	9.68%

Table 3.23.2 How often do you use Google Forms? Broken out by Type of institution

Type of institution	No Answer	Never really use it	Seldom use it	Sometimes use it	Often Use it	Very often use it
Academic Medical Library	0.00%	66.67%	8.33%	16.67%	0.00%	8.33%
Academic Scientific Library	20.00%	20.00%	30.00%	0.00%	20.00%	10.00%
Non-Educational Medical/Scientific Library	0.00%	88.89%	0.00%	0.00%	0.00%	11.11%

Table 3.23.3 How often do you use Google Forms? Broken out by Age range of the survey participant

Age range of the survey participant	No Answer	Never really use it	Seldom use it	Sometimes use it	Often Use it	Very often use it
Under 40	11.11%	33.33%	33.33%	0.00%	0.00%	22.22%
40-59	6.67%	53.33%	6.67%	13.33%	13.33%	6.67%
60 or Over	0.00%	100.00%	0.00%	0.00%	0.00%	0.00%

Table 3.23.4 How often do you use Google Forms? Broken out by Work specialization or title of the survey participant

Work specialization or title of the survey participant	No Answer	Never really use it	Seldom use it	Sometimes use it	Often Use it	Very often use it
reference or information literacy	10.00%	70.00%	0.00%	0.00%	10.00%	10.00%
research or subject specialist	7.14%	42.86%	28.57%	7.14%	7.14%	7.14%
other	0.00%	71.43%	0.00%	14.29%	0.00%	14.29%

Table 3.23.5 How often do you use Google Forms? Broken out by Compensation range of the survey participant

Compensation range of the survey participant	No Answer	Never really use it	Seldom use it	Sometimes use it	Often Use it	Very often use it
Less than $55,000	28.57%	42.86%	0.00%	0.00%	14.29%	14.29%
$55,000+ to $70,000	0.00%	61.54%	15.38%	7.69%	7.69%	7.69%
More than $70,000	0.00%	63.64%	18.18%	9.09%	0.00%	9.09%

Table 3.23.6 How often do you use Google Forms? Broken out by Gender of the survey participant

Gender of the survey participant	No Answer	Never really use it	Seldom use it	Sometimes use it	Often Use it	Very often use it
Male	14.29%	57.14%	14.29%	14.29%	0.00%	0.00%
Female	4.17%	58.33%	12.50%	4.17%	8.33%	12.50%

Table 3.23.7 How often do you use Google Forms? Broken out for medical and other scientific libraries

Your main subject focus is:	No Answer	Never really use it	Seldom use it	Sometimes use it	Often Use it	Very often use it
Medical, Biological or Pharmaceutical	4.55%	68.18%	4.55%	9.09%	4.55%	9.09%
Other Scientific	11.11%	33.33%	33.33%	0.00%	11.11%	11.11%

Table 3.24.1 How often do you use Google Slides?

	Never really use it	Seldom use it	Sometimes use it	Often Use it	Very often use it
Entire sample	70.97%	9.68%	9.68%	3.23%	6.45%

Table 3.24.2 How often do you use Google Slides? Broken out by Type of institution

Type of institution	Never really use it	Seldom use it	Sometimes use it	Often Use it	Very often use it
Academic Medical Library	83.33%	0.00%	16.67%	0.00%	0.00%
Academic Scientific Library	50.00%	10.00%	10.00%	10.00%	20.00%
Non-Educational Medical/Scientific Library	77.78%	22.22%	0.00%	0.00%	0.00%

Table 3.24.3 How often do you use Google Slides? Broken out by Age range of the survey participant

Age range of the survey participant	Never really use it	Seldom use it	Sometimes use it	Often Use it	Very often use it
Under 40	55.56%	11.11%	11.11%	0.00%	22.22%
40-59	73.33%	6.67%	13.33%	6.67%	0.00%
60 or Over	85.71%	14.29%	0.00%	0.00%	0.00%

Table 3.24.4 How often do you use Google Slides? Broken out by Work specialization or title of the survey participant

Work specialization or title of the survey participant	Never really use it	Seldom use it	Sometimes use it	Often Use it	Very often use it
reference or information literacy	60.00%	20.00%	10.00%	10.00%	0.00%
research or subject specialist	71.43%	7.14%	7.14%	0.00%	14.29%
other	85.71%	0.00%	14.29%	0.00%	0.00%

Table 3.24.5 How often do you use Google Slides? Broken out by Compensation range of the survey participant

Compensation range of the survey participant	Never really use it	Seldom use it	Sometimes use it	Often Use it	Very often use it
Less than $55,000	57.14%	14.29%	14.29%	14.29%	0.00%
$55,000+ to $70,000	76.92%	7.69%	7.69%	0.00%	7.69%
More than $70,000	72.73%	9.09%	9.09%	0.00%	9.09%

Table 3.24.6 How often do you use Google Slides? Broken out by Gender of the survey participant

Gender of the survey participant	Never really use it	Seldom use it	Sometimes use it	Often Use it	Very often use it
Male	85.71%	0.00%	14.29%	0.00%	0.00%
Female	66.67%	12.50%	8.33%	4.17%	8.33%

Table 3.24.7 How often do you use Google Slides? Broken out for medical and other scientific libraries

Your main subject focus is:	Never really use it	Seldom use it	Sometimes use it	Often Use it	Very often use it
Medical, Biological or Pharmaceutical	77.27%	9.09%	13.64%	0.00%	0.00%
Other Scientific	55.56%	11.11%	0.00%	11.11%	22.22%

Table 3.25.1 How often do you use Google Groups?

	No Answer	Never really use it	Seldom use it	Sometimes use it	Often Use it	Very often use it
Entire sample	6.45%	54.84%	19.35%	12.90%	3.23%	3.23%

Table 3.25.2 How often do you use Google Groups? Broken out by Type of institution

Type of institution	No Answer	Never really use it	Seldom use it	Sometimes use it	Often Use it	Very often use it
Academic Medical Library	0.00%	58.33%	33.33%	8.33%	0.00%	0.00%
Academic Scientific Library	20.00%	40.00%	20.00%	0.00%	10.00%	10.00%
Non-Educational Medical/Scientific Library	0.00%	66.67%	0.00%	33.33%	0.00%	0.00%

Table 3.25.3 How often do you use Google Groups? Broken out by Age range of the survey participant

Age range of the survey participant	No Answer	Never really use it	Seldom use it	Sometimes use it	Often Use it	Very often use it
Under 40	0.00%	55.56%	33.33%	0.00%	0.00%	11.11%
40-59	6.67%	60.00%	13.33%	13.33%	6.67%	0.00%
60 or Over	14.29%	42.86%	14.29%	28.57%	0.00%	0.00%

Table 3.25.4 How often do you use Google Groups? Broken out by Work specialization or title of the survey participant

Work specialization or title of the survey participant	No Answer	Never really use it	Seldom use it	Sometimes use it	Often Use it	Very often use it
reference or information literacy	20.00%	50.00%	10.00%	20.00%	0.00%	0.00%
research or subject specialist	0.00%	57.14%	28.57%	0.00%	7.14%	7.14%
other	0.00%	57.14%	14.29%	28.57%	0.00%	0.00%

Table 3.25.5 How often do you use Google Groups? Broken out by Compensation range of the survey participant

Compensation range of the survey participant	No Answer	Never really use it	Seldom use it	Sometimes use it	Often Use it	Very often use it
Less than $55,000	14.29%	57.14%	0.00%	14.29%	14.29%	0.00%
$55,000+ to $70,000	0.00%	61.54%	23.08%	7.69%	0.00%	7.69%
More than $70,000	9.09%	45.45%	27.27%	18.18%	0.00%	0.00%

Table 3.25.6 How often do you use Google Groups? Broken out by Gender of the survey participant

Gender of the survey participant	No Answer	Never really use it	Seldom use it	Sometimes use it	Often Use it	Very often use it
Male	14.29%	42.86%	28.57%	0.00%	14.29%	0.00%
Female	4.17%	58.33%	16.67%	16.67%	0.00%	4.17%

Table 3.25.7 How often do you use Google Groups? Broken out for medical and other scientific libraries

Your main subject focus is:	No Answer	Never really use it	Seldom use it	Sometimes use it	Often Use it	Very often use it
Medical, Biological or Pharmaceutical	0.00%	68.18%	18.18%	13.64%	0.00%	0.00%
Other Scientific	22.22%	22.22%	22.22%	11.11%	11.11%	11.11%

Table 3.26.1 How often do you use Google Analytics?

	No Answer	Never really use it	Seldom use it	Sometimes use it	Often Use it	Very often use it
Entire sample	3.23%	45.16%	22.58%	25.81%	0.00%	3.23%

Table 3.26.2 How often do you use Google Analytics? Broken out by Type of institution

Type of institution	No Answer	Never really use it	Seldom use it	Sometimes use it	Often Use it	Very often use it
Academic Medical Library	0.00%	41.67%	25.00%	33.33%	0.00%	0.00%
Academic Scientific Library	10.00%	30.00%	40.00%	20.00%	0.00%	0.00%
Non-Educational Medical/Scientific Library	0.00%	66.67%	0.00%	22.22%	0.00%	11.11%

Table 3.26.3 How often do you use Google Analytics? Broken out by Age range of the survey participant

Age range of the survey participant	No Answer	Never really use it	Seldom use it	Sometimes use it	Often Use it	Very often use it
Under 40	0.00%	22.22%	66.67%	11.11%	0.00%	0.00%
40-59	6.67%	53.33%	6.67%	26.67%	0.00%	6.67%
60 or Over	0.00%	57.14%	0.00%	42.86%	0.00%	0.00%

Table 3.26.4 How often do you use Google Analytics? Broken out by Work specialization or title of the survey participant

Work specialization or title of the survey participant	No Answer	Never really use it	Seldom use it	Sometimes use it	Often Use it	Very often use it
reference or information literacy	10.00%	60.00%	10.00%	10.00%	0.00%	10.00%
research or subject specialist	0.00%	28.57%	28.57%	42.86%	0.00%	0.00%
other	0.00%	57.14%	28.57%	14.29%	0.00%	0.00%

Table 3.26.5 How often do you use Google Analytics? Broken out by Compensation range of the survey participant

Compensation range of the survey participant	No Answer	Never really use it	Seldom use it	Sometimes use it	Often Use it	Very often use it
Less than $55,000	14.29%	42.86%	28.57%	14.29%	0.00%	0.00%
$55,000+ to $70,000	0.00%	38.46%	30.77%	23.08%	0.00%	7.69%
More than $70,000	0.00%	54.55%	9.09%	36.36%	0.00%	0.00%

Table 3.26.6 How often do you use Google Analytics? Broken out by Gender of the survey participant

Gender of the survey participant	No Answer	Never really use it	Seldom use it	Sometimes use it	Often Use it	Very often use it
Male	0.00%	28.57%	28.57%	42.86%	0.00%	0.00%
Female	4.17%	50.00%	20.83%	20.83%	0.00%	4.17%

Table 3.26.7 How often do you use Google Analytics? Broken out for medical and other scientific libraries

Your main subject focus is:	No Answer	Never really use it	Seldom use it	Sometimes use it	Often Use it	Very often use it
Medical, Biological or Pharmaceutical	0.00%	54.55%	18.18%	22.73%	0.00%	4.55%
Other Scientific	11.11%	22.22%	33.33%	33.33%	0.00%	0.00%

Table 3.27.1 How often do you use AdWords?

	No Answer	Never really use it	Seldom use it	Sometimes use it	Often Use it	Very often use it
Entire sample	3.23%	96.77%	0.00%	0.00%	0.00%	0.00%

Table 3.27.2 How often do you use AdWords? Broken out by Type of institution

Type of institution	No Answer	Never really use it	Seldom use it	Sometimes use it	Often Use it	Very often use it
Academic Medical Library	0.00%	100.00%	0.00%	0.00%	0.00%	0.00%
Academic Scientific Library	10.00%	90.00%	0.00%	0.00%	0.00%	0.00%
Non-Educational Medical/Scientific Library	0.00%	100.00%	0.00%	0.00%	0.00%	0.00%

Table 3.27.3 How often do you use AdWords? Broken out by Age range of the survey participant

Age range of the survey participant	No Answer	Never really use it	Seldom use it	Sometimes use it	Often Use it	Very often use it
Under 40	0.00%	100.00%	0.00%	0.00%	0.00%	0.00%
40-59	6.67%	93.33%	0.00%	0.00%	0.00%	0.00%
60 or Over	0.00%	100.00%	0.00%	0.00%	0.00%	0.00%

Table 3.27.4 How often do you use AdWords? Broken out by Work specialization or title of the survey participant

Work specialization or title of the survey participant	No Answer	Never really use it	Seldom use it	Sometimes use it	Often Use it	Very often use it
reference or information literacy	10.00%	90.00%	0.00%	0.00%	0.00%	0.00%
research or subject specialist	0.00%	100.00%	0.00%	0.00%	0.00%	0.00%
other	0.00%	100.00%	0.00%	0.00%	0.00%	0.00%

Table 3.27.5 How often do you use AdWords? Broken out by Compensation range of the survey participant

Compensation range of the survey participant	No Answer	Never really use it	Seldom use it	Sometimes use it	Often Use it	Very often use it
Less than $55,000	14.29%	85.71%	0.00%	0.00%	0.00%	0.00%
$55,000+ to $70,000	0.00%	100.00%	0.00%	0.00%	0.00%	0.00%
More than $70,000	0.00%	100.00%	0.00%	0.00%	0.00%	0.00%

Table 3.27.6 How often do you use AdWords? Broken out by Gender of the survey participant

Gender of the survey participant	No Answer	Never really use it	Seldom use it	Sometimes use it	Often Use it	Very often use it
Male	0.00%	100.00%	0.00%	0.00%	0.00%	0.00%
Female	4.17%	95.83%	0.00%	0.00%	0.00%	0.00%

Table 3.27.7 How often do you use AdWords? Broken out for medical and other scientific libraries

Your main subject focus is:	No Answer	Never really use it	Seldom use it	Sometimes use it	Often Use it	Very often use it
Medical, Biological or Pharmaceutical	0.00%	100.00%	0.00%	0.00%	0.00%	0.00%
Other Scientific	11.11%	88.89%	0.00%	0.00%	0.00%	0.00%

Table 3.28.1 How often do you use AdSense?

	No Answer	Never really use it	Seldom use it	Sometimes use it	Often Use it	Very often use it
Entire sample	3.23%	96.77%	0.00%	0.00%	0.00%	0.00%

Table 3.28.2 How often do you use AdSense? Broken out by Type of institution

Type of institution	No Answer	Never really use it	Seldom use it	Sometimes use it	Often Use it	Very often use it
Academic Medical Library	0.00%	100.00%	0.00%	0.00%	0.00%	0.00%
Academic Scientific Library	10.00%	90.00%	0.00%	0.00%	0.00%	0.00%
Non-Educational Medical/Scientific Library	0.00%	100.00%	0.00%	0.00%	0.00%	0.00%

Table 3.28.3 How often do you use AdSense? Broken out by Age range of the survey participant

Age range of the survey participant	No Answer	Never really use it	Seldom use it	Sometimes use it	Often Use it	Very often use it
Under 40	0.00%	100.00%	0.00%	0.00%	0.00%	0.00%
40-59	6.67%	93.33%	0.00%	0.00%	0.00%	0.00%
60 or Over	0.00%	100.00%	0.00%	0.00%	0.00%	0.00%

Table 3.28.4 How often do you use AdSense? Broken out by Work specialization or title of the survey participant

Work specialization or title of the survey participant	No Answer	Never really use it	Seldom use it	Sometimes use it	Often Use it	Very often use it
reference or information literacy	10.00%	90.00%	0.00%	0.00%	0.00%	0.00%
research or subject specialist	0.00%	100.00%	0.00%	0.00%	0.00%	0.00%
other	0.00%	100.00%	0.00%	0.00%	0.00%	0.00%

Table 3.28.5 How often do you use AdSense? Broken out by Compensation range of the survey participant

Compensation range of the survey participant	No Answer	Never really use it	Seldom use it	Sometimes use it	Often Use it	Very often use it
Less than $55,000	14.29%	85.71%	0.00%	0.00%	0.00%	0.00%
$55,000+ to $70,000	0.00%	100.00%	0.00%	0.00%	0.00%	0.00%
More than $70,000	0.00%	100.00%	0.00%	0.00%	0.00%	0.00%

Table 3.28.6 How often do you use AdSense? Broken out by Gender of the survey participant

Gender of the survey participant	No Answer	Never really use it	Seldom use it	Sometimes use it	Often Use it	Very often use it
Male	0.00%	100.00%	0.00%	0.00%	0.00%	0.00%
Female	4.17%	95.83%	0.00%	0.00%	0.00%	0.00%

Table 3.28.7 How often do you use AdSense? Broken out for medical and other scientific libraries

Your main subject focus is:	No Answer	Never really use it	Seldom use it	Sometimes use it	Often Use it	Very often use it
Medical, Biological or Pharmaceutical	0.00%	100.00%	0.00%	0.00%	0.00%	0.00%
Other Scientific	11.11%	88.89%	0.00%	0.00%	0.00%	0.00%

Table 3.29.1 How often do you use Blogger?

	No Answer	Never really use it	Seldom use it	Sometimes use it	Often Use it	Very often use it
Entire sample	3.23%	90.32%	3.23%	0.00%	3.23%	0.00%

Table 3.29.2 How often do you use Blogger? Broken out by Type of institution

Type of institution	No Answer	Never really use it	Seldom use it	Sometimes use it	Often Use it	Very often use it
Academic Medical Library	0.00%	91.67%	8.33%	0.00%	0.00%	0.00%
Academic Scientific Library	10.00%	90.00%	0.00%	0.00%	0.00%	0.00%
Non-Educational Medical/Scientific Library	0.00%	88.89%	0.00%	0.00%	11.11%	0.00%

Table 3.29.3 How often do you use Blogger? Broken out by Age range of the survey participant

Age range of the survey participant	No Answer	Never really use it	Seldom use it	Sometimes use it	Often Use it	Very often use it
Under 40	0.00%	100.00%	0.00%	0.00%	0.00%	0.00%
40-59	6.67%	80.00%	6.67%	0.00%	6.67%	0.00%
60 or Over	0.00%	100.00%	0.00%	0.00%	0.00%	0.00%

Table 3.29.4 How often do you use Blogger? Broken out by Work specialization or title of the survey participant

Work specialization or title of the survey participant	No Answer	Never really use it	Seldom use it	Sometimes use it	Often Use it	Very often use it
reference or information literacy	10.00%	80.00%	0.00%	0.00%	10.00%	0.00%
research or subject specialist	0.00%	100.00%	0.00%	0.00%	0.00%	0.00%
other	0.00%	85.71%	14.29%	0.00%	0.00%	0.00%

Table 3.29.5 How often do you use Blogger? Broken out by Compensation range of the survey participant

Compensation range of the survey participant	No Answer	Never really use it	Seldom use it	Sometimes use it	Often Use it	Very often use it
Less than $55,000	14.29%	85.71%	0.00%	0.00%	0.00%	0.00%
$55,000+ to $70,000	0.00%	92.31%	0.00%	0.00%	7.69%	0.00%
More than $70,000	0.00%	90.91%	9.09%	0.00%	0.00%	0.00%

Table 3.29.6 How often do you use Blogger? Broken out by Gender of the survey participant

Gender of the survey participant	No Answer	Never really use it	Seldom use it	Sometimes use it	Often Use it	Very often use it
Male	0.00%	100.00%	0.00%	0.00%	0.00%	0.00%
Female	4.17%	87.50%	4.17%	0.00%	4.17%	0.00%

Table 3.29.7 How often do you use Blogger? Broken out for medical and other scientific libraries

Your main subject focus is:	No Answer	Never really use it	Seldom use it	Sometimes use it	Often Use it	Very often use it
Medical, Biological or Pharmaceutical	0.00%	90.91%	4.55%	0.00%	4.55%	0.00%
Other Scientific	11.11%	88.89%	0.00%	0.00%	0.00%	0.00%

Table 3.30.1 How often do you use YouTube?

	No Answer	Never really use it	Seldom use it	Sometimes use it	Often Use it	Very often use it
Entire sample	3.23%	0.00%	16.13%	35.48%	25.81%	19.35%

Table 3.30.2 How often do you use YouTube? Broken out by Type of institution

Type of institution	No Answer	Never really use it	Seldom use it	Sometimes use it	Often Use it	Very often use it
Academic Medical Library	0.00%	0.00%	25.00%	25.00%	33.33%	16.67%
Academic Scientific Library	10.00%	0.00%	10.00%	40.00%	20.00%	20.00%
Non-Educational Medical/Scientific Library	0.00%	0.00%	11.11%	44.44%	22.22%	22.22%

Table 3.30.3 How often do you use YouTube? Broken out by Age range of the survey participant

Age range of the survey participant	No Answer	Never really use it	Seldom use it	Sometimes use it	Often Use it	Very often use it
Under 40	0.00%	0.00%	11.11%	22.22%	33.33%	33.33%
40-59	6.67%	0.00%	13.33%	33.33%	26.67%	20.00%
60 or Over	0.00%	0.00%	28.57%	57.14%	14.29%	0.00%

Table 3.30.4 How often do you use YouTube? Broken out by Work specialization or title of the survey participant

Work specialization or title of the survey participant	No Answer	Never really use it	Seldom use it	Sometimes use it	Often Use it	Very often use it
reference or information literacy	10.00%	0.00%	20.00%	30.00%	10.00%	30.00%
research or subject specialist	0.00%	0.00%	14.29%	35.71%	35.71%	14.29%
other	0.00%	0.00%	14.29%	42.86%	28.57%	14.29%

Table 3.30.5 How often do you use YouTube? Broken out by Compensation range of the survey participant

Compensation range of the survey participant	No Answer	Never really use it	Seldom use it	Sometimes use it	Often Use it	Very often use it
Less than $55,000	14.29%	0.00%	0.00%	28.57%	28.57%	28.57%
$55,000+ to $70,000	0.00%	0.00%	7.69%	30.77%	38.46%	23.08%
More than $70,000	0.00%	0.00%	36.36%	45.45%	9.09%	9.09%

Table 3.30.6 How often do you use YouTube? Broken out by Gender of the survey participant

Gender of the survey participant	No Answer	Never really use it	Seldom use it	Sometimes use it	Often Use it	Very often use it
Male	0.00%	0.00%	14.29%	42.86%	42.86%	0.00%
Female	4.17%	0.00%	16.67%	33.33%	20.83%	25.00%

Table 3.30.7 How often do you use YouTube? Broken out for medical and other scientific libraries

Your main subject focus is:	No Answer	Never really use it	Seldom use it	Sometimes use it	Often Use it	Very often use it
Medical, Biological or Pharmaceutical	0.00%	0.00%	18.18%	31.82%	31.82%	18.18%
Other Scientific	11.11%	0.00%	11.11%	44.44%	11.11%	22.22%

Table 4 When you do use the following features of Google how useful are they to you?

Table 4.1.1 When you do use Google Maps how useful is it to you?

	No Answer	Don't use this at all	Not very useful	Somewhat useful	Useful	Quite useful	Essential
Entire sample	3.23%	9.68%	0.00%	0.00%	9.68%	48.39%	29.03%

Table 4.1.2 When you do use Google Maps how useful is it to you? Broken out by Type of institution

Type of institution	No Answer	Don't use this at all	Not very useful	Somewhat useful	Useful	Quite useful	Essential
Academic Medical Library	0.00%	8.33%	0.00%	0.00%	0.00%	50.00%	41.67%
Academic Scientific Library	10.00%	0.00%	0.00%	0.00%	10.00%	60.00%	20.00%
Non-Educational Medical/Scientific Library	0.00%	22.22%	0.00%	0.00%	22.22%	33.33%	22.22%

Table 4.1.3 When you do use Google Maps how useful is it to you? Broken out by Age range of the survey participant

Age range of the survey participant	No Answer	Don't use this at all	Not very useful	Somewhat useful	Useful	Quite useful	Essential
Under 40	0.00%	11.11%	0.00%	0.00%	11.11%	44.44%	33.33%
40-59	6.67%	13.33%	0.00%	0.00%	6.67%	40.00%	33.33%
60 or Over	0.00%	0.00%	0.00%	0.00%	14.29%	71.43%	14.29%

Table 4.1.4 When you do use Google Maps how useful is it to you? Broken out by Work specialization or title of the survey participant

Work specialization or title of the survey participant	No Answer	Don't use this at all	Not very useful	Somewhat useful	Useful	Quite useful	Essential
reference or information literacy	10.00%	20.00%	0.00%	0.00%	10.00%	20.00%	40.00%
research or subject specialist	0.00%	7.14%	0.00%	0.00%	14.29%	57.14%	21.43%
other	0.00%	0.00%	0.00%	0.00%	0.00%	71.43%	28.57%

Table 4.1.5 When you do use Google Maps how useful is it to you? Broken out by Compensation range of the survey participant

Compensation range of the survey participant	No Answer	Don't use this at all	Not very useful	Somewhat useful	Useful	Quite useful	Essential
Less than $55,000	14.29%	14.29%	0.00%	0.00%	28.57%	0.00%	42.86%
$55,000+ to $70,000	0.00%	15.38%	0.00%	0.00%	7.69%	46.15%	30.77%
More than $70,000	0.00%	0.00%	0.00%	0.00%	0.00%	81.82%	18.18%

Table 4.1.6 When you do use Google Maps how useful is it to you? Broken out by Gender of the survey participant

Gender of the survey participant	No Answer	Don't use this at all	Not very useful	Somewhat useful	Useful	Quite useful	Essential
Male	0.00%	0.00%	0.00%	0.00%	14.29%	57.14%	28.57%
Female	4.17%	12.50%	0.00%	0.00%	8.33%	45.83%	29.17%

Table 4.1.7 When you do use Google Maps how useful is it to you? Broken out for medical and other scientific libraries

Your main subject focus is:	No Answer	Don't use this at all	Not very useful	Somewhat useful	Useful	Quite useful	Essential
Medical, Biological or Pharmaceutical	0.00%	13.64%	0.00%	0.00%	9.09%	40.91%	36.36%
Other Scientific	11.11%	0.00%	0.00%	0.00%	11.11%	66.67%	11.11%

Table 4.2.1 When you do use Google Advanced Search how useful is it to you?

	Don't use this at all	Not very useful	Somewhat useful	Useful	Quite useful	Essential
Entire sample	3.23%	9.68%	6.45%	29.03%	35.48%	16.13%

Table 4.2.2 When you do use Google Advanced Search how useful is it to you? Broken out by Type of institution

Type of institution	Don't use this at all	Not very useful	Somewhat useful	Useful	Quite useful	Essential
Academic Medical Library	0.00%	8.33%	0.00%	33.33%	41.67%	16.67%
Academic Scientific Library	0.00%	20.00%	10.00%	30.00%	40.00%	0.00%
Non-Educational Medical/Scientific Library	11.11%	0.00%	11.11%	22.22%	22.22%	33.33%

Table 4.2.3 When you do use Google Advanced Search how useful is it to you? Broken out by Age range of the survey participant

Age range of the survey participant	Don't use this at all	Not very useful	Somewhat useful	Useful	Quite useful	Essential
Under 40	0.00%	22.22%	11.11%	55.56%	11.11%	0.00%
40-59	0.00%	0.00%	0.00%	20.00%	46.67%	33.33%
60 or Over	14.29%	14.29%	14.29%	14.29%	42.86%	0.00%

Table 4.2.4 When you do use Google Advanced Search how useful is it to you? Broken out by Work specialization or title of the survey participant

Work specialization or title of the survey participant	Don't use this at all	Not very useful	Somewhat useful	Useful	Quite useful	Essential
reference or information literacy	0.00%	20.00%	10.00%	0.00%	40.00%	30.00%
research or subject specialist	0.00%	7.14%	7.14%	50.00%	28.57%	7.14%
other	14.29%	0.00%	0.00%	28.57%	42.86%	14.29%

Table 4.2.5 When you do use Google Advanced Search how useful is it to you? Broken out by Compensation range of the survey participant

Compensation range of the survey participant	Don't use this at all	Not very useful	Somewhat useful	Useful	Quite useful	Essential
Less than $55,000	0.00%	0.00%	14.29%	28.57%	28.57%	28.57%
$55,000+ to $70,000	0.00%	15.38%	7.69%	23.08%	30.77%	23.08%
More than $70,000	9.09%	9.09%	0.00%	36.36%	45.45%	0.00%

Table 4.2.6 When you do use Google Advanced Search how useful is it to you? Broken out by Gender of the survey participant

Gender of the survey participant	Don't use this at all	Not very useful	Somewhat useful	Useful	Quite useful	Essential
Male	0.00%	14.29%	14.29%	42.86%	28.57%	0.00%
Female	4.17%	8.33%	4.17%	25.00%	37.50%	20.83%

Table 4.2.7 When you do use Google Advanced Search how useful is it to you? Broken out for medical and other scientific libraries

Your main subject focus is:	Don't use this at all	Not very useful	Somewhat useful	Useful	Quite useful	Essential
Medical, Biological or Pharmaceutical	4.55%	4.55%	4.55%	27.27%	36.36%	22.73%
Other Scientific	0.00%	22.22%	11.11%	33.33%	33.33%	0.00%

Table 4.3.1 When you do use Google Alerts how useful is it to you?

	No Answer	Don't use this at all	Not very useful	Somewhat useful	Useful	Quite useful	Essential
Entire sample	6.45%	58.06%	3.23%	6.45%	22.58%	3.23%	0.00%

Table 4.3.2 When you do use Google Alerts how useful is it to you? Broken out by Type of institution

Type of institution	No Answer	Don't use this at all	Not very useful	Somewhat useful	Useful	Quite useful	Essential
Academic Medical Library	0.00%	50.00%	0.00%	8.33%	41.67%	0.00%	0.00%
Academic Scientific Library	20.00%	50.00%	10.00%	0.00%	10.00%	10.00%	0.00%
Non-Educational Medical/Scientific Library	0.00%	77.78%	0.00%	11.11%	11.11%	0.00%	0.00%

Table 4.3.3 When you do use Google Alerts how useful is it to you? Broken out by Age range of the survey participant

Age range of the survey participant	No Answer	Don't use this at all	Not very useful	Somewhat useful	Useful	Quite useful	Essential
Under 40	11.11%	66.67%	0.00%	0.00%	22.22%	0.00%	0.00%
40-59	6.67%	53.33%	0.00%	13.33%	20.00%	6.67%	0.00%
60 or Over	0.00%	57.14%	14.29%	0.00%	28.57%	0.00%	0.00%

Table 4.3.4 When you do use Google Alerts how useful is it to you? Broken out by Work specialization or title of the survey participant

Work specialization or title of the survey participant	No Answer	Don't use this at all	Not very useful	Somewhat useful	Useful	Quite useful	Essential
reference or information literacy	10.00%	70.00%	10.00%	0.00%	10.00%	0.00%	0.00%
research or subject specialist	7.14%	50.00%	0.00%	14.29%	21.43%	7.14%	0.00%
other	0.00%	57.14%	0.00%	0.00%	42.86%	0.00%	0.00%

Table 4.3.5 When you do use Google Alerts how useful is it to you? Broken out by Compensation range of the survey participant

Compensation range of the survey participant	No Answer	Don't use this at all	Not very useful	Somewhat useful	Useful	Quite useful	Essential
Less than $55,000	14.29%	57.14%	0.00%	0.00%	14.29%	14.29%	0.00%
$55,000+ to $70,000	7.69%	61.54%	0.00%	7.69%	23.08%	0.00%	0.00%
More than $70,000	0.00%	54.55%	9.09%	9.09%	27.27%	0.00%	0.00%

Table 4.3.6 When you do use Google Alerts how useful is it to you? Broken out by Gender of the survey participant

Gender of the survey participant	No Answer	Don't use this at all	Not very useful	Somewhat useful	Useful	Quite useful	Essential
Male	14.29%	28.57%	14.29%	28.57%	0.00%	14.29%	0.00%
Female	4.17%	66.67%	0.00%	0.00%	29.17%	0.00%	0.00%

Table 4.3.7 When you do use Google Alerts how useful is it to you? Broken out for medical and other scientific libraries

Your main subject focus is:	No Answer	Don't use this at all	Not very useful	Somewhat useful	Useful	Quite useful	Essential
Medical, Biological or Pharmaceutical	0.00%	63.64%	0.00%	9.09%	27.27%	0.00%	0.00%
Other Scientific	22.22%	44.44%	11.11%	0.00%	11.11%	11.11%	0.00%

Table 4.4.1 When you do use Google Notifications how useful is it to you?

	No Answer	Don't use this at all	Not very useful	Somewhat useful	Useful	Quite useful	Essential
Entire sample	6.45%	70.97%	6.45%	9.68%	6.45%	0.00%	0.00%

Table 4.4.2 When you do use Google Notifications how useful is it to you? Broken out by Type of institution

Type of institution	No Answer	Don't use this at all	Not very useful	Somewhat useful	Useful	Quite useful	Essential
Academic Medical Library	0.00%	75.00%	8.33%	8.33%	8.33%	0.00%	0.00%
Academic Scientific Library	20.00%	60.00%	10.00%	10.00%	0.00%	0.00%	0.00%
Non-Educational Medical/Scientific Library	0.00%	77.78%	0.00%	11.11%	11.11%	0.00%	0.00%

Table 4.4.3 When you do use Google Notifications how useful is it to you? Broken out by Age range of the survey participant

Age range of the survey participant	No Answer	Don't use this at all	Not very useful	Somewhat useful	Useful	Quite useful	Essential
Under 40	11.11%	88.89%	0.00%	0.00%	0.00%	0.00%	0.00%
40-59	6.67%	60.00%	0.00%	20.00%	13.33%	0.00%	0.00%
60 or Over	0.00%	71.43%	28.57%	0.00%	0.00%	0.00%	0.00%

Table 4.4.4 When you do use Google Notifications how useful is it to you? Broken out by Work specialization or title of the survey participant

Work specialization or title of the survey participant	No Answer	Don't use this at all	Not very useful	Somewhat useful	Useful	Quite useful	Essential
reference or information literacy	10.00%	80.00%	10.00%	0.00%	0.00%	0.00%	0.00%
research or subject specialist	7.14%	71.43%	0.00%	14.29%	7.14%	0.00%	0.00%
other	0.00%	57.14%	14.29%	14.29%	14.29%	0.00%	0.00%

Table 4.4.5 When you do use Google Notifications how useful is it to you? Broken out by Compensation range of the survey participant

Compensation range of the survey participant	No Answer	Don't use this at all	Not very useful	Somewhat useful	Useful	Quite useful	Essential
Less than $55,000	14.29%	57.14%	0.00%	14.29%	14.29%	0.00%	0.00%
$55,000+ to $70,000	7.69%	84.62%	0.00%	7.69%	0.00%	0.00%	0.00%
More than $70,000	0.00%	63.64%	18.18%	9.09%	9.09%	0.00%	0.00%

Table 4.4.6 When you do use Google Notifications how useful is it to you? Broken out by Gender of the survey participant

Gender of the survey participant	No Answer	Don't use this at all	Not very useful	Somewhat useful	Useful	Quite useful	Essential
Male	14.29%	42.86%	14.29%	28.57%	0.00%	0.00%	0.00%
Female	4.17%	79.17%	4.17%	4.17%	8.33%	0.00%	0.00%

Table 4.4.7 When you do use Google Notifications how useful is it to you? Broken out for medical and other scientific libraries

Your main subject focus is:	No Answer	Don't use this at all	Not very useful	Somewhat useful	Useful	Quite useful	Essential
Medical, Biological or Pharmaceutical	0.00%	77.27%	4.55%	9.09%	9.09%	0.00%	0.00%
Other Scientific	22.22%	55.56%	11.11%	11.11%	0.00%	0.00%	0.00%

Table 4.5.1 When you do use Google Images how useful is it to you?

	No Answer	Don't use this at all	Not very useful	Somewhat useful	Useful	Quite useful	Essential
Entire sample	6.45%	3.23%	0.00%	16.13%	29.03%	35.48%	9.68%

Table 4.5.2 When you do use Google Images how useful is it to you? Broken out by Type of institution

Type of institution	No Answer	Don't use this at all	Not very useful	Somewhat useful	Useful	Quite useful	Essential
Academic Medical Library	0.00%	0.00%	0.00%	8.33%	25.00%	50.00%	16.67%
Academic Scientific Library	20.00%	10.00%	0.00%	10.00%	20.00%	40.00%	0.00%
Non-Educational Medical/Scientific Library	0.00%	0.00%	0.00%	33.33%	44.44%	11.11%	11.11%

Table 4.5.3 When you do use Google Images how useful is it to you? Broken out by Age range of the survey participant

Age range of the survey participant	No Answer	Don't use this at all	Not very useful	Somewhat useful	Useful	Quite useful	Essential
Under 40	11.11%	11.11%	0.00%	22.22%	11.11%	33.33%	11.11%
40-59	6.67%	0.00%	0.00%	13.33%	33.33%	33.33%	13.33%
60 or Over	0.00%	0.00%	0.00%	14.29%	42.86%	42.86%	0.00%

Table 4.5.4 When you do use Google Images how useful is it to you? Broken out by Work specialization or title of the survey participant

Work specialization or title of the survey participant	No Answer	Don't use this at all	Not very useful	Somewhat useful	Useful	Quite useful	Essential
reference or information literacy	10.00%	0.00%	0.00%	30.00%	20.00%	30.00%	10.00%
research or subject specialist	7.14%	7.14%	0.00%	14.29%	28.57%	35.71%	7.14%
other	0.00%	0.00%	0.00%	0.00%	42.86%	42.86%	14.29%

Table 4.5.5 When you do use Google Images how useful is it to you? Broken out by Compensation range of the survey participant

Compensation range of the survey participant	No Answer	Don't use this at all	Not very useful	Somewhat useful	Useful	Quite useful	Essential
Less than $55,000	14.29%	0.00%	0.00%	0.00%	42.86%	28.57%	14.29%
$55,000+ to $70,000	7.69%	7.69%	0.00%	30.77%	15.38%	30.77%	7.69%
More than $70,000	0.00%	0.00%	0.00%	9.09%	36.36%	45.45%	9.09%

Table 4.5.6 When you do use Google Images how useful is it to you? Broken out by Gender of the survey participant

Gender of the survey participant	No Answer	Don't use this at all	Not very useful	Somewhat useful	Useful	Quite useful	Essential
Male	14.29%	0.00%	0.00%	28.57%	28.57%	14.29%	14.29%
Female	4.17%	4.17%	0.00%	12.50%	29.17%	41.67%	8.33%

Table 4.5.7 When you do use Google Images how useful is it to you? Broken out for medical and other scientific libraries

Your main subject focus is:	No Answer	Don't use this at all	Not very useful	Somewhat useful	Useful	Quite useful	Essential
Medical, Biological or Pharmaceutical	0.00%	0.00%	0.00%	18.18%	31.82%	36.36%	13.64%
Other Scientific	22.22%	11.11%	0.00%	11.11%	22.22%	33.33%	0.00%

Table 4.6.1 When you do use Google Photos how useful is it to you?

	No Answer	Don't use this at all	Not very useful	Somewhat useful	Useful	Quite useful	Essential
Entire sample	6.45%	58.06%	3.23%	3.23%	12.90%	9.68%	6.45%

Table 4.6.2 When you do use Google Photos how useful is it to you? Broken out by Type of institution

Type of institution	No Answer	Don't use this at all	Not very useful	Somewhat useful	Useful	Quite useful	Essential
Academic Medical Library	0.00%	58.33%	8.33%	0.00%	8.33%	25.00%	0.00%
Academic Scientific Library	20.00%	40.00%	0.00%	10.00%	20.00%	0.00%	10.00%
Non-Educational Medical/Scientific Library	0.00%	77.78%	0.00%	0.00%	11.11%	0.00%	11.11%

Table 4.6.3 When you do use Google Photos how useful is it to you? Broken out by Age range of the survey participant

Age range of the survey participant	No Answer	Don't use this at all	Not very useful	Somewhat useful	Useful	Quite useful	Essential
Under 40	11.11%	66.67%	0.00%	0.00%	11.11%	0.00%	11.11%
40-59	6.67%	46.67%	6.67%	0.00%	20.00%	13.33%	6.67%
60 or Over	0.00%	71.43%	0.00%	14.29%	0.00%	14.29%	0.00%

Table 4.6.4 When you do use Google Photos how useful is it to you? Broken out by Work specialization or title of the survey participant

Work specialization or title of the survey participant	No Answer	Don't use this at all	Not very useful	Somewhat useful	Useful	Quite useful	Essential
reference or information literacy	10.00%	60.00%	0.00%	10.00%	10.00%	0.00%	10.00%
research or subject specialist	7.14%	57.14%	7.14%	0.00%	21.43%	0.00%	7.14%
other	0.00%	57.14%	0.00%	0.00%	0.00%	42.86%	0.00%

Table 4.6.5 When you do use Google Photos how useful is it to you? Broken out by Compensation range of the survey participant

Compensation range of the survey participant	No Answer	Don't use this at all	Not very useful	Somewhat useful	Useful	Quite useful	Essential
Less than $55,000	14.29%	42.86%	0.00%	0.00%	42.86%	0.00%	0.00%
$55,000+ to $70,000	7.69%	69.23%	0.00%	0.00%	0.00%	7.69%	15.38%
More than $70,000	0.00%	54.55%	9.09%	9.09%	9.09%	18.18%	0.00%

Table 4.6.6 When you do use Google Photos how useful is it to you? Broken out by Gender of the survey participant

Gender of the survey participant	No Answer	Don't use this at all	Not very useful	Somewhat useful	Useful	Quite useful	Essential
Male	14.29%	42.86%	14.29%	14.29%	14.29%	0.00%	0.00%
Female	4.17%	62.50%	0.00%	0.00%	12.50%	12.50%	8.33%

Table 4.6.7 When you do use Google Photos how useful is it to you? Broken out for medical and other scientific libraries

Your main subject focus is:	No Answer	Don't use this at all	Not very useful	Somewhat useful	Useful	Quite useful	Essential
Medical, Biological or Pharmaceutical	0.00%	63.64%	4.55%	0.00%	13.64%	13.64%	4.55%
Other Scientific	22.22%	44.44%	0.00%	11.11%	11.11%	0.00%	11.11%

Table 4.7.1 When you do use Google Calendar how useful is it to you?

	No Answer	Don't use this at all	Not very useful	Somewhat useful	Useful	Quite useful	Essential
Entire sample	3.23%	41.94%	6.45%	12.90%	12.90%	9.68%	12.90%

Table 4.7.2 When you do use Google Calendar how useful is it to you? Broken out by Type of institution

Type of institution	No Answer	Don't use this at all	Not very useful	Somewhat useful	Useful	Quite useful	Essential
Academic Medical Library	8.33%	41.67%	8.33%	8.33%	16.67%	16.67%	0.00%
Academic Scientific Library	0.00%	10.00%	10.00%	20.00%	10.00%	10.00%	40.00%
Non-Educational Medical/Scientific Library	0.00%	77.78%	0.00%	11.11%	11.11%	0.00%	0.00%

Table 4.7.3 When you do use Google Calendar how useful is it to you? Broken out by Age range of the survey participant

Age range of the survey participant	No Answer	Don't use this at all	Not very useful	Somewhat useful	Useful	Quite useful	Essential
Under 40	0.00%	33.33%	0.00%	11.11%	11.11%	22.22%	22.22%
40-59	0.00%	53.33%	13.33%	6.67%	13.33%	6.67%	6.67%
60 or Over	14.29%	28.57%	0.00%	28.57%	14.29%	0.00%	14.29%

Table 4.7.4 When you do use Google Calendar how useful is it to you? Broken out by Work specialization or title of the survey participant

Work specialization or title of the survey participant	No Answer	Don't use this at all	Not very useful	Somewhat useful	Useful	Quite useful	Essential
reference or information literacy	0.00%	30.00%	0.00%	20.00%	10.00%	10.00%	30.00%
research or subject specialist	7.14%	35.71%	14.29%	14.29%	7.14%	14.29%	7.14%
other	0.00%	71.43%	0.00%	0.00%	28.57%	0.00%	0.00%

Table 4.7.5 When you do use Google Calendar how useful is it to you? Broken out by Compensation range of the survey participant

Compensation range of the survey participant	No Answer	Don't use this at all	Not very useful	Somewhat useful	Useful	Quite useful	Essential
Less than $55,000	0.00%	42.86%	14.29%	14.29%	0.00%	0.00%	28.57%
$55,000+ to $70,000	7.69%	38.46%	0.00%	15.38%	23.08%	7.69%	7.69%
More than $70,000	0.00%	45.45%	9.09%	9.09%	9.09%	18.18%	9.09%

Table 4.7.6 When you do use Google Calendar how useful is it to you? Broken out by Gender of the survey participant

Gender of the survey participant	No Answer	Don't use this at all	Not very useful	Somewhat useful	Useful	Quite useful	Essential
Male	0.00%	42.86%	28.57%	0.00%	14.29%	0.00%	14.29%
Female	4.17%	41.67%	0.00%	16.67%	12.50%	12.50%	12.50%

Table 4.7.7 When you do use Google Calendar how useful is it to you? Broken out for medical and other scientific libraries

Your main subject focus is:	No Answer	Don't use this at all	Not very useful	Somewhat useful	Useful	Quite useful	Essential
Medical, Biological or Pharmaceutical	4.55%	50.00%	4.55%	13.64%	13.64%	9.09%	4.55%
Other Scientific	0.00%	22.22%	11.11%	11.11%	11.11%	11.11%	33.33%

Table 4.8.1 When you do use Chrome how useful is it to you?

	Don't use this at all	Not very useful	Somewhat useful	Useful	Quite useful	Essential
Entire sample	0.00%	0.00%	6.45%	19.35%	32.26%	41.94%

Table 4.8.2 When you do use Chrome how useful is it to you? Broken out by Type of institution

Type of institution	Don't use this at all	Not very useful	Somewhat useful	Useful	Quite useful	Essential
Academic Medical Library	0.00%	0.00%	0.00%	8.33%	25.00%	66.67%
Academic Scientific Library	0.00%	0.00%	20.00%	20.00%	20.00%	40.00%
Non-Educational Medical/Scientific Library	0.00%	0.00%	0.00%	33.33%	55.56%	11.11%

Table 4.8.3 When you do use Chrome how useful is it to you? Broken out by Age range of the survey participant

Age range of the survey participant	Don't use this at all	Not very useful	Somewhat useful	Useful	Quite useful	Essential
Under 40	0.00%	0.00%	11.11%	11.11%	44.44%	33.33%
40-59	0.00%	0.00%	6.67%	26.67%	13.33%	53.33%
60 or Over	0.00%	0.00%	0.00%	14.29%	57.14%	28.57%

Table 4.8.4 When you do use Chrome how useful is it to you? Broken out by Work specialization or title of the survey participant

Work specialization or title of the survey participant	Don't use this at all	Not very useful	Somewhat useful	Useful	Quite useful	Essential
reference or information literacy	0.00%	0.00%	10.00%	10.00%	40.00%	40.00%
research or subject specialist	0.00%	0.00%	7.14%	28.57%	28.57%	35.71%
other	0.00%	0.00%	0.00%	14.29%	28.57%	57.14%

Table 4.8.5 When you do use Chrome how useful is it to you? Broken out by Compensation range of the survey participant

Compensation range of the survey participant	Don't use this at all	Not very useful	Somewhat useful	Useful	Quite useful	Essential
Less than $55,000	0.00%	0.00%	28.57%	14.29%	14.29%	42.86%
$55,000+ to $70,000	0.00%	0.00%	0.00%	23.08%	46.15%	30.77%
More than $70,000	0.00%	0.00%	0.00%	18.18%	27.27%	54.55%

Table 4.8.6 When you do use Chrome how useful is it to you? Broken out by Gender of the survey participant

Gender of the survey participant	Don't use this at all	Not very useful	Somewhat useful	Useful	Quite useful	Essential
Male	0.00%	0.00%	14.29%	14.29%	57.14%	14.29%
Female	0.00%	0.00%	4.17%	20.83%	25.00%	50.00%

Table 4.8.7 When you do use Chrome how useful is it to you? Broken out for medical and other scientific libraries

Your main subject focus is:	Don't use this at all	Not very useful	Somewhat useful	Useful	Quite useful	Essential
Medical, Biological or Pharmaceutical	0.00%	0.00%	4.55%	22.73%	31.82%	40.91%
Other Scientific	0.00%	0.00%	11.11%	11.11%	33.33%	44.44%

Table 4.9.1 When you do use Google Books how useful is it to you?

	No Answer	Don't use this at all	Not very useful	Somewhat useful	Useful	Quite useful	Essential
Entire sample	9.68%	12.90%	3.23%	22.58%	22.58%	19.35%	9.68%

Table 4.9.2 When you do use Google Books how useful is it to you? Broken out by Type of institution

Type of institution	No Answer	Don't use this at all	Not very useful	Somewhat useful	Useful	Quite useful	Essential
Academic Medical Library	0.00%	16.67%	0.00%	25.00%	16.67%	33.33%	8.33%
Academic Scientific Library	20.00%	10.00%	10.00%	20.00%	30.00%	0.00%	10.00%
Non-Educational Medical/Scientific Library	11.11%	11.11%	0.00%	22.22%	22.22%	22.22%	11.11%

Table 4.9.3 When you do use Google Books how useful is it to you? Broken out by Age range of the survey participant

Age range of the survey participant	No Answer	Don't use this at all	Not very useful	Somewhat useful	Useful	Quite useful	Essential
Under 40	11.11%	22.22%	0.00%	11.11%	33.33%	11.11%	11.11%
40-59	6.67%	13.33%	0.00%	20.00%	20.00%	26.67%	13.33%
60 or Over	14.29%	0.00%	14.29%	42.86%	14.29%	14.29%	0.00%

Table 4.9.4 When you do use Google Books how useful is it to you? Broken out by Work specialization or title of the survey participant

Work specialization or title of the survey participant	No Answer	Don't use this at all	Not very useful	Somewhat useful	Useful	Quite useful	Essential
reference or information literacy	20.00%	10.00%	10.00%	30.00%	20.00%	0.00%	10.00%
research or subject specialist	7.14%	14.29%	0.00%	7.14%	28.57%	28.57%	14.29%
other	0.00%	14.29%	0.00%	42.86%	14.29%	28.57%	0.00%

Table 4.9.5 When you do use Google Books how useful is it to you? Broken out by Compensation range of the survey participant

Compensation range of the survey participant	No Answer	Don't use this at all	Not very useful	Somewhat useful	Useful	Quite useful	Essential
Less than $55,000	28.57%	14.29%	0.00%	14.29%	28.57%	14.29%	0.00%
$55,000+ to $70,000	7.69%	23.08%	0.00%	23.08%	15.38%	15.38%	15.38%
More than $70,000	0.00%	0.00%	9.09%	27.27%	27.27%	27.27%	9.09%

Table 4.9.6 When you do use Google Books how useful is it to you? Broken out by Gender of the survey participant

Gender of the survey participant	No Answer	Don't use this at all	Not very useful	Somewhat useful	Useful	Quite useful	Essential
Male	14.29%	14.29%	14.29%	0.00%	14.29%	28.57%	14.29%
Female	8.33%	12.50%	0.00%	29.17%	25.00%	16.67%	8.33%

Table 4.9.7 When you do use Google Books how useful is it to you? Broken out for medical and other scientific libraries

Your main subject focus is:	No Answer	Don't use this at all	Not very useful	Somewhat useful	Useful	Quite useful	Essential
Medical, Biological or Pharmaceutical	4.55%	18.18%	0.00%	22.73%	18.18%	27.27%	9.09%
Other Scientific	22.22%	0.00%	11.11%	22.22%	33.33%	0.00%	11.11%

Table 4.10.1 When you do use Google Scholar how useful is it to you?

	Don't use this at all	Not very useful	Somewhat useful	Useful	Quite useful	Essential
Entire sample	0.00%	3.23%	6.45%	6.45%	29.03%	54.84%

Table 4.10.2 When you do use Google Scholar how useful is it to you? Broken out by Type of institution

Type of institution	Don't use this at all	Not very useful	Somewhat useful	Useful	Quite useful	Essential
Academic Medical Library	0.00%	0.00%	8.33%	16.67%	16.67%	58.33%
Academic Scientific Library	0.00%	10.00%	0.00%	0.00%	50.00%	40.00%
Non-Educational Medical/Scientific Library	0.00%	0.00%	11.11%	0.00%	22.22%	66.67%

Table 4.10.3 When you do use Google Scholar how useful is it to you? Broken out by Age range of the survey participant

Age range of the survey participant	Don't use this at all	Not very useful	Somewhat useful	Useful	Quite useful	Essential
Under 40	0.00%	0.00%	11.11%	11.11%	33.33%	44.44%
40-59	0.00%	0.00%	0.00%	0.00%	33.33%	66.67%
60 or Over	0.00%	14.29%	14.29%	14.29%	14.29%	42.86%

Table 4.10.4 When you do use Google Scholar how useful is it to you? Broken out by Work specialization or title of the survey participant

Work specialization or title of the survey participant	Don't use this at all	Not very useful	Somewhat useful	Useful	Quite useful	Essential
reference or information literacy	0.00%	10.00%	10.00%	10.00%	20.00%	50.00%
research or subject specialist	0.00%	0.00%	7.14%	0.00%	35.71%	57.14%
other	0.00%	0.00%	0.00%	14.29%	28.57%	57.14%

Table 4.10.5 When you do use Google Scholar how useful is it to you? Broken out by Compensation range of the survey participant

Compensation range of the survey participant	Don't use this at all	Not very useful	Somewhat useful	Useful	Quite useful	Essential
Less than $55,000	0.00%	0.00%	14.29%	0.00%	42.86%	42.86%
$55,000+ to $70,000	0.00%	0.00%	7.69%	7.69%	7.69%	76.92%
More than $70,000	0.00%	9.09%	0.00%	9.09%	45.45%	36.36%

Table 4.10.6 When you do use Google Scholar how useful is it to you? Broken out by Gender of the survey participant

Gender of the survey participant	Don't use this at all	Not very useful	Somewhat useful	Useful	Quite useful	Essential
Male	0.00%	14.29%	14.29%	0.00%	28.57%	42.86%
Female	0.00%	0.00%	4.17%	8.33%	29.17%	58.33%

Table 4.10.7 When you do use Google Scholar how useful is it to you? Broken out for medical and other scientific libraries

Your main subject focus is:	Don't use this at all	Not very useful	Somewhat useful	Useful	Quite useful	Essential
Medical, Biological or Pharmaceutical	0.00%	0.00%	9.09%	9.09%	18.18%	63.64%
Other Scientific	0.00%	11.11%	0.00%	0.00%	55.56%	33.33%

Table 4.11.1 When you do use Google Scholar My Citations how useful is it to you?

	No Answer	Don't use this at all	Not very useful	Somewhat useful	Useful	Quite useful	Essential
Entire sample	3.23%	48.39%	3.23%	9.68%	12.90%	12.90%	9.68%

Table 4.11.2 When you do use Google Scholar My Citations how useful is it to you? Broken out by Type of institution

Type of institution	No Answer	Don't use this at all	Not very useful	Somewhat useful	Useful	Quite useful	Essential
Academic Medical Library	0.00%	66.67%	0.00%	0.00%	16.67%	8.33%	8.33%
Academic Scientific Library	10.00%	10.00%	10.00%	20.00%	10.00%	20.00%	20.00%
Non-Educational Medical/Scientific Library	0.00%	66.67%	0.00%	11.11%	11.11%	11.11%	0.00%

Table 4.11.3 When you do use Google Scholar My Citations how useful is it to you? Broken out by Age range of the survey participant

Age range of the survey participant	No Answer	Don't use this at all	Not very useful	Somewhat useful	Useful	Quite useful	Essential
Under 40	11.11%	44.44%	11.11%	0.00%	11.11%	0.00%	22.22%
40-59	0.00%	46.67%	0.00%	13.33%	13.33%	20.00%	6.67%
60 or Over	0.00%	57.14%	0.00%	14.29%	14.29%	14.29%	0.00%

Table 4.11.4 When you do use Google Scholar My Citations how useful is it to you? Broken out by Work specialization or title of the survey participant

Work specialization or title of the survey participant	No Answer	Don't use this at all	Not very useful	Somewhat useful	Useful	Quite useful	Essential
reference or information literacy	0.00%	30.00%	10.00%	20.00%	20.00%	20.00%	0.00%
research or subject specialist	7.14%	42.86%	0.00%	7.14%	14.29%	7.14%	21.43%
other	0.00%	85.71%	0.00%	0.00%	0.00%	14.29%	0.00%

Table 4.11.5 When you do use Google Scholar My Citations how useful is it to you? Broken out by Compensation range of the survey participant

Compensation range of the survey participant	No Answer	Don't use this at all	Not very useful	Somewhat useful	Useful	Quite useful	Essential
Less than $55,000	0.00%	42.86%	14.29%	14.29%	14.29%	14.29%	0.00%
$55,000+ to $70,000	7.69%	61.54%	0.00%	7.69%	7.69%	7.69%	7.69%
More than $70,000	0.00%	36.36%	0.00%	9.09%	18.18%	18.18%	18.18%

Table 4.11.6 When you do use Google Scholar My Citations how useful is it to you? Broken out by Gender of the survey participant

Gender of the survey participant	No Answer	Don't use this at all	Not very useful	Somewhat useful	Useful	Quite useful	Essential
Male	14.29%	28.57%	0.00%	28.57%	14.29%	0.00%	14.29%
Female	0.00%	54.17%	4.17%	4.17%	12.50%	16.67%	8.33%

Table 4.11.7 When you do use Google Scholar My Citations how useful is it to you? Broken out for medical and other scientific libraries

Your main subject focus is:	No Answer	Don't use this at all	Not very useful	Somewhat useful	Useful	Quite useful	Essential
Medical, Biological or Pharmaceutical	0.00%	68.18%	4.55%	4.55%	13.64%	4.55%	4.55%
Other Scientific	11.11%	0.00%	0.00%	22.22%	11.11%	33.33%	22.22%

Table 4.12.1 When you do use Google Translate how useful is it to you?

	No Answer	Don't use this at all	Not very useful	Somewhat useful	Useful	Quite useful	Essential
Entire sample	6.45%	19.35%	3.23%	6.45%	29.03%	29.03%	6.45%

Table 4.12.2 When you do use Google Translate how useful is it to you? Broken out by Type of institution

Type of institution	No Answer	Don't use this at all	Not very useful	Somewhat useful	Useful	Quite useful	Essential
Academic Medical Library	0.00%	8.33%	0.00%	0.00%	41.67%	41.67%	8.33%
Academic Scientific Library	20.00%	20.00%	10.00%	10.00%	20.00%	10.00%	10.00%
Non-Educational Medical/Scientific Library	0.00%	33.33%	0.00%	11.11%	22.22%	33.33%	0.00%

Table 4.12.3 When you do use Google Translate how useful is it to you? Broken out by Age range of the survey participant

Age range of the survey participant	No Answer	Don't use this at all	Not very useful	Somewhat useful	Useful	Quite useful	Essential
Under 40	11.11%	11.11%	11.11%	0.00%	33.33%	11.11%	22.22%
40-59	6.67%	20.00%	0.00%	6.67%	33.33%	33.33%	0.00%
60 or Over	0.00%	28.57%	0.00%	14.29%	14.29%	42.86%	0.00%

Table 4.12.4 When you do use Google Translate how useful is it to you? Broken out by Work specialization or title of the survey participant

Work specialization or title of the survey participant	No Answer	Don't use this at all	Not very useful	Somewhat useful	Useful	Quite useful	Essential
reference or information literacy	10.00%	40.00%	10.00%	10.00%	10.00%	20.00%	0.00%
research or subject specialist	7.14%	7.14%	0.00%	7.14%	35.71%	35.71%	7.14%
other	0.00%	14.29%	0.00%	0.00%	42.86%	28.57%	14.29%

Table 4.12.5 When you do use Google Translate how useful is it to you? Broken out by Compensation range of the survey participant

Compensation range of the survey participant	No Answer	Don't use this at all	Not very useful	Somewhat useful	Useful	Quite useful	Essential
Less than $55,000	14.29%	14.29%	14.29%	0.00%	14.29%	28.57%	14.29%
$55,000+ to $70,000	7.69%	23.08%	0.00%	7.69%	30.77%	23.08%	7.69%
More than $70,000	0.00%	18.18%	0.00%	9.09%	36.36%	36.36%	0.00%

Table 4.12.6 When you do use Google Translate how useful is it to you? Broken out by Gender of the survey participant

Gender of the survey participant	No Answer	Don't use this at all	Not very useful	Somewhat useful	Useful	Quite useful	Essential
Male	14.29%	0.00%	0.00%	28.57%	28.57%	28.57%	0.00%
Female	4.17%	25.00%	4.17%	0.00%	29.17%	29.17%	8.33%

Table 4.12.7 When you do use Google Translate how useful is it to you? Broken out for medical and other scientific libraries

Your main subject focus is:	No Answer	Don't use this at all	Not very useful	Somewhat useful	Useful	Quite useful	Essential
Medical, Biological or Pharmaceutical	0.00%	22.73%	4.55%	4.55%	31.82%	31.82%	4.55%
Other Scientific	22.22%	11.11%	0.00%	11.11%	22.22%	22.22%	11.11%

Table 4.13.1 When you do use Google Public Data Explorer how useful is it to you?

	No Answer	Don't use this at all	Not very useful	Somewhat useful	Useful	Quite useful	Essential
Entire sample	6.45%	80.65%	0.00%	6.45%	0.00%	6.45%	0.00%

Table 4.13.2 When you do use Google Public Data Explorer how useful is it to you? Broken out by Type of institution

Type of institution	No Answer	Don't use this at all	Not very useful	Somewhat useful	Useful	Quite useful	Essential
Academic Medical Library	0.00%	83.33%	0.00%	0.00%	0.00%	16.67%	0.00%
Academic Scientific Library	20.00%	70.00%	0.00%	10.00%	0.00%	0.00%	0.00%
Non-Educational Medical/Scientific Library	0.00%	88.89%	0.00%	11.11%	0.00%	0.00%	0.00%

Table 4.13.3 When you do use Google Public Data Explorer how useful is it to you? Broken out by Age range of the survey participant

Age range of the survey participant	No Answer	Don't use this at all	Not very useful	Somewhat useful	Useful	Quite useful	Essential
Under 40	11.11%	77.78%	0.00%	11.11%	0.00%	0.00%	0.00%
40-59	6.67%	80.00%	0.00%	6.67%	0.00%	6.67%	0.00%
60 or Over	0.00%	85.71%	0.00%	0.00%	0.00%	14.29%	0.00%

Table 4.13.4 When you do use Google Public Data Explorer how useful is it to you? Broken out by Work specialization or title of the survey participant

Work specialization or title of the survey participant	No Answer	Don't use this at all	Not very useful	Somewhat useful	Useful	Quite useful	Essential
reference or information literacy	10.00%	70.00%	0.00%	20.00%	0.00%	0.00%	0.00%
research or subject specialist	7.14%	78.57%	0.00%	0.00%	0.00%	14.29%	0.00%
other	0.00%	100.00%	0.00%	0.00%	0.00%	0.00%	0.00%

Table 4.13.5 When you do use Google Public Data Explorer how useful is it to you? Broken out by Compensation range of the survey participant

Compensation range of the survey participant	No Answer	Don't use this at all	Not very useful	Somewhat useful	Useful	Quite useful	Essential
Less than $55,000	14.29%	71.43%	0.00%	14.29%	0.00%	0.00%	0.00%
$55,000+ to $70,000	7.69%	76.92%	0.00%	7.69%	0.00%	7.69%	0.00%
More than $70,000	0.00%	90.91%	0.00%	0.00%	0.00%	9.09%	0.00%

Table 4.13.6 When you do use Google Public Data Explorer how useful is it to you? Broken out by Gender of the survey participant

Gender of the survey participant	No Answer	Don't use this at all	Not very useful	Somewhat useful	Useful	Quite useful	Essential
Male	14.29%	71.43%	0.00%	0.00%	0.00%	14.29%	0.00%
Female	4.17%	83.33%	0.00%	8.33%	0.00%	4.17%	0.00%

Table 4.13.7 When you do use Google Public Data Explorer how useful is it to you? Broken out for medical and other scientific libraries

Your main subject focus is:	No Answer	Don't use this at all	Not very useful	Somewhat useful	Useful	Quite useful	Essential
Medical, Biological or Pharmaceutical	0.00%	81.82%	0.00%	9.09%	0.00%	9.09%	0.00%
Other Scientific	22.22%	77.78%	0.00%	0.00%	0.00%	0.00%	0.00%

Table 4.14.1 When you do use Google Drive how useful is it to you?

	Don't use this at all	Not very useful	Somewhat useful	Useful	Quite useful	Essential
Entire sample	32.26%	0.00%	12.90%	9.68%	16.13%	29.03%

Table 4.14.2 When you do use Google Drive how useful is it to you? Broken out by Type of institution

Type of institution	Don't use this at all	Not very useful	Somewhat useful	Useful	Quite useful	Essential
Academic Medical Library	25.00%	0.00%	0.00%	16.67%	33.33%	25.00%
Academic Scientific Library	10.00%	0.00%	20.00%	10.00%	10.00%	50.00%
Non-Educational Medical/Scientific Library	66.67%	0.00%	22.22%	0.00%	0.00%	11.11%

Table 4.14.3 When you do use Google Drive how useful is it to you? Broken out by Age range of the survey participant

Age range of the survey participant	Don't use this at all	Not very useful	Somewhat useful	Useful	Quite useful	Essential
Under 40	0.00%	0.00%	11.11%	22.22%	11.11%	55.56%
40-59	40.00%	0.00%	20.00%	6.67%	20.00%	13.33%
60 or Over	57.14%	0.00%	0.00%	0.00%	14.29%	28.57%

Table 4.14.4 When you do use Google Drive how useful is it to you? Broken out by Work specialization or title of the survey participant

Work specialization or title of the survey participant	Don't use this at all	Not very useful	Somewhat useful	Useful	Quite useful	Essential
reference or information literacy	30.00%	0.00%	10.00%	0.00%	20.00%	40.00%
research or subject specialist	21.43%	0.00%	21.43%	21.43%	14.29%	21.43%
other	57.14%	0.00%	0.00%	0.00%	14.29%	28.57%

Table 4.14.5 When you do use Google Drive how useful is it to you? Broken out by Compensation range of the survey participant

Compensation range of the survey participant	Don't use this at all	Not very useful	Somewhat useful	Useful	Quite useful	Essential
Less than $55,000	28.57%	0.00%	14.29%	0.00%	0.00%	57.14%
$55,000+ to $70,000	23.08%	0.00%	23.08%	15.38%	15.38%	23.08%
More than $70,000	45.45%	0.00%	0.00%	9.09%	27.27%	18.18%

Table 4.14.6 When you do use Google Drive how useful is it to you? Broken out by Gender of the survey participant

Gender of the survey participant	Don't use this at all	Not very useful	Somewhat useful	Useful	Quite useful	Essential
Male	42.86%	0.00%	14.29%	28.57%	14.29%	0.00%
Female	29.17%	0.00%	12.50%	4.17%	16.67%	37.50%

Table 4.14.7 When you do use Google Drive how useful is it to you? Broken out for medical and other scientific libraries

Your main subject focus is:	Don't use this at all	Not very useful	Somewhat useful	Useful	Quite useful	Essential
Medical, Biological or Pharmaceutical	36.36%	0.00%	13.64%	9.09%	18.18%	22.73%
Other Scientific	22.22%	0.00%	11.11%	11.11%	11.11%	44.44%

Table 4.15.1 When you do use Google Earth how useful is it to you?

	No Answer	Don't use this at all	Not very useful	Somewhat useful	Useful	Quite useful	Essential
Entire sample	3.23%	32.26%	9.68%	19.35%	22.58%	12.90%	0.00%

Table 4.15.2 When you do use Google Earth how useful is it to you? Broken out by Type of institution

Type of institution	No Answer	Don't use this at all	Not very useful	Somewhat useful	Useful	Quite useful	Essential
Academic Medical Library	0.00%	33.33%	0.00%	8.33%	25.00%	33.33%	0.00%
Academic Scientific Library	10.00%	30.00%	20.00%	30.00%	10.00%	0.00%	0.00%
Non-Educational Medical/Scientific Library	0.00%	33.33%	11.11%	22.22%	33.33%	0.00%	0.00%

Table 4.15.3 When you do use Google Earth how useful is it to you? Broken out by Age range of the survey participant

Age range of the survey participant	No Answer	Don't use this at all	Not very useful	Somewhat useful	Useful	Quite useful	Essential
Under 40	0.00%	44.44%	11.11%	22.22%	11.11%	11.11%	0.00%
40-59	6.67%	26.67%	0.00%	26.67%	33.33%	6.67%	0.00%
60 or Over	0.00%	28.57%	28.57%	0.00%	14.29%	28.57%	0.00%

Table 4.15.4 When you do use Google Earth how useful is it to you? Broken out by Work specialization or title of the survey participant

Work specialization or title of the survey participant	No Answer	Don't use this at all	Not very useful	Somewhat useful	Useful	Quite useful	Essential
reference or information literacy	10.00%	40.00%	20.00%	0.00%	20.00%	10.00%	0.00%
research or subject specialist	0.00%	21.43%	7.14%	35.71%	14.29%	21.43%	0.00%
other	0.00%	42.86%	0.00%	14.29%	42.86%	0.00%	0.00%

Table 4.15.5 When you do use Google Earth how useful is it to you? Broken out by Compensation range of the survey participant

Compensation range of the survey participant	No Answer	Don't use this at all	Not very useful	Somewhat useful	Useful	Quite useful	Essential
Less than $55,000	14.29%	57.14%	14.29%	14.29%	0.00%	0.00%	0.00%
$55,000+ to $70,000	0.00%	23.08%	7.69%	15.38%	30.77%	23.08%	0.00%
More than $70,000	0.00%	27.27%	9.09%	27.27%	27.27%	9.09%	0.00%

Table 4.15.6 When you do use Google Earth how useful is it to you? Broken out by Gender of the survey participant

Gender of the survey participant	No Answer	Don't use this at all	Not very useful	Somewhat useful	Useful	Quite useful	Essential
Male	0.00%	0.00%	28.57%	42.86%	14.29%	14.29%	0.00%
Female	4.17%	41.67%	4.17%	12.50%	25.00%	12.50%	0.00%

Table 4.15.7 When you do use Google Earth how useful is it to you? Broken out for medical and other scientific libraries

Your main subject focus is:	No Answer	Don't use this at all	Not very useful	Somewhat useful	Useful	Quite useful	Essential
Medical, Biological or Pharmaceutical	0.00%	40.91%	4.55%	9.09%	27.27%	18.18%	0.00%
Other Scientific	11.11%	11.11%	22.22%	44.44%	11.11%	0.00%	0.00%

Table 4.16.1 When you do use Google Sky how useful is it to you?

	No Answer	Don't use this at all	Not very useful	Somewhat useful	Useful	Quite useful	Essential
Entire sample	3.23%	70.97%	3.23%	16.13%	6.45%	0.00%	0.00%

Table 4.16.2 When you do use Google Sky how useful is it to you? Broken out by Type of institution

Type of institution	No Answer	Don't use this at all	Not very useful	Somewhat useful	Useful	Quite useful	Essential
Academic Medical Library	0.00%	83.33%	0.00%	8.33%	8.33%	0.00%	0.00%
Academic Scientific Library	10.00%	50.00%	10.00%	20.00%	10.00%	0.00%	0.00%
Non-Educational Medical/Scientific Library	0.00%	77.78%	0.00%	22.22%	0.00%	0.00%	0.00%

Table 4.16.3 When you do use Google Sky how useful is it to you? Broken out by Age range of the survey participant

Age range of the survey participant	No Answer	Don't use this at all	Not very useful	Somewhat useful	Useful	Quite useful	Essential
Under 40	0.00%	77.78%	11.11%	11.11%	0.00%	0.00%	0.00%
40-59	6.67%	53.33%	0.00%	26.67%	13.33%	0.00%	0.00%
60 or Over	0.00%	100.00%	0.00%	0.00%	0.00%	0.00%	0.00%

Table 4.16.4 When you do use Google Sky how useful is it to you? Broken out by Work specialization or title of the survey participant

Work specialization or title of the survey participant	No Answer	Don't use this at all	Not very useful	Somewhat useful	Useful	Quite useful	Essential
reference or information literacy	10.00%	70.00%	0.00%	10.00%	10.00%	0.00%	0.00%
research or subject specialist	0.00%	71.43%	7.14%	14.29%	7.14%	0.00%	0.00%
other	0.00%	71.43%	0.00%	28.57%	0.00%	0.00%	0.00%

Table 4.16.5 When you do use Google Sky how useful is it to you? Broken out by Compensation range of the survey participant

Compensation range of the survey participant	No Answer	Don't use this at all	Not very useful	Somewhat useful	Useful	Quite useful	Essential
Less than $55,000	14.29%	71.43%	0.00%	14.29%	0.00%	0.00%	0.00%
$55,000+ to $70,000	0.00%	69.23%	7.69%	23.08%	0.00%	0.00%	0.00%
More than $70,000	0.00%	72.73%	0.00%	9.09%	18.18%	0.00%	0.00%

Table 4.16.6 When you do use Google Sky how useful is it to you? Broken out by Gender of the survey participant

Gender of the survey participant	No Answer	Don't use this at all	Not very useful	Somewhat useful	Useful	Quite useful	Essential
Male	0.00%	71.43%	14.29%	14.29%	0.00%	0.00%	0.00%
Female	4.17%	70.83%	0.00%	16.67%	8.33%	0.00%	0.00%

Table 4.16.7 When you do use Google Sky how useful is it to you? Broken out for medical and other scientific libraries

Your main subject focus is:	No Answer	Don't use this at all	Not very useful	Somewhat useful	Useful	Quite useful	Essential
Medical, Biological or Pharmaceutical	0.00%	86.36%	0.00%	9.09%	4.55%	0.00%	0.00%
Other Scientific	11.11%	33.33%	11.11%	33.33%	11.11%	0.00%	0.00%

Table 4.17.1 When you do use Google+ how useful is it to you?

	No Answer	Don't use this at all	Not very useful	Somewhat useful	Useful	Quite useful	Essential
Entire sample	9.68%	67.74%	3.23%	6.45%	3.23%	6.45%	3.23%

Table 4.17.2 When you do use Google+ how useful is it to you? Broken out by Type of institution

Type of institution	No Answer	Don't use this at all	Not very useful	Somewhat useful	Useful	Quite useful	Essential
Academic Medical Library	0.00%	66.67%	8.33%	0.00%	0.00%	16.67%	8.33%
Academic Scientific Library	30.00%	50.00%	0.00%	10.00%	10.00%	0.00%	0.00%
Non-Educational Medical/Scientific Library	0.00%	88.89%	0.00%	11.11%	0.00%	0.00%	0.00%

Table 4.17.3 When you do use Google+ how useful is it to you? Broken out by Age range of the survey participant

Age range of the survey participant	No Answer	Don't use this at all	Not very useful	Somewhat useful	Useful	Quite useful	Essential
Under 40	11.11%	55.56%	0.00%	11.11%	11.11%	11.11%	0.00%
40-59	13.33%	66.67%	6.67%	6.67%	0.00%	0.00%	6.67%
60 or Over	0.00%	85.71%	0.00%	0.00%	0.00%	14.29%	0.00%

Table 4.17.4 When you do use Google+ how useful is it to you? Broken out by Work specialization or title of the survey participant

Work specialization or title of the survey participant	No Answer	Don't use this at all	Not very useful	Somewhat useful	Useful	Quite useful	Essential
reference or information literacy	20.00%	60.00%	0.00%	10.00%	0.00%	10.00%	0.00%
research or subject specialist	7.14%	71.43%	7.14%	7.14%	7.14%	0.00%	0.00%
other	0.00%	71.43%	0.00%	0.00%	0.00%	14.29%	14.29%

Table 4.17.5 When you do use Google+ how useful is it to you? Broken out by Compensation range of the survey participant

Compensation range of the survey participant	No Answer	Don't use this at all	Not very useful	Somewhat useful	Useful	Quite useful	Essential
Less than $55,000	14.29%	71.43%	0.00%	0.00%	0.00%	14.29%	0.00%
$55,000+ to $70,000	7.69%	61.54%	0.00%	15.38%	0.00%	7.69%	7.69%
More than $70,000	9.09%	72.73%	9.09%	0.00%	9.09%	0.00%	0.00%

Table 4.17.6 When you do use Google+ how useful is it to you? Broken out by Gender of the survey participant

Gender of the survey participant	No Answer	Don't use this at all	Not very useful	Somewhat useful	Useful	Quite useful	Essential
Male	14.29%	71.43%	14.29%	0.00%	0.00%	0.00%	0.00%
Female	8.33%	66.67%	0.00%	8.33%	4.17%	8.33%	4.17%

Table 4.17.7 When you do use Google+ how useful is it to you? Broken out for medical and other scientific libraries

Your main subject focus is:	No Answer	Don't use this at all	Not very useful	Somewhat useful	Useful	Quite useful	Essential
Medical, Biological or Pharmaceutical	0.00%	77.27%	4.55%	4.55%	0.00%	9.09%	4.55%
Other Scientific	33.33%	44.44%	0.00%	11.11%	11.11%	0.00%	0.00%

Table 4.18.1 When you do use Google Hangouts how useful is it to you?

	No Answer	Don't use this at all	Not very useful	Somewhat useful	Useful	Quite useful	Essential
Entire sample	6.45%	64.52%	3.23%	3.23%	9.68%	9.68%	3.23%

Table 4.18.2 When you do use Google Hangouts how useful is it to you? Broken out by Type of institution

Type of institution	No Answer	Don't use this at all	Not very useful	Somewhat useful	Useful	Quite useful	Essential
Academic Medical Library	0.00%	66.67%	8.33%	0.00%	0.00%	16.67%	8.33%
Academic Scientific Library	20.00%	40.00%	0.00%	0.00%	30.00%	10.00%	0.00%
Non-Educational Medical/Scientific Library	0.00%	88.89%	0.00%	11.11%	0.00%	0.00%	0.00%

Table 4.18.3 When you do use Google Hangouts how useful is it to you? Broken out by Age range of the survey participant

Age range of the survey participant	No Answer	Don't use this at all	Not very useful	Somewhat useful	Useful	Quite useful	Essential
Under 40	11.11%	55.56%	0.00%	0.00%	22.22%	11.11%	0.00%
40-59	6.67%	66.67%	6.67%	6.67%	6.67%	0.00%	6.67%
60 or Over	0.00%	71.43%	0.00%	0.00%	0.00%	28.57%	0.00%

Table 4.18.4 When you do use Google Hangouts how useful is it to you? Broken out by Work specialization or title of the survey participant

Work specialization or title of the survey participant	No Answer	Don't use this at all	Not very useful	Somewhat useful	Useful	Quite useful	Essential
reference or information literacy	10.00%	60.00%	0.00%	0.00%	10.00%	20.00%	0.00%
research or subject specialist	7.14%	64.29%	7.14%	0.00%	14.29%	7.14%	0.00%
other	0.00%	71.43%	0.00%	14.29%	0.00%	0.00%	14.29%

Table 4.18.5 When you do use Google Hangouts how useful is it to you? Broken out by Compensation range of the survey participant

Compensation range of the survey participant	No Answer	Don't use this at all	Not very useful	Somewhat useful	Useful	Quite useful	Essential
Less than $55,000	14.29%	71.43%	0.00%	0.00%	0.00%	14.29%	0.00%
$55,000+ to $70,000	7.69%	61.54%	0.00%	0.00%	7.69%	15.38%	7.69%
More than $70,000	0.00%	63.64%	9.09%	9.09%	18.18%	0.00%	0.00%

Table 4.18.6 When you do use Google Hangouts how useful is it to you? Broken out by Gender of the survey participant

Gender of the survey participant	No Answer	Don't use this at all	Not very useful	Somewhat useful	Useful	Quite useful	Essential
Male	14.29%	71.43%	14.29%	0.00%	0.00%	0.00%	0.00%
Female	4.17%	62.50%	0.00%	4.17%	12.50%	12.50%	4.17%

Table 4.18.7 When you do use Google Hangouts how useful is it to you? Broken out for medical and other scientific libraries

Your main subject focus is:	No Answer	Don't use this at all	Not very useful	Somewhat useful	Useful	Quite useful	Essential
Medical, Biological or Pharmaceutical	0.00%	77.27%	4.55%	0.00%	0.00%	13.64%	4.55%
Other Scientific	22.22%	33.33%	0.00%	11.11%	33.33%	0.00%	0.00%

Table 4.19.1 When you do use Gmail how useful is it to you?

	No Answer	Don't use this at all	Not very useful	Somewhat useful	Useful	Quite useful	Essential
Entire sample	3.23%	19.35%	3.23%	6.45%	6.45%	16.13%	45.16%

Table 4.19.2 When you do use Gmail how useful is it to you? Broken out by Type of institution

Type of institution	No Answer	Don't use this at all	Not very useful	Somewhat useful	Useful	Quite useful	Essential
Academic Medical Library	0.00%	16.67%	8.33%	0.00%	8.33%	25.00%	41.67%
Academic Scientific Library	10.00%	0.00%	0.00%	20.00%	10.00%	20.00%	40.00%
Non-Educational Medical/Scientific Library	0.00%	44.44%	0.00%	0.00%	0.00%	0.00%	55.56%

Table 4.19.3 When you do use Gmail how useful is it to you? Broken out by Age range of the survey participant

Age range of the survey participant	No Answer	Don't use this at all	Not very useful	Somewhat useful	Useful	Quite useful	Essential
Under 40	0.00%	11.11%	0.00%	0.00%	22.22%	33.33%	33.33%
40-59	6.67%	26.67%	0.00%	6.67%	0.00%	13.33%	46.67%
60 or Over	0.00%	14.29%	14.29%	14.29%	0.00%	0.00%	57.14%

Table 4.19.4 When you do use Gmail how useful is it to you? Broken out by Work specialization or title of the survey participant

Work specialization or title of the survey participant	No Answer	Don't use this at all	Not very useful	Somewhat useful	Useful	Quite useful	Essential
reference or information literacy	10.00%	10.00%	10.00%	10.00%	0.00%	10.00%	50.00%
research or subject specialist	0.00%	28.57%	0.00%	7.14%	14.29%	14.29%	35.71%
other	0.00%	14.29%	0.00%	0.00%	0.00%	28.57%	57.14%

Table 4.19.5 When you do use Gmail how useful is it to you? Broken out by Compensation range of the survey participant

Compensation range of the survey participant	No Answer	Don't use this at all	Not very useful	Somewhat useful	Useful	Quite useful	Essential
Less than $55,000	0.00%	28.57%	0.00%	0.00%	0.00%	28.57%	42.86%
$55,000+ to $70,000	0.00%	15.38%	7.69%	7.69%	7.69%	15.38%	46.15%
More than $70,000	9.09%	18.18%	0.00%	9.09%	9.09%	9.09%	45.45%

Table 4.19.6 When you do use Gmail how useful is it to you? Broken out by Gender of the survey participant

Gender of the survey participant	No Answer	Don't use this at all	Not very useful	Somewhat useful	Useful	Quite useful	Essential
Male	0.00%	28.57%	0.00%	14.29%	14.29%	28.57%	14.29%
Female	4.17%	16.67%	4.17%	4.17%	4.17%	12.50%	54.17%

Table 4.19.7 When you do use Gmail how useful is it to you? Broken out for medical and other scientific libraries

Your main subject focus is:	No Answer	Don't use this at all	Not very useful	Somewhat useful	Useful	Quite useful	Essential
Medical, Biological or Pharmaceutical	0.00%	22.73%	4.55%	4.55%	4.55%	13.64%	50.00%
Other Scientific	11.11%	11.11%	0.00%	11.11%	11.11%	22.22%	33.33%

Table 4.20.1 When you do use Google Bookmarks how useful is it to you?

	No Answer	Don't use this at all	Not very useful	Somewhat useful	Useful	Quite useful	Essential
Entire sample	9.68%	64.52%	3.23%	3.23%	12.90%	3.23%	3.23%

Table 4.20.2 When you do use Google Bookmarks how useful is it to you? Broken out by Type of institution

Type of institution	No Answer	Don't use this at all	Not very useful	Somewhat useful	Useful	Quite useful	Essential
Academic Medical Library	0.00%	75.00%	0.00%	0.00%	16.67%	8.33%	0.00%
Academic Scientific Library	20.00%	60.00%	10.00%	0.00%	10.00%	0.00%	0.00%
Non-Educational Medical/Scientific Library	11.11%	55.56%	0.00%	11.11%	11.11%	0.00%	11.11%

Table 4.20.3 When you do use Google Bookmarks how useful is it to you? Broken out by Age range of the survey participant

Age range of the survey participant	No Answer	Don't use this at all	Not very useful	Somewhat useful	Useful	Quite useful	Essential
Under 40	22.22%	66.67%	11.11%	0.00%	0.00%	0.00%	0.00%
40-59	6.67%	53.33%	0.00%	6.67%	20.00%	6.67%	6.67%
60 or Over	0.00%	85.71%	0.00%	0.00%	14.29%	0.00%	0.00%

Table 4.20.4 When you do use Google Bookmarks how useful is it to you? Broken out by Work specialization or title of the survey participant

Work specialization or title of the survey participant	No Answer	Don't use this at all	Not very useful	Somewhat useful	Useful	Quite useful	Essential
reference or information literacy	10.00%	70.00%	0.00%	0.00%	10.00%	0.00%	10.00%
research or subject specialist	14.29%	71.43%	7.14%	0.00%	7.14%	0.00%	0.00%
other	0.00%	42.86%	0.00%	14.29%	28.57%	14.29%	0.00%

Table 4.20.5 When you do use Google Bookmarks how useful is it to you? Broken out by Compensation range of the survey participant

Compensation range of the survey participant	No Answer	Don't use this at all	Not very useful	Somewhat useful	Useful	Quite useful	Essential
Less than $55,000	14.29%	85.71%	0.00%	0.00%	0.00%	0.00%	0.00%
$55,000+ to $70,000	15.38%	53.85%	7.69%	0.00%	7.69%	7.69%	7.69%
More than $70,000	0.00%	63.64%	0.00%	9.09%	27.27%	0.00%	0.00%

Table 4.20.6 When you do use Google Bookmarks how useful is it to you? Broken out by Gender of the survey participant

Gender of the survey participant	No Answer	Don't use this at all	Not very useful	Somewhat useful	Useful	Quite useful	Essential
Male	14.29%	85.71%	0.00%	0.00%	0.00%	0.00%	0.00%
Female	8.33%	58.33%	4.17%	4.17%	16.67%	4.17%	4.17%

Table 4.20.7 When you do use Google Bookmarks how useful is it to you? Broken out for medical and other scientific libraries

Your main subject focus is:	No Answer	Don't use this at all	Not very useful	Somewhat useful	Useful	Quite useful	Essential
Medical, Biological or Pharmaceutical	4.55%	72.73%	0.00%	0.00%	13.64%	4.55%	4.55%
Other Scientific	22.22%	44.44%	11.11%	11.11%	11.11%	0.00%	0.00%

Table 4.21.1 When you do use Google Patent Search how useful is it to you?

	No Answer	Don't use this at all	Not very useful	Somewhat useful	Useful	Quite useful	Essential
Entire sample	6.45%	61.29%	3.23%	3.23%	6.45%	19.35%	0.00%

Table 4.21.2 When you do use Google Patent Search how useful is it to you? Broken out by Type of institution

Type of institution	No Answer	Don't use this at all	Not very useful	Somewhat useful	Useful	Quite useful	Essential
Academic Medical Library	0.00%	83.33%	0.00%	0.00%	0.00%	16.67%	0.00%
Academic Scientific Library	20.00%	40.00%	0.00%	10.00%	20.00%	10.00%	0.00%
Non-Educational Medical/Scientific Library	0.00%	55.56%	11.11%	0.00%	0.00%	33.33%	0.00%

Table 4.21.3 When you do use Google Patent Search how useful is it to you? Broken out by Age range of the survey participant

Age range of the survey participant	No Answer	Don't use this at all	Not very useful	Somewhat useful	Useful	Quite useful	Essential
Under 40	11.11%	55.56%	0.00%	11.11%	11.11%	11.11%	0.00%
40-59	6.67%	60.00%	0.00%	0.00%	6.67%	26.67%	0.00%
60 or Over	0.00%	71.43%	14.29%	0.00%	0.00%	14.29%	0.00%

Table 4.21.4 When you do use Google Patent Search how useful is it to you? Broken out by Work specialization or title of the survey participant

Work specialization or title of the survey participant	No Answer	Don't use this at all	Not very useful	Somewhat useful	Useful	Quite useful	Essential
reference or information literacy	10.00%	60.00%	10.00%	10.00%	0.00%	10.00%	0.00%
research or subject specialist	7.14%	50.00%	0.00%	0.00%	14.29%	28.57%	0.00%
other	0.00%	85.71%	0.00%	0.00%	0.00%	14.29%	0.00%

Table 4.21.5 When you do use Google Patent Search how useful is it to you? Broken out by Compensation range of the survey participant

Compensation range of the survey participant	No Answer	Don't use this at all	Not very useful	Somewhat useful	Useful	Quite useful	Essential
Less than $55,000	14.29%	28.57%	14.29%	14.29%	14.29%	14.29%	0.00%
$55,000+ to $70,000	7.69%	61.54%	0.00%	0.00%	7.69%	23.08%	0.00%
More than $70,000	0.00%	81.82%	0.00%	0.00%	0.00%	18.18%	0.00%

Table 4.21.6 When you do use Google Patent Search how useful is it to you? Broken out by Gender of the survey participant

Gender of the survey participant	No Answer	Don't use this at all	Not very useful	Somewhat useful	Useful	Quite useful	Essential
Male	14.29%	57.14%	0.00%	0.00%	14.29%	14.29%	0.00%
Female	4.17%	62.50%	4.17%	4.17%	4.17%	20.83%	0.00%

Table 4.21.7 When you do use Google Patent Search how useful is it to you? Broken out for medical and other scientific libraries

Your main subject focus is:	No Answer	Don't use this at all	Not very useful	Somewhat useful	Useful	Quite useful	Essential
Medical, Biological or Pharmaceutical	0.00%	68.18%	4.55%	4.55%	0.00%	22.73%	0.00%
Other Scientific	22.22%	44.44%	0.00%	0.00%	22.22%	11.11%	0.00%

Table 4.22.1 When you do use Google Forms how useful is it to you?

	No Answer	Don't use this at all	Not very useful	Somewhat useful	Useful	Quite useful	Essential
Entire sample	3.23%	61.29%	3.23%	6.45%	9.68%	3.23%	12.90%

Table 4.22.2 When you do use Google Forms how useful is it to you? Broken out by Type of institution

Type of institution	No Answer	Don't use this at all	Not very useful	Somewhat useful	Useful	Quite useful	Essential
Academic Medical Library	0.00%	75.00%	0.00%	0.00%	8.33%	0.00%	16.67%
Academic Scientific Library	10.00%	20.00%	10.00%	20.00%	20.00%	10.00%	10.00%
Non-Educational Medical/Scientific Library	0.00%	88.89%	0.00%	0.00%	0.00%	0.00%	11.11%

Table 4.22.3 When you do use Google Forms how useful is it to you? Broken out by Age range of the survey participant

Age range of the survey participant	No Answer	Don't use this at all	Not very useful	Somewhat useful	Useful	Quite useful	Essential
Under 40	0.00%	33.33%	11.11%	11.11%	11.11%	11.11%	22.22%
40-59	6.67%	60.00%	0.00%	6.67%	13.33%	0.00%	13.33%
60 or Over	0.00%	100.00%	0.00%	0.00%	0.00%	0.00%	0.00%

Table 4.22.4 When you do use Google Forms how useful is it to you? Broken out by Work specialization or title of the survey participant

Work specialization or title of the survey participant	No Answer	Don't use this at all	Not very useful	Somewhat useful	Useful	Quite useful	Essential
reference or information literacy	10.00%	60.00%	0.00%	10.00%	0.00%	10.00%	10.00%
research or subject specialist	0.00%	57.14%	7.14%	7.14%	21.43%	0.00%	7.14%
other	0.00%	71.43%	0.00%	0.00%	0.00%	0.00%	28.57%

Table 4.22.5 When you do use Google Forms how useful is it to you? Broken out by Compensation range of the survey participant

Compensation range of the survey participant	No Answer	Don't use this at all	Not very useful	Somewhat useful	Useful	Quite useful	Essential
Less than $55,000	14.29%	57.14%	0.00%	0.00%	0.00%	14.29%	14.29%
$55,000+ to $70,000	0.00%	61.54%	7.69%	7.69%	7.69%	0.00%	15.38%
More than $70,000	0.00%	63.64%	0.00%	9.09%	18.18%	0.00%	9.09%

Table 4.22.6 When you do use Google Forms how useful is it to you? Broken out by Gender of the survey participant

Gender of the survey participant	No Answer	Don't use this at all	Not very useful	Somewhat useful	Useful	Quite useful	Essential
Male	0.00%	71.43%	0.00%	14.29%	14.29%	0.00%	0.00%
Female	4.17%	58.33%	4.17%	4.17%	8.33%	4.17%	16.67%

Table 4.22.7 When you do use Google Forms how useful is it to you? Broken out for medical and other scientific libraries

Your main subject focus is:	No Answer	Don't use this at all	Not very useful	Somewhat useful	Useful	Quite useful	Essential
Medical, Biological or Pharmaceutical	0.00%	72.73%	0.00%	0.00%	9.09%	4.55%	13.64%
Other Scientific	11.11%	33.33%	11.11%	22.22%	11.11%	0.00%	11.11%

Table 4.23.1 When you do use Google Slides how useful is it to you?

	No Answer	Don't use this at all	Not very useful	Somewhat useful	Useful	Quite useful	Essential
Entire sample	3.23%	70.97%	6.45%	3.23%	6.45%	6.45%	3.23%

Table 4.23.2 When you do use Google Slides how useful is it to you? Broken out by Type of institution

Type of institution	No Answer	Don't use this at all	Not very useful	Somewhat useful	Useful	Quite useful	Essential
Academic Medical Library	0.00%	83.33%	0.00%	0.00%	8.33%	0.00%	8.33%
Academic Scientific Library	10.00%	50.00%	10.00%	10.00%	0.00%	20.00%	0.00%
Non-Educational Medical/Scientific Library	0.00%	77.78%	11.11%	0.00%	11.11%	0.00%	0.00%

Table 4.23.3 When you do use Google Slides how useful is it to you? Broken out by Age range of the survey participant

Age range of the survey participant	No Answer	Don't use this at all	Not very useful	Somewhat useful	Useful	Quite useful	Essential
Under 40	11.11%	55.56%	11.11%	11.11%	0.00%	11.11%	0.00%
40-59	0.00%	73.33%	0.00%	0.00%	13.33%	6.67%	6.67%
60 or Over	0.00%	85.71%	14.29%	0.00%	0.00%	0.00%	0.00%

Table 4.23.4 When you do use Google Slides how useful is it to you? Broken out by Work specialization or title of the survey participant

Work specialization or title of the survey participant	No Answer	Don't use this at all	Not very useful	Somewhat useful	Useful	Quite useful	Essential
reference or information literacy	0.00%	60.00%	10.00%	10.00%	10.00%	10.00%	0.00%
research or subject specialist	7.14%	71.43%	7.14%	0.00%	7.14%	7.14%	0.00%
other	0.00%	85.71%	0.00%	0.00%	0.00%	0.00%	14.29%

Table 4.23.5 When you do use Google Slides how useful is it to you? Broken out by Compensation range of the survey participant

Compensation range of the survey participant	No Answer	Don't use this at all	Not very useful	Somewhat useful	Useful	Quite useful	Essential
Less than $55,000	0.00%	57.14%	14.29%	14.29%	0.00%	14.29%	0.00%
$55,000+ to $70,000	7.69%	69.23%	7.69%	0.00%	7.69%	0.00%	7.69%
More than $70,000	0.00%	81.82%	0.00%	0.00%	9.09%	9.09%	0.00%

Table 4.23.6 When you do use Google Slides how useful is it to you? Broken out by Gender of the survey participant

Gender of the survey participant	No Answer	Don't use this at all	Not very useful	Somewhat useful	Useful	Quite useful	Essential
Male	14.29%	71.43%	0.00%	0.00%	14.29%	0.00%	0.00%
Female	0.00%	70.83%	8.33%	4.17%	4.17%	8.33%	4.17%

Table 4.23.7 When you do use Google Slides how useful is it to you? Broken out for medical and other scientific libraries

Your main subject focus is:	No Answer	Don't use this at all	Not very useful	Somewhat useful	Useful	Quite useful	Essential
Medical, Biological or Pharmaceutical	0.00%	77.27%	4.55%	4.55%	9.09%	0.00%	4.55%
Other Scientific	11.11%	55.56%	11.11%	0.00%	0.00%	22.22%	0.00%

Table 4.24.1 When you do use Google Groups how useful is it to you?

	No Answer	Don't use this at all	Not very useful	Somewhat useful	Useful	Quite useful	Essential
Entire sample	6.45%	67.74%	0.00%	3.23%	12.90%	6.45%	3.23%

Table 4.24.2 When you do use Google Groups how useful is it to you? Broken out by Type of institution

Type of institution	No Answer	Don't use this at all	Not very useful	Somewhat useful	Useful	Quite useful	Essential
Academic Medical Library	0.00%	75.00%	0.00%	0.00%	25.00%	0.00%	0.00%
Academic Scientific Library	20.00%	60.00%	0.00%	0.00%	0.00%	20.00%	0.00%
Non-Educational Medical/Scientific Library	0.00%	66.67%	0.00%	11.11%	11.11%	0.00%	11.11%

Table 4.24.3 When you do use Google Groups how useful is it to you? Broken out by Age range of the survey participant

Age range of the survey participant	No Answer	Don't use this at all	Not very useful	Somewhat useful	Useful	Quite useful	Essential
Under 40	11.11%	66.67%	0.00%	0.00%	11.11%	11.11%	0.00%
40-59	6.67%	66.67%	0.00%	6.67%	13.33%	6.67%	0.00%
60 or Over	0.00%	71.43%	0.00%	0.00%	14.29%	0.00%	14.29%

Table 4.24.4 When you do use Google Groups how useful is it to you? Broken out by Work specialization or title of the survey participant

Work specialization or title of the survey participant	No Answer	Don't use this at all	Not very useful	Somewhat useful	Useful	Quite useful	Essential
reference or information literacy	10.00%	70.00%	0.00%	0.00%	10.00%	0.00%	10.00%
research or subject specialist	7.14%	64.29%	0.00%	0.00%	14.29%	14.29%	0.00%
other	0.00%	71.43%	0.00%	14.29%	14.29%	0.00%	0.00%

Table 4.24.5 When you do use Google Groups how useful is it to you? Broken out by Compensation range of the survey participant

Compensation range of the survey participant	No Answer	Don't use this at all	Not very useful	Somewhat useful	Useful	Quite useful	Essential
Less than $55,000	14.29%	57.14%	0.00%	0.00%	0.00%	14.29%	14.29%
$55,000+ to $70,000	7.69%	69.23%	0.00%	0.00%	15.38%	7.69%	0.00%
More than $70,000	0.00%	72.73%	0.00%	9.09%	18.18%	0.00%	0.00%

Table 4.24.6 When you do use Google Groups how useful is it to you? Broken out by Gender of the survey participant

Gender of the survey participant	No Answer	Don't use this at all	Not very useful	Somewhat useful	Useful	Quite useful	Essential
Male	14.29%	42.86%	0.00%	0.00%	28.57%	14.29%	0.00%
Female	4.17%	75.00%	0.00%	4.17%	8.33%	4.17%	4.17%

Table 4.24.7 When you do use Google Groups how useful is it to you? Broken out for medical and other scientific libraries

Your main subject focus is:	No Answer	Don't use this at all	Not very useful	Somewhat useful	Useful	Quite useful	Essential
Medical, Biological or Pharmaceutical	0.00%	77.27%	0.00%	0.00%	18.18%	0.00%	4.55%
Other Scientific	22.22%	44.44%	0.00%	11.11%	0.00%	22.22%	0.00%

Table 4.25.1 When you do use Google Analytics how useful is it to you?

	No Answer	Don't use this at all	Not very useful	Somewhat useful	Useful	Quite useful	Essential
Entire sample	9.68%	54.84%	3.23%	6.45%	12.90%	9.68%	3.23%

Table 4.25.2 When you do use Google Analytics how useful is it to you? Broken out by Type of institution

Type of institution	No Answer	Don't use this at all	Not very useful	Somewhat useful	Useful	Quite useful	Essential
Academic Medical Library	8.33%	50.00%	0.00%	8.33%	16.67%	16.67%	0.00%
Academic Scientific Library	20.00%	50.00%	10.00%	0.00%	20.00%	0.00%	0.00%
Non-Educational Medical/Scientific Library	0.00%	66.67%	0.00%	11.11%	0.00%	11.11%	11.11%

Table 4.25.3 When you do use Google Analytics how useful is it to you? Broken out by Age range of the survey participant

Age range of the survey participant	No Answer	Don't use this at all	Not very useful	Somewhat useful	Useful	Quite useful	Essential
Under 40	11.11%	55.56%	11.11%	0.00%	22.22%	0.00%	0.00%
40-59	6.67%	53.33%	0.00%	13.33%	13.33%	6.67%	6.67%
60 or Over	14.29%	57.14%	0.00%	0.00%	0.00%	28.57%	0.00%

Table 4.25.4 When you do use Google Analytics how useful is it to you? Broken out by Work specialization or title of the survey participant

Work specialization or title of the survey participant	No Answer	Don't use this at all	Not very useful	Somewhat useful	Useful	Quite useful	Essential
reference or information literacy	10.00%	70.00%	0.00%	0.00%	0.00%	10.00%	10.00%
research or subject specialist	7.14%	35.71%	7.14%	7.14%	28.57%	14.29%	0.00%
other	14.29%	71.43%	0.00%	14.29%	0.00%	0.00%	0.00%

Table 4.25.5 When you do use Google Analytics how useful is it to you? Broken out by Compensation range of the survey participant

Compensation range of the survey participant	No Answer	Don't use this at all	Not very useful	Somewhat useful	Useful	Quite useful	Essential
Less than $55,000	14.29%	71.43%	0.00%	0.00%	14.29%	0.00%	0.00%
$55,000+ to $70,000	7.69%	46.15%	7.69%	0.00%	7.69%	23.08%	7.69%
More than $70,000	9.09%	54.55%	0.00%	18.18%	18.18%	0.00%	0.00%

Table 4.25.6 When you do use Google Analytics how useful is it to you? Broken out by Gender of the survey participant

Gender of the survey participant	No Answer	Don't use this at all	Not very useful	Somewhat useful	Useful	Quite useful	Essential
Male	14.29%	28.57%	0.00%	14.29%	28.57%	14.29%	0.00%
Female	8.33%	62.50%	4.17%	4.17%	8.33%	8.33%	4.17%

Table 4.25.7 When you do use Google Analytics how useful is it to you? Broken out for medical and other scientific libraries

Your main subject focus is:	No Answer	Don't use this at all	Not very useful	Somewhat useful	Useful	Quite useful	Essential
Medical, Biological or Pharmaceutical	4.55%	63.64%	0.00%	4.55%	9.09%	13.64%	4.55%
Other Scientific	22.22%	33.33%	11.11%	11.11%	22.22%	0.00%	0.00%

Table 4.26.1 When you do use Blogger how useful is it to you?

	No Answer	Don't use this at all	Not very useful	Somewhat useful	Useful	Quite useful	Essential
Entire sample	6.45%	83.87%	3.23%	0.00%	0.00%	6.45%	0.00%

Table 4.26.2 When you do use Blogger how useful is it to you? Broken out by Type of institution

Type of institution	No Answer	Don't use this at all	Not very useful	Somewhat useful	Useful	Quite useful	Essential
Academic Medical Library	0.00%	91.67%	0.00%	0.00%	0.00%	8.33%	0.00%
Academic Scientific Library	20.00%	70.00%	10.00%	0.00%	0.00%	0.00%	0.00%
Non-Educational Medical/Scientific Library	0.00%	88.89%	0.00%	0.00%	0.00%	11.11%	0.00%

Table 4.26.3 When you do use Blogger how useful is it to you? Broken out by Age range of the survey participant

Age range of the survey participant	No Answer	Don't use this at all	Not very useful	Somewhat useful	Useful	Quite useful	Essential
Under 40	11.11%	77.78%	11.11%	0.00%	0.00%	0.00%	0.00%
40-59	6.67%	80.00%	0.00%	0.00%	0.00%	13.33%	0.00%
60 or Over	0.00%	100.00%	0.00%	0.00%	0.00%	0.00%	0.00%

Table 4.26.4 When you do use Blogger how useful is it to you? Broken out by Work specialization or title of the survey participant

Work specialization or title of the survey participant	No Answer	Don't use this at all	Not very useful	Somewhat useful	Useful	Quite useful	Essential
reference or information literacy	10.00%	80.00%	0.00%	0.00%	0.00%	10.00%	0.00%
research or subject specialist	7.14%	85.71%	7.14%	0.00%	0.00%	0.00%	0.00%
other	0.00%	85.71%	0.00%	0.00%	0.00%	14.29%	0.00%

Table 4.26.5 When you do use Blogger how useful is it to you? Broken out by Compensation range of the survey participant

Compensation range of the survey participant	No Answer	Don't use this at all	Not very useful	Somewhat useful	Useful	Quite useful	Essential
Less than $55,000	14.29%	85.71%	0.00%	0.00%	0.00%	0.00%	0.00%
$55,000+ to $70,000	7.69%	76.92%	7.69%	0.00%	0.00%	7.69%	0.00%
More than $70,000	0.00%	90.91%	0.00%	0.00%	0.00%	9.09%	0.00%

Table 4.26.6 When you do use Blogger how useful is it to you? Broken out by Gender of the survey participant

Gender of the survey participant	No Answer	Don't use this at all	Not very useful	Somewhat useful	Useful	Quite useful	Essential
Male	14.29%	85.71%	0.00%	0.00%	0.00%	0.00%	0.00%
Female	4.17%	83.33%	4.17%	0.00%	0.00%	8.33%	0.00%

Table 4.26.7 When you do use Blogger how useful is it to you? Broken out for medical and other scientific libraries

Your main subject focus is:	No Answer	Don't use this at all	Not very useful	Somewhat useful	Useful	Quite useful	Essential
Medical, Biological or Pharmaceutical	0.00%	90.91%	0.00%	0.00%	0.00%	9.09%	0.00%
Other Scientific	22.22%	66.67%	11.11%	0.00%	0.00%	0.00%	0.00%

Table 4.27.1 When you do use YouTube how useful is it to you?

	No Answer	Don't use this at all	Not very useful	Somewhat useful	Useful	Quite useful	Essential
Entire sample	6.45%	3.23%	3.23%	9.68%	25.81%	22.58%	29.03%

Table 4.27.2 When you do use YouTube how useful is it to you? Broken out by Type of institution

Type of institution	No Answer	Don't use this at all	Not very useful	Somewhat useful	Useful	Quite useful	Essential
Academic Medical Library	8.33%	8.33%	0.00%	0.00%	16.67%	16.67%	50.00%
Academic Scientific Library	10.00%	0.00%	0.00%	10.00%	20.00%	40.00%	20.00%
Non-Educational Medical/Scientific Library	0.00%	0.00%	11.11%	22.22%	44.44%	11.11%	11.11%

Table 4.27.3 When you do use YouTube how useful is it to you? Broken out by Age range of the survey participant

Age range of the survey participant	No Answer	Don't use this at all	Not very useful	Somewhat useful	Useful	Quite useful	Essential
Under 40	0.00%	0.00%	11.11%	11.11%	11.11%	33.33%	33.33%
40-59	13.33%	0.00%	0.00%	6.67%	40.00%	13.33%	26.67%
60 or Over	0.00%	14.29%	0.00%	14.29%	14.29%	28.57%	28.57%

Table 4.27.4 When you do use YouTube how useful is it to you? Broken out by Work specialization or title of the survey participant

Work specialization or title of the survey participant	No Answer	Don't use this at all	Not very useful	Somewhat useful	Useful	Quite useful	Essential
reference or information literacy	10.00%	0.00%	0.00%	0.00%	40.00%	30.00%	20.00%
research or subject specialist	7.14%	7.14%	7.14%	7.14%	21.43%	28.57%	21.43%
other	0.00%	0.00%	0.00%	28.57%	14.29%	0.00%	57.14%

Table 4.27.5 When you do use YouTube how useful is it to you? Broken out by Compensation range of the survey participant

Compensation range of the survey participant	No Answer	Don't use this at all	Not very useful	Somewhat useful	Useful	Quite useful	Essential
Less than $55,000	14.29%	0.00%	0.00%	0.00%	14.29%	42.86%	28.57%
$55,000+ to $70,000	0.00%	0.00%	7.69%	0.00%	38.46%	23.08%	30.77%
More than $70,000	9.09%	9.09%	0.00%	27.27%	18.18%	9.09%	27.27%

Table 4.27.6 When you do use YouTube how useful is it to you? Broken out by Gender of the survey participant

Gender of the survey participant	No Answer	Don't use this at all	Not very useful	Somewhat useful	Useful	Quite useful	Essential
Male	14.29%	14.29%	0.00%	0.00%	14.29%	57.14%	0.00%
Female	4.17%	0.00%	4.17%	12.50%	29.17%	12.50%	37.50%

Table 4.27.7 When you do use YouTube how useful is it to you? Broken out for medical and other scientific libraries

Your main subject focus is:	No Answer	Don't use this at all	Not very useful	Somewhat useful	Useful	Quite useful	Essential
Medical, Biological or Pharmaceutical	4.55%	4.55%	4.55%	4.55%	31.82%	18.18%	31.82%
Other Scientific	11.11%	0.00%	0.00%	22.22%	11.11%	33.33%	22.22%

For those Google features that you labeled "Quite Useful" or "Essential" what were these features and what do you use them for?

Academic Medical Library

1) Advanced search operators - AND / OR SITE; ALLINTITLE
2) Chrome is my preferred search tool. Use Gmail for personal email - I do have yahoo & Hotmail accounts but use those primarily to park sale mail
3) Chrome is one of my most frequently used browsers and I rely on Gmail for my personal email. What are trying to ask here - specifics? For so many features?
4) I use them for work and leisure. Google maps is used for when I travel for work and pleasure. YouTube is used both for work and leisure.
5) Google maps: finding things; students I work with create maps of activity for research. Advanced search: to modify searches in specific ways Images: looking for images/helping users look for images on specific things, filtering, looking up usage rights. Chrome--need at least two browsers and this is a very good, usable one. Google Scholar--very helpful in scholarly/research literature searching, especially hard to find things, tests and instruments, devices. Great linking integrated with our electronic journals. Gmail: very good alternative to university provided account; YouTube--search for examples for teaching, search for instructions for teaching, putting up outreach videos, etc.
6) I'm always on YouTube, looking up music videos, listening to music, uploading tutorials for my job, etc. I use Google Forms for most if not all my forms and of course, to have that, I need a Gmail account. Google maps, images and Chrome as the web browsers are my go-to favorites.

Academic Scientific Library

1) Mostly personal life stuff, but I use them almost every day. For work, I use Drive and Scholar almost daily.
2) Larger storage, easy to use
3) I use Google Maps less for research than for practical reasons, like navigating to a meeting location. I use Google Scholar Citations as an addendum to my resume, helpful for tracking my own publications (although I have just signed up with ORCID and may use that instead in the future). I use Google Drive all day every day. I like that I can access my working files from anywhere with an internet connection. I now save nothing to my standard hard or network drives. I use Google Images to find illustrative images for reports, documents, communications, etc. The best part is being able to filter by usage license. And I use Google Scholar to round out database searching. It's also popular with the students I teach.
4) I use 'directions' in Maps. In Scholar I use citations links, the 'cite', and 'Import to endnote' features. In images I use the limit to images that can be freely shared

5) Google Maps, directions for various purposes Google Advanced Search - trying to restrict search to pertinent items google scholar - way to limit search and remove extraneous items Google Drive shared items, class schedules
6) My alumni email and calendar are Google based

Non-Educational Medical/Scientific Library

1) Assuming the usage is for work and not for personal, Chrome is important because it's the only browser I'm allowed to use at work besides IE, and Google scholar is the only way I can access citations besides PubMed. It would be helpful if I knew this was for work only for work and personal use
2) Google Scholar is very useful since it seems to search article text and comes up with useful content I might miss in PubMed. I also use its "cited by" feature which is very useful.
3) Maps - finding directions or locating a place, advanced search - finding more than one search term, and Chrome - browser
4) Work related communication
5) Gmail I use for everything except personal correspondence. Google Maps I typically use to get directions to places I need to get to (or to see where they are) Advanced Search and Scholar I use when I'm looking for information. Books gives me a look at resources I might not have physically available. Translate I've used to read some web pages or compose messages to someone in a foreign country.
6) Google Scholar is used for forward citation searching and Google advanced for determining search syntax to create complex grey lit search strategies. Google books help to preview content before purchase or requesting it through other libraries. Google translate is used for determining foreign language article titles, search terms. Patent search is the easiest access point to this kind of info and has assisted with searches related to electronic cigarettes, vaping. You tube is essential for learning new skills/self-training as needed.
7) Maps - planning routes when travelling; checking where places are: Scholar - literature searching; checking full text availability; Chrome - as a back up to IE when IE bugs mean websites don't display or work properly. Analytics - for personal use (own website)
8) I use them in my teaching of resources, to learn things myself (tutorials on you tube), to do my research, to share information with colleagues and to help staff, students and faculty.
9) Finds literature not in my other databases

Table 5 Approximately how much time in the past month have you personally spent (in hours or fractions thereof) using the following Google features in connection with your work? If you have not used the feature in the past month put in a zero.

Table 5.1.1 Approximately how much time in the past month have you personally spent (in hours or fractions thereof) using Google Maps in connection with your work? If you have not used the feature in the past month put in a zero.

	Mean	Median	Minimum	Maximum
Entire sample	1.94	0.50	0.00	30.00

Table 5.1.2 Approximately how much time in the past month have you personally spent (in hours or fractions thereof) using Google Maps in connection with your work? If you have not used the feature in the past month put in a zero. Broken out by Type of institution

Type of institution	Mean	Median	Minimum	Maximum
Academic Medical Library	1.01	1.00	0.10	2.00
Academic Scientific Library	3.72	0.50	0.00	30.00
Non-Educational Medical/Scientific Library	0.88	0.25	0.00	3.00

Table 5.1.3 Approximately how much time in the past month have you personally spent (in hours or fractions thereof) using Google Maps in connection with your work? If you have not used the feature in the past month put in a zero. Broken out by Age range of the survey participant

Age range of the survey participant	Mean	Median	Minimum	Maximum
Under 40	4.86	0.50	0.00	30.00
40-59	0.96	0.38	0.00	3.00
60 or Over	0.50	0.50	0.00	1.00

Table 5.1.4 Approximately how much time in the past month have you personally spent (in hours or fractions thereof) using Google Maps in connection with your work? If you have not used the feature in the past month put in a zero. Broken out by Work specialization or title of the survey participant

Work specialization or title of the survey participant	Mean	Median	Minimum	Maximum
reference or information literacy	0.28	0.14	0.00	1.00
research or subject specialist	3.50	0.50	0.00	30.00
other	1.29	1.50	0.00	2.50

Table 5.1.5 Approximately how much time in the past month have you personally spent (in hours or fractions thereof) using Google Maps in connection with your work? If you have not used the feature in the past month put in a zero. Broken out by Compensation range of the survey participant

Compensation range of the survey participant	Mean	Median	Minimum	Maximum
Less than $55,000	0.52	0.05	0.00	2.00
$55,000+ to $70,000	3.97	0.75	0.00	30.00
More than $70,000	0.64	0.50	0.00	2.00

Table 5.1.6 Approximately how much time in the past month have you personally spent (in hours or fractions thereof) using Google Maps in connection with your work? If you have not used the feature in the past month put in a zero. Broken out by Gender of the survey participant

Gender of the survey participant	Mean	Median	Minimum	Maximum
Male	0.75	0.00	0.00	3.00
Female	2.17	0.50	0.00	30.00

Table 5.1.7 Approximately how much time in the past month have you personally spent (in hours or fractions thereof) using Google Maps in connection with your work? If you have not used the feature in the past month put in a zero. Broken out for medical and other scientific libraries

Your main subject focus is:	Mean	Median	Minimum	Maximum
Medical, Biological or Pharmaceutical	0.99	1.00	0.00	3.00
Other Scientific	3.97	0.38	0.00	30.00

Table 5.2.1 Approximately how much time in the past month have you personally spent (in hours or fractions thereof) using Google Advanced Search in connection with your work? If you have not used the feature in the past month put in a zero.

	Mean	Median	Minimum	Maximum
Entire sample	1.85	1.00	0.00	16.00

Table 5.2.2 Approximately how much time in the past month have you personally spent (in hours or fractions thereof) using Google Advanced Search in connection with your work? If you have not used the feature in the past month put in a zero. Broken out by Type of institution

Type of institution	Mean	Median	Minimum	Maximum
Academic Medical Library	1.43	2.00	0.00	3.00
Academic Scientific Library	0.94	0.00	0.00	5.00
Non-Educational Medical/Scientific Library	3.08	1.00	0.00	16.00

Table 5.2.3 Approximately how much time in the past month have you personally spent (in hours or fractions thereof) using Google Advanced Search in connection with your work? If you have not used the feature in the past month put in a zero. Broken out by Age range of the survey participant

Age range of the survey participant	Mean	Median	Minimum	Maximum
Under 40	1.43	0.00	0.00	5.00
40-59	2.65	1.00	0.00	16.00
60 or Over	0.75	0.50	0.00	2.00

Table 5.2.4 Approximately how much time in the past month have you personally spent (in hours or fractions thereof) using Google Advanced Search in connection with your work? If you have not used the feature in the past month put in a zero. Broken out by Work specialization or title of the survey participant

Work specialization or title of the survey participant	Mean	Median	Minimum	Maximum
reference or information literacy	3.25	1.25	0.00	16.00
research or subject specialist	1.39	1.00	0.00	5.00
other	0.83	0.50	0.00	3.00

Table 5.2.5 Approximately how much time in the past month have you personally spent (in hours or fractions thereof) using Google Advanced Search in connection with your work? If you have not used the feature in the past month put in a zero. Broken out by Compensation range of the survey participant

Compensation range of the survey participant	Mean	Median	Minimum	Maximum
Less than $55,000	2.42	1.75	0.00	5.00
$55,000+ to $70,000	2.43	0.63	0.00	16.00
More than $70,000	0.83	0.50	0.00	3.00

Table 5.2.6 Approximately how much time in the past month have you personally spent (in hours or fractions thereof) using Google Advanced Search in connection with your work? If you have not used the feature in the past month put in a zero. Broken out by Gender of the survey participant

Gender of the survey participant	Mean	Median	Minimum	Maximum
Male	0.31	0.13	0.00	1.00
Female	2.14	1.00	0.00	16.00

Table 5.2.7 Approximately how much time in the past month have you personally spent (in hours or fractions thereof) using Google Advanced Search in connection with your work? If you have not used the feature in the past month put in a zero. Broken out for medical and other scientific libraries

Your main subject focus is:	Mean	Median	Minimum	Maximum
Medical, Biological or Pharmaceutical	2.46	1.50	0.00	16.00
Other Scientific	0.56	0.25	0.00	2.00

Table 5.3.1 Approximately how much time in the past month have you personally spent (in hours or fractions thereof) using Google Alerts in connection with your work? If you have not used the feature in the past month put in a zero.

	Mean	Median	Minimum	Maximum
Entire sample	0.12	0.00	0.00	1.00

Table 5.3.2 Approximately how much time in the past month have you personally spent (in hours or fractions thereof) using Google Alerts in connection with your work? If you have not used the feature in the past month put in a zero. Broken out by Type of institution

Type of institution	Mean	Median	Minimum	Maximum
Academic Medical Library	0.02	0.00	0.00	0.17
Academic Scientific Library	0.29	0.00	0.00	1.00
Non-Educational Medical/Scientific Library	0.06	0.00	0.00	0.50

Table 5.3.3 Approximately how much time in the past month have you personally spent (in hours or fractions thereof) using Google Alerts in connection with your work? If you have not used the feature in the past month put in a zero. Broken out by Age range of the survey participant

Age range of the survey participant	Mean	Median	Minimum	Maximum
Under 40	0.17	0.00	0.00	1.00
40-59	0.14	0.00	0.00	1.00
60 or Over	0.03	0.00	0.00	0.17

Table 5.3.4 Approximately how much time in the past month have you personally spent (in hours or fractions thereof) using Google Alerts in connection with your work? If you have not used the feature in the past month put in a zero. Broken out by Work specialization or title of the survey participant

Work specialization or title of the survey participant	Mean	Median	Minimum	Maximum
reference or information literacy	0.00	0.00	0.00	0.00
research or subject specialist	0.27	0.00	0.00	1.00
other	0.00	0.00	0.00	0.00

Table 5.3.5 Approximately how much time in the past month have you personally spent (in hours or fractions thereof) using Google Alerts in connection with your work? If you have not used the feature in the past month put in a zero. Broken out by Compensation range of the survey participant

Compensation range of the survey participant	Mean	Median	Minimum	Maximum
Less than $55,000	0.17	0.00	0.00	1.00
$55,000+ to $70,000	0.19	0.00	0.00	1.00
More than $70,000	0.00	0.00	0.00	0.00

Table 5.3.6 Approximately how much time in the past month have you personally spent (in hours or fractions thereof) using Google Alerts in connection with your work? If you have not used the feature in the past month put in a zero. Broken out by Gender of the survey participant

Gender of the survey participant	Mean	Median	Minimum	Maximum
Male	0.50	0.50	0.00	1.00
Female	0.06	0.00	0.00	1.00

Table 5.3.7 Approximately how much time in the past month have you personally spent (in hours or fractions thereof) using Google Alerts in connection with your work? If you have not used the feature in the past month put in a zero. Broken out for medical and other scientific libraries

Your main subject focus is:	Mean	Median	Minimum	Maximum
Medical, Biological or Pharmaceutical	0.04	0.00	0.00	0.50
Other Scientific	0.33	0.00	0.00	1.00

Table 5.4.1 Approximately how much time in the past month have you personally spent (in hours or fractions thereof) using Google Notifications in connection with your work? If you have not used the feature in the past month put in a zero.

	Mean	Median	Minimum	Maximum
Entire sample	0.05	0.00	0.00	1.00

Table 5.4.2 Approximately how much time in the past month have you personally spent (in hours or fractions thereof) using Google Notifications in connection with your work? If you have not used the feature in the past month put in a zero. Broken out by Type of institution

Type of institution	Mean	Median	Minimum	Maximum
Academic Medical Library	0.00	0.00	0.00	0.00
Academic Scientific Library	0.14	0.00	0.00	1.00
Non-Educational Medical/Scientific Library	0.00	0.00	0.00	0.00

Table 5.4.3 Approximately how much time in the past month have you personally spent (in hours or fractions thereof) using Google Notifications in connection with your work? If you have not used the feature in the past month put in a zero. Broken out by Age range of the survey participant

Age range of the survey participant	Mean	Median	Minimum	Maximum
Under 40	0.17	0.00	0.00	1.00
40-59	0.00	0.00	0.00	0.00
60 or Over	0.00	0.00	0.00	0.00

Table 5.4.4 Approximately how much time in the past month have you personally spent (in hours or fractions thereof) using Google Notifications in connection with your work? If you have not used the feature in the past month put in a zero. Broken out by Work specialization or title of the survey participant

Work specialization or title of the survey participant	Mean	Median	Minimum	Maximum
reference or information literacy	0.00	0.00	0.00	0.00
research or subject specialist	0.11	0.00	0.00	1.00
other	0.00	0.00	0.00	0.00

Table 5.4.5 Approximately how much time in the past month have you personally spent (in hours or fractions thereof) using Google Notifications in connection with your work? If you have not used the feature in the past month put in a zero. Broken out by Compensation range of the survey participant

Compensation range of the survey participant	Mean	Median	Minimum	Maximum
Less than $55,000	0.00	0.00	0.00	0.00
$55,000+ to $70,000	0.13	0.00	0.00	1.00
More than $70,000	0.00	0.00	0.00	0.00

Table 5.4.6 Approximately how much time in the past month have you personally spent (in hours or fractions thereof) using Google Notifications in connection with your work? If you have not used the feature in the past month put in a zero. Broken out by Gender of the survey participant

Gender of the survey participant	Mean	Median	Minimum	Maximum
Male	0.00	0.00	0.00	0.00
Female	0.05	0.00	0.00	1.00

Table 5.4.7 Approximately how much time in the past month have you personally spent (in hours or fractions thereof) using Google Notifications in connection with your work? If you have not used the feature in the past month put in a zero. Broken out for medical and other scientific libraries

Your main subject focus is:	Mean	Median	Minimum	Maximum
Medical, Biological or Pharmaceutical	0.00	0.00	0.00	0.00
Other Scientific	0.17	0.00	0.00	1.00

Table 5.5.1 Approximately how much time in the past month have you personally spent (in hours or fractions thereof) using Google Images in connection with your work? If you have not used the feature in the past month put in a zero.

	Mean	Median	Minimum	Maximum
Entire sample	1.73	1.00	0.00	6.00

Table 5.5.2 Approximately how much time in the past month have you personally spent (in hours or fractions thereof) using Google Images in connection with your work? If you have not used the feature in the past month put in a zero. Broken out by Type of institution

Type of institution	Mean	Median	Minimum	Maximum
Academic Medical Library	1.81	2.00	0.00	6.00
Academic Scientific Library	1.93	2.00	0.00	4.00
Non-Educational Medical/Scientific Library	1.52	1.00	0.00	5.00

Table 5.5.3 Approximately how much time in the past month have you personally spent (in hours or fractions thereof) using Google Images in connection with your work? If you have not used the feature in the past month put in a zero. Broken out by Age range of the survey participant

Age range of the survey participant	Mean	Median	Minimum	Maximum
Under 40	2.42	1.50	0.50	6.00
40-59	1.76	1.00	0.00	5.00
60 or Over	1.00	1.00	0.00	2.00

Table 5.5.4 Approximately how much time in the past month have you personally spent (in hours or fractions thereof) using Google Images in connection with your work? If you have not used the feature in the past month put in a zero. Broken out by Work specialization or title of the survey participant

Work specialization or title of the survey participant	Mean	Median	Minimum	Maximum
reference or information literacy	1.20	1.00	0.00	3.20
research or subject specialist	1.65	1.00	0.50	4.00
other	2.50	2.00	0.00	6.00

Table 5.5.5 Approximately how much time in the past month have you personally spent (in hours or fractions thereof) using Google Images in connection with your work? If you have not used the feature in the past month put in a zero. Broken out by Compensation range of the survey participant

Compensation range of the survey participant	Mean	Median	Minimum	Maximum
Less than $55,000	2.12	2.00	0.20	6.00
$55,000+ to $70,000	1.47	1.00	0.00	4.00
More than $70,000	1.75	1.25	0.00	5.00

Table 5.5.6 Approximately how much time in the past month have you personally spent (in hours or fractions thereof) using Google Images in connection with your work? If you have not used the feature in the past month put in a zero. Broken out by Gender of the survey participant

Gender of the survey participant	Mean	Median	Minimum	Maximum
Male	1.00	1.00	0.00	2.00
Female	1.85	1.50	0.00	6.00

Table 5.5.7 Approximately how much time in the past month have you personally spent (in hours or fractions thereof) using Google Images in connection with your work? If you have not used the feature in the past month put in a zero. Broken out for medical and other scientific libraries

Your main subject focus is:	Mean	Median	Minimum	Maximum
Medical, Biological or Pharmaceutical	1.61	1.00	0.00	6.00
Other Scientific	2.08	1.50	0.00	5.00

Table 5.6.1 Approximately how much time in the past month have you personally spent (in hours or fractions thereof) using Google Calendar in connection with your work? If you have not used the feature in the past month put in a zero.

	Mean	Median	Minimum	Maximum
Entire sample	2.39	0.00	0.00	40.00

Table 5.6.2 Approximately how much time in the past month have you personally spent (in hours or fractions thereof) using Google Calendar in connection with your work? If you have not used the feature in the past month put in a zero. Broken out by Type of institution

Type of institution	Mean	Median	Minimum	Maximum
Academic Medical Library	0.50	0.00	0.00	2.00
Academic Scientific Library	6.25	1.00	0.00	40.00
Non-Educational Medical/Scientific Library	0.22	0.00	0.00	2.00

Table 5.6.3 Approximately how much time in the past month have you personally spent (in hours or fractions thereof) using Google Calendar in connection with your work? If you have not used the feature in the past month put in a zero. Broken out by Age range of the survey participant

Age range of the survey participant	Mean	Median	Minimum	Maximum
Under 40	6.71	0.00	0.00	40.00
40-59	0.18	0.00	0.00	1.00
60 or Over	1.20	2.00	0.00	2.00

Table 5.6.4 Approximately how much time in the past month have you personally spent (in hours or fractions thereof) using Google Calendar in connection with your work? If you have not used the feature in the past month put in a zero. Broken out by Work specialization or title of the survey participant

Work specialization or title of the survey participant	Mean	Median	Minimum	Maximum
reference or information literacy	0.57	0.00	0.00	2.00
research or subject specialist	4.90	0.50	0.00	40.00
other	0.33	0.00	0.00	2.00

Table 5.6.5 Approximately how much time in the past month have you personally spent (in hours or fractions thereof) using Google Calendar in connection with your work? If you have not used the feature in the past month put in a zero. Broken out by Compensation range of the survey participant

Compensation range of the survey participant	Mean	Median	Minimum	Maximum
Less than $55,000	0.33	0.00	0.00	2.00
$55,000+ to $70,000	0.78	0.00	0.00	6.00
More than $70,000	5.75	1.00	0.00	40.00

Table 5.6.6 Approximately how much time in the past month have you personally spent (in hours or fractions thereof) using Google Calendar in connection with your work? If you have not used the feature in the past month put in a zero. Broken out by Gender of the survey participant

Gender of the survey participant	Mean	Median	Minimum	Maximum
Male	0.50	0.00	0.00	2.00
Female	2.79	0.00	0.00	40.00

Table 5.6.7 Approximately how much time in the past month have you personally spent (in hours or fractions thereof) using Google Calendar in connection with your work? If you have not used the feature in the past month put in a zero. Broken out for medical and other scientific libraries

Your main subject focus is:	Mean	Median	Minimum	Maximum
Medical, Biological or Pharmaceutical	0.38	0.00	0.00	2.00
Other Scientific	7.00	1.00	0.00	40.00

Table 5.7.1 Approximately how much time in the past month have you personally spent (in hours or fractions thereof) using Chrome in connection with your work? If you have not used the feature in the past month put in a zero.

	Mean	Median	Minimum	Maximum
Entire sample	39.83	32.00	0.00	160.00

Table 5.7.2 Approximately how much time in the past month have you personally spent (in hours or fractions thereof) using Chrome in connection with your work? If you have not used the feature in the past month put in a zero. Broken out by Type of institution

Type of institution	Mean	Median	Minimum	Maximum
Academic Medical Library	47.43	50.00	1.00	160.00
Academic Scientific Library	46.25	32.50	0.00	160.00
Non-Educational Medical/Scientific Library	26.75	26.00	0.00	80.00

Table 5.7.3 Approximately how much time in the past month have you personally spent (in hours or fractions thereof) using Chrome in connection with your work? If you have not used the feature in the past month put in a zero. Broken out by Age range of the survey participant

Age range of the survey participant	Mean	Median	Minimum	Maximum
Under 40	73.00	67.50	3.00	160.00
40-59	17.09	4.00	0.00	60.00
60 or Over	48.33	37.50	1.00	160.00

Table 5.7.4 Approximately how much time in the past month have you personally spent (in hours or fractions thereof) using Chrome in connection with your work? If you have not used the feature in the past month put in a zero. Broken out by Work specialization or title of the survey participant

Work specialization or title of the survey participant	Mean	Median	Minimum	Maximum
reference or information literacy	16.43	3.00	1.00	40.00
research or subject specialist	53.80	50.00	0.00	160.00
other	43.83	22.00	0.00	160.00

Table 5.7.5 Approximately how much time in the past month have you personally spent (in hours or fractions thereof) using Chrome in connection with your work? If you have not used the feature in the past month put in a zero. Broken out by Compensation range of the survey participant

Compensation range of the survey participant	Mean	Median	Minimum	Maximum
Less than $55,000	19.17	11.50	0.00	55.00
$55,000+ to $70,000	35.13	28.50	0.00	90.00
More than $70,000	57.78	40.00	2.00	160.00

Table 5.7.6 Approximately how much time in the past month have you personally spent (in hours or fractions thereof) using Chrome in connection with your work? If you have not used the feature in the past month put in a zero. Broken out by Gender of the survey participant

Gender of the survey participant	Mean	Median	Minimum	Maximum
Male	14.33	3.00	0.00	40.00
Female	43.65	33.50	0.00	160.00

Table 5.7.7 Approximately how much time in the past month have you personally spent (in hours or fractions thereof) using Chrome in connection with your work? If you have not used the feature in the past month put in a zero. Broken out for medical and other scientific libraries

Your main subject focus is:	Mean	Median	Minimum	Maximum
Medical, Biological or Pharmaceutical	33.38	22.50	0.00	160.00
Other Scientific	54.57	40.00	0.00	160.00

Table 5.8.1 Approximately how much time in the past month have you personally spent (in hours or fractions thereof) using Google Books in connection with your work? If you have not used the feature in the past month put in a zero.

	Mean	Median	Minimum	Maximum
Entire sample	1.37	0.75	0.00	7.00

Table 5.8.2 Approximately how much time in the past month have you personally spent (in hours or fractions thereof) using Google Books in connection with your work? If you have not used the feature in the past month put in a zero. Broken out by Type of institution

Type of institution	Mean	Median	Minimum	Maximum
Academic Medical Library	1.02	0.05	0.00	5.00
Academic Scientific Library	1.36	0.50	0.00	7.00
Non-Educational Medical/Scientific Library	1.62	1.00	0.00	5.00

Table 5.8.3 Approximately how much time in the past month have you personally spent (in hours or fractions thereof) using Google Books in connection with your work? If you have not used the feature in the past month put in a zero. Broken out by Age range of the survey participant

Age range of the survey participant	Mean	Median	Minimum	Maximum
Under 40	1.58	0.75	0.00	7.00
40-59	1.29	1.00	0.00	5.00
60 or Over	1.30	0.00	0.00	5.00

Table 5.8.4 Approximately how much time in the past month have you personally spent (in hours or fractions thereof) using Google Books in connection with your work? If you have not used the feature in the past month put in a zero. Broken out by Work specialization or title of the survey participant

Work specialization or title of the survey participant	Mean	Median	Minimum	Maximum
reference or information literacy	1.20	1.00	0.00	4.80
research or subject specialist	1.31	1.00	0.00	7.00
other	1.67	0.00	0.00	5.00

Table 5.8.5 Approximately how much time in the past month have you personally spent (in hours or fractions thereof) using Google Books in connection with your work? If you have not used the feature in the past month put in a zero. Broken out by Compensation range of the survey participant

Compensation range of the survey participant	Mean	Median	Minimum	Maximum
Less than $55,000	0.77	1.00	0.00	1.50
$55,000+ to $70,000	1.76	0.63	0.00	7.00
More than $70,000	1.44	0.25	0.00	5.00

Table 5.8.6 Approximately how much time in the past month have you personally spent (in hours or fractions thereof) using Google Books in connection with your work? If you have not used the feature in the past month put in a zero. Broken out by Gender of the survey participant

Gender of the survey participant	Mean	Median	Minimum	Maximum
Male	0.42	0.25	0.00	1.00
Female	1.52	1.00	0.00	7.00

Table 5.8.7 Approximately how much time in the past month have you personally spent (in hours or fractions thereof) using Google Books in connection with your work? If you have not used the feature in the past month put in a zero. Broken out for medical and other scientific libraries

Your main subject focus is:	Mean	Median	Minimum	Maximum
Medical, Biological or Pharmaceutical	1.04	0.63	0.00	5.00
Other Scientific	2.25	0.75	0.00	7.00

Table 5.9.1 Approximately how much time in the past month have you personally spent (in hours or fractions thereof) using Google Scholar in connection with your work? If you have not used the feature in the past month put in a zero.

	Mean	Median	Minimum	Maximum
Entire sample	11.19	2.50	0.00	80.00

Table 5.9.2 Approximately how much time in the past month have you personally spent (in hours or fractions thereof) using Google Scholar in connection with your work? If you have not used the feature in the past month put in a zero. Broken out by Type of institution

Type of institution	Mean	Median	Minimum	Maximum
Academic Medical Library	7.50	2.00	0.50	25.00
Academic Scientific Library	7.02	2.00	0.20	25.00
Non-Educational Medical/Scientific Library	18.22	10.00	0.00	80.00

Table 5.9.3 Approximately how much time in the past month have you personally spent (in hours or fractions thereof) using Google Scholar in connection with your work? If you have not used the feature in the past month put in a zero. Broken out by Age range of the survey participant

Age range of the survey participant	Mean	Median	Minimum	Maximum
Under 40	19.57	8.00	1.00	80.00
40-59	8.46	3.00	0.00	32.00
60 or Over	6.87	2.25	0.20	20.00

Table 5.9.4 Approximately how much time in the past month have you personally spent (in hours or fractions thereof) using Google Scholar in connection with your work? If you have not used the feature in the past month put in a zero. Broken out by Work specialization or title of the survey participant

Work specialization or title of the survey participant	Mean	Median	Minimum	Maximum
reference or information literacy	7.96	2.25	0.20	32.00
research or subject specialist	15.45	5.00	1.00	80.00
other	7.67	2.00	0.00	25.00

Table 5.9.5 Approximately how much time in the past month have you personally spent (in hours or fractions thereof) using Google Scholar in connection with your work? If you have not used the feature in the past month put in a zero. Broken out by Compensation range of the survey participant

Compensation range of the survey participant	Mean	Median	Minimum	Maximum
Less than $55,000	8.42	6.00	1.00	25.00
$55,000+ to $70,000	20.10	18.25	0.00	80.00
More than $70,000	3.13	2.00	0.20	16.00

Table 5.9.6 Approximately how much time in the past month have you personally spent (in hours or fractions thereof) using Google Scholar in connection with your work? If you have not used the feature in the past month put in a zero. Broken out by Gender of the survey participant

Gender of the survey participant	Mean	Median	Minimum	Maximum
Male	2.80	3.00	0.20	5.00
Female	12.79	2.50	0.00	80.00

Table 5.9.7 Approximately how much time in the past month have you personally spent (in hours or fractions thereof) using Google Scholar in connection with your work? If you have not used the feature in the past month put in a zero. Broken out for medical and other scientific libraries

Your main subject focus is:	Mean	Median	Minimum	Maximum
Medical, Biological or Pharmaceutical	14.62	8.00	0.00	80.00
Other Scientific	3.90	2.00	0.20	19.00

Table 5.10.1 Approximately how much time in the past month have you personally spent (in hours or fractions thereof) using Google Translate in connection with your work? If you have not used the feature in the past month put in a zero.

	Mean	Median	Minimum	Maximum
Entire sample	1.25	0.00	0.00	12.00

Table 5.10.2 Approximately how much time in the past month have you personally spent (in hours or fractions thereof) using Google Translate in connection with your work? If you have not used the feature in the past month put in a zero. Broken out by Type of institution

Type of institution	Mean	Median	Minimum	Maximum
Academic Medical Library	2.36	1.00	0.00	12.00
Academic Scientific Library	1.64	0.00	0.00	10.00
Non-Educational Medical/Scientific Library	0.08	0.00	0.00	0.50

Table 5.10.3 Approximately how much time in the past month have you personally spent (in hours or fractions thereof) using Google Translate in connection with your work? If you have not used the feature in the past month put in a zero. Broken out by Age range of the survey participant

Age range of the survey participant	Mean	Median	Minimum	Maximum
Under 40	3.75	0.25	0.00	12.00
40-59	0.34	0.00	0.00	1.00
60 or Over	0.42	0.00	0.00	2.00

Table 5.10.4 Approximately how much time in the past month have you personally spent (in hours or fractions thereof) using Google Translate in connection with your work? If you have not used the feature in the past month put in a zero. Broken out by Work specialization or title of the survey participant

Work specialization or title of the survey participant	Mean	Median	Minimum	Maximum
reference or information literacy	0.00	0.00	0.00	0.00
research or subject specialist	1.35	0.50	0.00	10.00
other	2.54	0.63	0.00	12.00

Table 5.10.5 Approximately how much time in the past month have you personally spent (in hours or fractions thereof) using Google Translate in connection with your work? If you have not used the feature in the past month put in a zero. Broken out by Compensation range of the survey participant

Compensation range of the survey participant	Mean	Median	Minimum	Maximum
Less than $55,000	2.25	0.25	0.00	12.00
$55,000+ to $70,000	1.17	0.00	0.00	10.00
More than $70,000	0.59	0.38	0.00	2.00

Table 5.10.6 Approximately how much time in the past month have you personally spent (in hours or fractions thereof) using Google Translate in connection with your work? If you have not used the feature in the past month put in a zero. Broken out by Gender of the survey participant

Gender of the survey participant	Mean	Median	Minimum	Maximum
Male	0.33	0.00	0.00	1.00
Female	1.39	0.00	0.00	12.00

Table 5.10.7 Approximately how much time in the past month have you personally spent (in hours or fractions thereof) using Google Translate in connection with your work? If you have not used the feature in the past month put in a zero. Broken out for medical and other scientific libraries

Your main subject focus is:	Mean	Median	Minimum	Maximum
Medical, Biological or Pharmaceutical	1.00	0.00	0.00	12.00
Other Scientific	1.96	0.38	0.00	10.00

Table 5.12.1 Approximately how much time in the past month have you personally spent (in hours or fractions thereof) using Google Public Data Explorer in connection with your work? If you have not used the feature in the past month put in a zero.

	Mean	Median	Minimum	Maximum
Entire sample	0.05	0.00	0.00	1.00

Table 5.12.2 Approximately how much time in the past month have you personally spent (in hours or fractions thereof) using Google Public Data Explorer in connection with your work? If you have not used the feature in the past month put in a zero. Broken out by Type of institution

Type of institution	Mean	Median	Minimum	Maximum
Academic Medical Library	0.00	0.00	0.00	0.00
Academic Scientific Library	0.14	0.00	0.00	1.00
Non-Educational Medical/Scientific Library	0.00	0.00	0.00	0.00

Table 5.12.3 Approximately how much time in the past month have you personally spent (in hours or fractions thereof) using Google Public Data Explorer in connection with your work? If you have not used the feature in the past month put in a zero. Broken out by Age range of the survey participant

Age range of the survey participant	Mean	Median	Minimum	Maximum
Under 40	0.17	0.00	0.00	1.00
40-59	0.00	0.00	0.00	0.00
60 or Over	0.00	0.00	0.00	0.00

Table 5.12.4 Approximately how much time in the past month have you personally spent (in hours or fractions thereof) using Google Public Data Explorer in connection with your work? If you have not used the feature in the past month put in a zero. Broken out by Work specialization or title of the survey participant

Work specialization or title of the survey participant	Mean	Median	Minimum	Maximum
reference or information literacy	0.14	0.00	0.00	1.00
research or subject specialist	0.00	0.00	0.00	0.00
other	0.00	0.00	0.00	0.00

Table 5.12.5 Approximately how much time in the past month have you personally spent (in hours or fractions thereof) using Google Public Data Explorer in connection with your work? If you have not used the feature in the past month put in a zero. Broken out by Compensation range of the survey participant

Compensation range of the survey participant	Mean	Median	Minimum	Maximum
Less than $55,000	0.17	0.00	0.00	1.00
$55,000+ to $70,000	0.00	0.00	0.00	0.00
More than $70,000	0.00	0.00	0.00	0.00

Table 5.12.6 Approximately how much time in the past month have you personally spent (in hours or fractions thereof) using Google Public Data Explorer in connection with your work? If you have not used the feature in the past month put in a zero. Broken out by Gender of the survey participant

Gender of the survey participant	Mean	Median	Minimum	Maximum
Male	0.00	0.00	0.00	0.00
Female	0.05	0.00	0.00	1.00

Table 5.12.7 Approximately how much time in the past month have you personally spent (in hours or fractions thereof) using Google Public Data Explorer in connection with your work? If you have not used the feature in the past month put in a zero. Broken out for medical and other scientific libraries

Your main subject focus is:	Mean	Median	Minimum	Maximum
Medical, Biological or Pharmaceutical	0.06	0.00	0.00	1.00
Other Scientific	0.00	0.00	0.00	0.00

Table 5.13.1 Approximately how much time in the past month have you personally spent (in hours or fractions thereof) using Google Drive in connection with your work? If you have not used the feature in the past month put in a zero.

	Mean	Median	Minimum	Maximum
Entire sample	8.56	0.00	0.00	80.00

Table 5.13.2 Approximately how much time in the past month have you personally spent (in hours or fractions thereof) using Google Drive in connection with your work? If you have not used the feature in the past month put in a zero. Broken out by Type of institution

Type of institution	Mean	Median	Minimum	Maximum
Academic Medical Library	5.43	1.00	0.00	30.00
Academic Scientific Library	15.67	4.00	0.00	80.00
Non-Educational Medical/Scientific Library	3.89	0.00	0.00	35.00

Table 5.13.3 Approximately how much time in the past month have you personally spent (in hours or fractions thereof) using Google Drive in connection with your work? If you have not used the feature in the past month put in a zero. Broken out by Age range of the survey participant

Age range of the survey participant	Mean	Median	Minimum	Maximum
Under 40	23.71	15.00	0.00	80.00
40-59	0.67	0.00	0.00	4.00
60 or Over	6.67	0.00	0.00	35.00

Table 5.13.4 Approximately how much time in the past month have you personally spent (in hours or fractions thereof) using Google Drive in connection with your work? If you have not used the feature in the past month put in a zero. Broken out by Work specialization or title of the survey participant

Work specialization or title of the survey participant	Mean	Median	Minimum	Maximum
reference or information literacy	6.38	0.00	0.00	35.00
research or subject specialist	12.00	2.00	0.00	80.00
other	5.17	0.00	0.00	30.00

Table 5.13.5 Approximately how much time in the past month have you personally spent (in hours or fractions thereof) using Google Drive in connection with your work? If you have not used the feature in the past month put in a zero. Broken out by Compensation range of the survey participant

Compensation range of the survey participant	Mean	Median	Minimum	Maximum
Less than $55,000	14.00	9.50	0.00	35.00
$55,000+ to $70,000	3.60	0.00	0.00	30.00
More than $70,000	10.44	1.00	0.00	80.00

Table 5.13.6 Approximately how much time in the past month have you personally spent (in hours or fractions thereof) using Google Drive in connection with your work? If you have not used the feature in the past month put in a zero. Broken out by Gender of the survey participant

Gender of the survey participant	Mean	Median	Minimum	Maximum
Male	1.25	0.50	0.00	4.00
Female	9.95	0.00	0.00	80.00

Table 5.13.7 Approximately how much time in the past month have you personally spent (in hours or fractions thereof) using Google Drive in connection with your work? If you have not used the feature in the past month put in a zero. Broken out for medical and other scientific libraries

Your main subject focus is:	Mean	Median	Minimum	Maximum
Medical, Biological or Pharmaceutical	5.18	0.00	0.00	35.00
Other Scientific	15.75	2.50	0.00	80.00

Table 5.14.1 Approximately how much time in the past month have you personally spent (in hours or fractions thereof) using Google Earth in connection with your work? If you have not used the feature in the past month put in a zero.

	Mean	Median	Minimum	Maximum
Entire sample	0.18	0.00	0.00	2.50

Table 5.14.2 Approximately how much time in the past month have you personally spent (in hours or fractions thereof) using Google Earth in connection with your work? If you have not used the feature in the past month put in a zero. Broken out by Type of institution

Type of institution	Mean	Median	Minimum	Maximum
Academic Medical Library	0.21	0.00	0.00	1.00
Academic Scientific Library	0.00	0.00	0.00	0.00
Non-Educational Medical/Scientific Library	0.31	0.00	0.00	2.50

Table 5.14.3 Approximately how much time in the past month have you personally spent (in hours or fractions thereof) using Google Earth in connection with your work? If you have not used the feature in the past month put in a zero. Broken out by Age range of the survey participant

Age range of the survey participant	Mean	Median	Minimum	Maximum
Under 40	0.00	0.00	0.00	0.00
40-59	0.11	0.00	0.00	1.00
60 or Over	0.49	0.10	0.00	2.50

Table 5.14.4 Approximately how much time in the past month have you personally spent (in hours or fractions thereof) using Google Earth in connection with your work? If you have not used the feature in the past month put in a zero. Broken out by Work specialization or title of the survey participant

Work specialization or title of the survey participant	Mean	Median	Minimum	Maximum
reference or information literacy	0.39	0.00	0.00	2.50
research or subject specialist	0.13	0.00	0.00	1.00
other	0.04	0.00	0.00	0.25

Table 5.14.5 Approximately how much time in the past month have you personally spent (in hours or fractions thereof) using Google Earth in connection with your work? If you have not used the feature in the past month put in a zero. Broken out by Compensation range of the survey participant

Compensation range of the survey participant	Mean	Median	Minimum	Maximum
Less than $55,000	0.42	0.00	0.00	2.50
$55,000+ to $70,000	0.05	0.00	0.00	0.25
More than $70,000	0.16	0.00	0.00	1.00

Table 5.14.6 Approximately how much time in the past month have you personally spent (in hours or fractions thereof) using Google Earth in connection with your work? If you have not used the feature in the past month put in a zero. Broken out by Gender of the survey participant

Gender of the survey participant	Mean	Median	Minimum	Maximum
Male	0.00	0.00	0.00	0.00
Female	0.21	0.00	0.00	2.50

Table 5.14.7 Approximately how much time in the past month have you personally spent (in hours or fractions thereof) using Google Earth in connection with your work? If you have not used the feature in the past month put in a zero. Broken out for medical and other scientific libraries

Your main subject focus is:	Mean	Median	Minimum	Maximum
Medical, Biological or Pharmaceutical	0.23	0.00	0.00	2.50
Other Scientific	0.04	0.00	0.00	0.25

Table 5.15.1 Approximately how much time in the past month have you personally spent (in hours or fractions thereof) using Google Sky in connection with your work? If you have not used the feature in the past month put in a zero.

	Mean	Median	Minimum	Maximum
Entire sample	0.01	0.00	0.00	0.25

Table 5.15.2 Approximately how much time in the past month have you personally spent (in hours or fractions thereof) using Google Sky in connection with your work? If you have not used the feature in the past month put in a zero. Broken out by Type of institution

Type of institution	Mean	Median	Minimum	Maximum
Academic Medical Library	0.00	0.00	0.00	0.00
Academic Scientific Library	0.00	0.00	0.00	0.00
Non-Educational Medical/Scientific Library	0.03	0.00	0.00	0.25

Table 5.15.3 Approximately how much time in the past month have you personally spent (in hours or fractions thereof) using Google Sky in connection with your work? If you have not used the feature in the past month put in a zero. Broken out by Age range of the survey participant

Age range of the survey participant	Mean	Median	Minimum	Maximum
Under 40	0.00	0.00	0.00	0.00
40-59	0.02	0.00	0.00	0.25
60 or Over	0.00	0.00	0.00	0.00

Table 5.15.4 Approximately how much time in the past month have you personally spent (in hours or fractions thereof) using Google Sky in connection with your work? If you have not used the feature in the past month put in a zero. Broken out by Work specialization or title of the survey participant

Work specialization or title of the survey participant	Mean	Median	Minimum	Maximum
reference or information literacy	0.00	0.00	0.00	0.00
research or subject specialist	0.00	0.00	0.00	0.00
other	0.04	0.00	0.00	0.25

Table 5.15.5 Approximately how much time in the past month have you personally spent (in hours or fractions thereof) using Google Sky in connection with your work? If you have not used the feature in the past month put in a zero. Broken out by Compensation range of the survey participant

Compensation range of the survey participant	Mean	Median	Minimum	Maximum
Less than $55,000	0.00	0.00	0.00	0.00
$55,000+ to $70,000	0.00	0.00	0.00	0.00
More than $70,000	0.03	0.00	0.00	0.25

Table 5.15.6 Approximately how much time in the past month have you personally spent (in hours or fractions thereof) using Google Sky in connection with your work? If you have not used the feature in the past month put in a zero. Broken out by Gender of the survey participant

Gender of the survey participant	Mean	Median	Minimum	Maximum
Male	0.00	0.00	0.00	0.00
Female	0.01	0.00	0.00	0.25

Table 5.15.7 Approximately how much time in the past month have you personally spent (in hours or fractions thereof) using Google Sky in connection with your work? If you have not used the feature in the past month put in a zero. Broken out for medical and other scientific libraries

Your main subject focus is:	Mean	Median	Minimum	Maximum
Medical, Biological or Pharmaceutical	0.00	0.00	0.00	0.00
Other Scientific	0.04	0.00	0.00	0.25

Table 5.16.1 Approximately how much time in the past month have you personally spent (in hours or fractions thereof) using Google+ in connection with your work? If you have not used the feature in the past month put in a zero.

	Mean	Median	Minimum	Maximum
Entire sample	0.09	0.00	0.00	2.00

Table 5.16.2 Approximately how much time in the past month have you personally spent (in hours or fractions thereof) using Google+ in connection with your work? If you have not used the feature in the past month put in a zero. Broken out by Type of institution

Type of institution	Mean	Median	Minimum	Maximum
Academic Medical Library	0.00	0.00	0.00	0.00
Academic Scientific Library	0.00	0.00	0.00	0.00
Non-Educational Medical/Scientific Library	0.22	0.00	0.00	2.00

Table 5.16.3 Approximately how much time in the past month have you personally spent (in hours or fractions thereof) using Google+ in connection with your work? If you have not used the feature in the past month put in a zero. Broken out by Age range of the survey participant

Age range of the survey participant	Mean	Median	Minimum	Maximum
Under 40	0.00	0.00	0.00	0.00
40-59	0.18	0.00	0.00	2.00
60 or Over	0.00	0.00	0.00	0.00

Table 5.16.4 Approximately how much time in the past month have you personally spent (in hours or fractions thereof) using Google+ in connection with your work? If you have not used the feature in the past month put in a zero. Broken out by Work specialization or title of the survey participant

Work specialization or title of the survey participant	Mean	Median	Minimum	Maximum
reference or information literacy	0.29	0.00	0.00	2.00
research or subject specialist	0.00	0.00	0.00	0.00
other	0.00	0.00	0.00	0.00

Table 5.16.5 Approximately how much time in the past month have you personally spent (in hours or fractions thereof) using Google+ in connection with your work? If you have not used the feature in the past month put in a zero. Broken out by Compensation range of the survey participant

Compensation range of the survey participant	Mean	Median	Minimum	Maximum
Less than $55,000	0.00	0.00	0.00	0.00
$55,000+ to $70,000	0.25	0.00	0.00	2.00
More than $70,000	0.00	0.00	0.00	0.00

Table 5.16.6 Approximately how much time in the past month have you personally spent (in hours or fractions thereof) using Google+ in connection with your work? If you have not used the feature in the past month put in a zero. Broken out by Gender of the survey participant

Gender of the survey participant	Mean	Median	Minimum	Maximum
Male	0.00	0.00	0.00	0.00
Female	0.11	0.00	0.00	2.00

Table 5.16.7 Approximately how much time in the past month have you personally spent (in hours or fractions thereof) using Google+ in connection with your work? If you have not used the feature in the past month put in a zero. Broken out for medical and other scientific libraries

Your main subject focus is:	Mean	Median	Minimum	Maximum
Medical, Biological or Pharmaceutical	0.13	0.00	0.00	2.00
Other Scientific	0.00	0.00	0.00	0.00

Table 5.17.1 Approximately how much time in the past month have you personally spent (in hours or fractions thereof) using Google Hangouts in connection with your work? If you have not used the feature in the past month put in a zero.

	Mean	Median	Minimum	Maximum
Entire sample	0.40	0.00	0.00	6.00

Table 5.17.2 Approximately how much time in the past month have you personally spent (in hours or fractions thereof) using Google Hangouts in connection with your work? If you have not used the feature in the past month put in a zero. Broken out by Type of institution

Type of institution	Mean	Median	Minimum	Maximum
Academic Medical Library	0.29	0.00	0.00	2.00
Academic Scientific Library	1.00	0.00	0.00	6.00
Non-Educational Medical/Scientific Library	0.03	0.00	0.00	0.25

Table 5.17.3 Approximately how much time in the past month have you personally spent (in hours or fractions thereof) using Google Hangouts in connection with your work? If you have not used the feature in the past month put in a zero. Broken out by Age range of the survey participant

Age range of the survey participant	Mean	Median	Minimum	Maximum
Under 40	1.17	0.00	0.00	6.00
40-59	0.02	0.00	0.00	0.25
60 or Over	0.33	0.00	0.00	2.00

Table 5.17.4 Approximately how much time in the past month have you personally spent (in hours or fractions thereof) using Google Hangouts in connection with your work? If you have not used the feature in the past month put in a zero. Broken out by Work specialization or title of the survey participant

Work specialization or title of the survey participant	Mean	Median	Minimum	Maximum
reference or information literacy	0.00	0.00	0.00	0.00
research or subject specialist	0.90	0.00	0.00	6.00
other	0.04	0.00	0.00	0.25

Table 5.17.5 Approximately how much time in the past month have you personally spent (in hours or fractions thereof) using Google Hangouts in connection with your work? If you have not used the feature in the past month put in a zero. Broken out by Compensation range of the survey participant

Compensation range of the survey participant	Mean	Median	Minimum	Maximum
Less than $55,000	0.00	0.00	0.00	0.00
$55,000+ to $70,000	0.89	0.00	0.00	6.00
More than $70,000	0.16	0.00	0.00	1.00

Table 5.17.6 Approximately how much time in the past month have you personally spent (in hours or fractions thereof) using Google Hangouts in connection with your work? If you have not used the feature in the past month put in a zero. Broken out by Gender of the survey participant

Gender of the survey participant	Mean	Median	Minimum	Maximum
Male	0.00	0.00	0.00	0.00
Female	0.46	0.00	0.00	6.00

Table 5.17.7 Approximately how much time in the past month have you personally spent (in hours or fractions thereof) using Google Hangouts in connection with your work? If you have not used the feature in the past month put in a zero. Broken out for medical and other scientific libraries

Your main subject focus is:	Mean	Median	Minimum	Maximum
Medical, Biological or Pharmaceutical	0.12	0.00	0.00	2.00
Other Scientific	1.21	0.13	0.00	6.00

Table 5.18.1 Approximately how much time in the past month have you personally spent (in hours or fractions thereof) using Gmail in connection with your work? If you have not used the feature in the past month put in a zero.

	Mean	Median	Minimum	Maximum
Entire sample	13.44	0.25	0.00	80.00

Table 5.18.2 Approximately how much time in the past month have you personally spent (in hours or fractions thereof) using Gmail in connection with your work? If you have not used the feature in the past month put in a zero. Broken out by Type of institution

Type of institution	Mean	Median	Minimum	Maximum
Academic Medical Library	10.29	0.00	0.00	40.00
Academic Scientific Library	19.06	1.25	0.00	80.00
Non-Educational Medical/Scientific Library	10.89	0.00	0.00	50.00

Table 5.18.3 Approximately how much time in the past month have you personally spent (in hours or fractions thereof) using Gmail in connection with your work? If you have not used the feature in the past month put in a zero. Broken out by Age range of the survey participant

Age range of the survey participant	Mean	Median	Minimum	Maximum
Under 40	25.79	30.00	0.00	80.00
40-59	4.36	0.00	0.00	40.00
60 or Over	15.67	2.00	0.00	50.00

Table 5.18.4 Approximately how much time in the past month have you personally spent (in hours or fractions thereof) using Gmail in connection with your work? If you have not used the feature in the past month put in a zero. Broken out by Work specialization or title of the survey participant

Work specialization or title of the survey participant	Mean	Median	Minimum	Maximum
reference or information literacy	13.43	2.00	0.00	50.00
research or subject specialist	13.86	0.00	0.00	80.00
other	12.67	3.00	0.00	40.00

Table 5.18.5 Approximately how much time in the past month have you personally spent (in hours or fractions thereof) using Gmail in connection with your work? If you have not used the feature in the past month put in a zero. Broken out by Compensation range of the survey participant

Compensation range of the survey participant	Mean	Median	Minimum	Maximum
Less than $55,000	13.33	0.00	0.00	50.00
$55,000+ to $70,000	8.05	1.25	0.00	40.00
More than $70,000	20.25	1.00	0.00	80.00

Table 5.18.6 Approximately how much time in the past month have you personally spent (in hours or fractions thereof) using Gmail in connection with your work? If you have not used the feature in the past month put in a zero. Broken out by Gender of the survey participant

Gender of the survey participant	Mean	Median	Minimum	Maximum
Male	0.63	0.25	0.00	2.00
Female	16.00	1.00	0.00	80.00

Table 5.18.7 Approximately how much time in the past month have you personally spent (in hours or fractions thereof) using Gmail in connection with your work? If you have not used the feature in the past month put in a zero. Broken out for medical and other scientific libraries

Your main subject focus is:	Mean	Median	Minimum	Maximum
Medical, Biological or Pharmaceutical	10.00	0.00	0.00	50.00
Other Scientific	21.79	2.00	0.00	80.00

Table 5.19.1 Approximately how much time in the past month have you personally spent (in hours or fractions thereof) using Google Bookmarks in connection with your work? If you have not used the feature in the past month put in a zero.

	Mean	Median	Minimum	Maximum
Entire sample	0.06	0.00	0.00	1.00

Table 5.19.2 Approximately how much time in the past month have you personally spent (in hours or fractions thereof) using Google Bookmarks in connection with your work? If you have not used the feature in the past month put in a zero. Broken out by Type of institution

Type of institution	Mean	Median	Minimum	Maximum
Academic Medical Library	0.17	0.00	0.00	1.00
Academic Scientific Library	0.00	0.00	0.00	0.00
Non-Educational Medical/Scientific Library	0.03	0.00	0.00	0.25

Table 5.19.3 Approximately how much time in the past month have you personally spent (in hours or fractions thereof) using Google Bookmarks in connection with your work? If you have not used the feature in the past month put in a zero. Broken out by Age range of the survey participant

Age range of the survey participant	Mean	Median	Minimum	Maximum
Under 40	0.00	0.00	0.00	0.00
40-59	0.11	0.00	0.00	1.00
60 or Over	0.00	0.00	0.00	0.00

Table 5.19.4 Approximately how much time in the past month have you personally spent (in hours or fractions thereof) using Google Bookmarks in connection with your work? If you have not used the feature in the past month put in a zero. Broken out by Work specialization or title of the survey participant

Work specialization or title of the survey participant	Mean	Median	Minimum	Maximum
reference or information literacy	0.00	0.00	0.00	0.00
research or subject specialist	0.11	0.00	0.00	1.00
other	0.04	0.00	0.00	0.25

Table 5.19.5 Approximately how much time in the past month have you personally spent (in hours or fractions thereof) using Google Bookmarks in connection with your work? If you have not used the feature in the past month put in a zero. Broken out by Compensation range of the survey participant

Compensation range of the survey participant	Mean	Median	Minimum	Maximum
Less than $55,000	0.00	0.00	0.00	0.00
$55,000+ to $70,000	0.00	0.00	0.00	0.00
More than $70,000	0.16	0.00	0.00	1.00

Table 5.19.6 Approximately how much time in the past month have you personally spent (in hours or fractions thereof) using Google Bookmarks in connection with your work? If you have not used the feature in the past month put in a zero. Broken out by Gender of the survey participant

Gender of the survey participant	Mean	Median	Minimum	Maximum
Male	0.00	0.00	0.00	0.00
Female	0.07	0.00	0.00	1.00

Table 5.19.7 Approximately how much time in the past month have you personally spent (in hours or fractions thereof) using Google Bookmarks in connection with your work? If you have not used the feature in the past month put in a zero. Broken out for medical and other scientific libraries

Your main subject focus is:	Mean	Median	Minimum	Maximum
Medical, Biological or Pharmaceutical	0.06	0.00	0.00	1.00
Other Scientific	0.04	0.00	0.00	0.25

Table 5.20.1 Approximately how much time in the past month have you personally spent (in hours or fractions thereof) using Google Patent Search in connection with your work? If you have not used the feature in the past month put in a zero.

	Mean	Median	Minimum	Maximum
Entire sample	0.24	0.00	0.00	3.00

Table 5.20.2 Approximately how much time in the past month have you personally spent (in hours or fractions thereof) using Google Patent Search in connection with your work? If you have not used the feature in the past month put in a zero. Broken out by Type of institution

Type of institution	Mean	Median	Minimum	Maximum
Academic Medical Library	0.01	0.00	0.00	0.10
Academic Scientific Library	0.43	0.00	0.00	3.00
Non-Educational Medical/Scientific Library	0.28	0.00	0.00	2.50

Table 5.20.3 Approximately how much time in the past month have you personally spent (in hours or fractions thereof) using Google Patent Search in connection with your work? If you have not used the feature in the past month put in a zero. Broken out by Age range of the survey participant

Age range of the survey participant	Mean	Median	Minimum	Maximum
Under 40	0.50	0.00	0.00	3.00
40-59	0.00	0.00	0.00	0.00
60 or Over	0.43	0.00	0.00	2.50

Table 5.20.4 Approximately how much time in the past month have you personally spent (in hours or fractions thereof) using Google Patent Search in connection with your work? If you have not used the feature in the past month put in a zero. Broken out by Work specialization or title of the survey participant

Work specialization or title of the survey participant	Mean	Median	Minimum	Maximum
reference or information literacy	0.36	0.00	0.00	2.50
research or subject specialist	0.31	0.00	0.00	3.00
other	0.00	0.00	0.00	0.00

Table 5.20.5 Approximately how much time in the past month have you personally spent (in hours or fractions thereof) using Google Patent Search in connection with your work? If you have not used the feature in the past month put in a zero. Broken out by Compensation range of the survey participant

Compensation range of the survey participant	Mean	Median	Minimum	Maximum
Less than $55,000	0.42	0.00	0.00	2.50
$55,000+ to $70,000	0.34	0.00	0.00	3.00
More than $70,000	0.00	0.00	0.00	0.00

Table 5.20.6 Approximately how much time in the past month have you personally spent (in hours or fractions thereof) using Google Patent Search in connection with your work? If you have not used the feature in the past month put in a zero. Broken out by Gender of the survey participant

Gender of the survey participant	Mean	Median	Minimum	Maximum
Male	0.00	0.00	0.00	0.00
Female	0.28	0.00	0.00	3.00

Table 5.20.7 Approximately how much time in the past month have you personally spent (in hours or fractions thereof) using Google Patent Search in connection with your work? If you have not used the feature in the past month put in a zero. Broken out for medical and other scientific libraries

Your main subject focus is:	Mean	Median	Minimum	Maximum
Medical, Biological or Pharmaceutical	0.15	0.00	0.00	2.50
Other Scientific	0.50	0.00	0.00	3.00

Table 5.21.1 Approximately how much time in the past month have you personally spent (in hours or fractions thereof) using Google Forms in connection with your work? If you have not used the feature in the past month put in a zero.

	Mean	Median	Minimum	Maximum
Entire sample	2.41	0.00	0.00	40.00

Table 5.21.2 Approximately how much time in the past month have you personally spent (in hours or fractions thereof) using Google Forms in connection with your work? If you have not used the feature in the past month put in a zero. Broken out by Type of institution

Type of institution	Mean	Median	Minimum	Maximum
Academic Medical Library	6.67	0.00	0.00	40.00
Academic Scientific Library	1.86	0.00	0.00	10.00
Non-Educational Medical/Scientific Library	0.00	0.00	0.00	0.00

Table 5.21.3 Approximately how much time in the past month have you personally spent (in hours or fractions thereof) using Google Forms in connection with your work? If you have not used the feature in the past month put in a zero. Broken out by Age range of the survey participant

Age range of the survey participant	Mean	Median	Minimum	Maximum
Under 40	8.83	1.50	0.00	40.00
40-59	0.00	0.00	0.00	0.00
60 or Over	0.00	0.00	0.00	0.00

Table 5.21.4 Approximately how much time in the past month have you personally spent (in hours or fractions thereof) using Google Forms in connection with your work? If you have not used the feature in the past month put in a zero. Broken out by Work specialization or title of the survey participant

Work specialization or title of the survey participant	Mean	Median	Minimum	Maximum
reference or information literacy	1.43	0.00	0.00	10.00
research or subject specialist	0.33	0.00	0.00	2.00
other	6.67	0.00	0.00	40.00

Table 5.21.5 Approximately how much time in the past month have you personally spent (in hours or fractions thereof) using Google Forms in connection with your work? If you have not used the feature in the past month put in a zero. Broken out by Compensation range of the survey participant

Compensation range of the survey participant	Mean	Median	Minimum	Maximum
Less than $55,000	8.33	0.00	0.00	40.00
$55,000+ to $70,000	0.00	0.00	0.00	0.00
More than $70,000	0.38	0.00	0.00	2.00

Table 5.21.6 Approximately how much time in the past month have you personally spent (in hours or fractions thereof) using Google Forms in connection with your work? If you have not used the feature in the past month put in a zero. Broken out by Gender of the survey participant

Gender of the survey participant	Mean	Median	Minimum	Maximum
Male	0.00	0.00	0.00	0.00
Female	2.79	0.00	0.00	40.00

Table 5.21.7 Approximately how much time in the past month have you personally spent (in hours or fractions thereof) using Google Forms in connection with your work? If you have not used the feature in the past month put in a zero. Broken out for medical and other scientific libraries

Your main subject focus is:	Mean	Median	Minimum	Maximum
Medical, Biological or Pharmaceutical	3.13	0.00	0.00	40.00
Other Scientific	0.50	0.00	0.00	2.00

Table 5.22.1 Approximately how much time in the past month have you personally spent (in hours or fractions thereof) using Google Slides in connection with your work? If you have not used the feature in the past month put in a zero.

	Mean	Median	Minimum	Maximum
Entire sample	0.07	0.00	0.00	1.00

Table 5.22.2 Approximately how much time in the past month have you personally spent (in hours or fractions thereof) using Google Slides in connection with your work? If you have not used the feature in the past month put in a zero. Broken out by Type of institution

Type of institution	Mean	Median	Minimum	Maximum
Academic Medical Library	0.00	0.00	0.00	0.00
Academic Scientific Library	0.21	0.00	0.00	1.00
Non-Educational Medical/Scientific Library	0.00	0.00	0.00	0.00

Table 5.22.3 Approximately how much time in the past month have you personally spent (in hours or fractions thereof) using Google Slides in connection with your work? If you have not used the feature in the past month put in a zero. Broken out by Age range of the survey participant

Age range of the survey participant	Mean	Median	Minimum	Maximum
Under 40	0.25	0.00	0.00	1.00
40-59	0.00	0.00	0.00	0.00
60 or Over	0.00	0.00	0.00	0.00

Table 5.22.4 Approximately how much time in the past month have you personally spent (in hours or fractions thereof) using Google Slides in connection with your work? If you have not used the feature in the past month put in a zero. Broken out by Work specialization or title of the survey participant

Work specialization or title of the survey participant	Mean	Median	Minimum	Maximum
reference or information literacy	0.00	0.00	0.00	0.00
research or subject specialist	0.17	0.00	0.00	1.00
other	0.00	0.00	0.00	0.00

Table 5.22.5 Approximately how much time in the past month have you personally spent (in hours or fractions thereof) using Google Slides in connection with your work? If you have not used the feature in the past month put in a zero. Broken out by Compensation range of the survey participant

Compensation range of the survey participant	Mean	Median	Minimum	Maximum
Less than $55,000	0.00	0.00	0.00	0.00
$55,000+ to $70,000	0.00	0.00	0.00	0.00
More than $70,000	0.19	0.00	0.00	1.00

Table 5.22.6 Approximately how much time in the past month have you personally spent (in hours or fractions thereof) using Google Slides in connection with your work? If you have not used the feature in the past month put in a zero. Broken out by Gender of the survey participant

Gender of the survey participant	Mean	Median	Minimum	Maximum
Male	0.00	0.00	0.00	0.00
Female	0.08	0.00	0.00	1.00

Table 5.22.7 Approximately how much time in the past month have you personally spent (in hours or fractions thereof) using Google Slides in connection with your work? If you have not used the feature in the past month put in a zero. Broken out for medical and other scientific libraries

Your main subject focus is:	Mean	Median	Minimum	Maximum
Medical, Biological or Pharmaceutical	0.00	0.00	0.00	0.00
Other Scientific	0.25	0.00	0.00	1.00

Table 5.23.1 Approximately how much time in the past month have you personally spent (in hours or fractions thereof) using Google Groups in connection with your work? If you have not used the feature in the past month put in a zero.

	Mean	Median	Minimum	Maximum
Entire sample	0.40	0.00	0.00	4.00

Table 5.23.2 Approximately how much time in the past month have you personally spent (in hours or fractions thereof) using Google Groups in connection with your work? If you have not used the feature in the past month put in a zero. Broken out by Type of institution

Type of institution	Mean	Median	Minimum	Maximum
Academic Medical Library	0.17	0.00	0.00	1.00
Academic Scientific Library	0.57	0.00	0.00	4.00
Non-Educational Medical/Scientific Library	0.42	0.00	0.00	3.50

Table 5.23.3 Approximately how much time in the past month have you personally spent (in hours or fractions thereof) using Google Groups in connection with your work? If you have not used the feature in the past month put in a zero. Broken out by Age range of the survey participant

Age range of the survey participant	Mean	Median	Minimum	Maximum
Under 40	0.00	0.00	0.00	0.00
40-59	0.39	0.00	0.00	4.00
60 or Over	0.90	0.00	0.00	3.50

Table 5.23.4 Approximately how much time in the past month have you personally spent (in hours or fractions thereof) using Google Groups in connection with your work? If you have not used the feature in the past month put in a zero. Broken out by Work specialization or title of the survey participant

Work specialization or title of the survey participant	Mean	Median	Minimum	Maximum
reference or information literacy	0.50	0.00	0.00	3.50
research or subject specialist	0.44	0.00	0.00	4.00
other	0.21	0.00	0.00	1.00

Table 5.23.5 Approximately how much time in the past month have you personally spent (in hours or fractions thereof) using Google Groups in connection with your work? If you have not used the feature in the past month put in a zero. Broken out by Compensation range of the survey participant

Compensation range of the survey participant	Mean	Median	Minimum	Maximum
Less than $55,000	1.25	0.00	0.00	4.00
$55,000+ to $70,000	0.00	0.00	0.00	0.00
More than $70,000	0.16	0.00	0.00	1.00

Table 5.23.6 Approximately how much time in the past month have you personally spent (in hours or fractions thereof) using Google Groups in connection with your work? If you have not used the feature in the past month put in a zero. Broken out by Gender of the survey participant

Gender of the survey participant	Mean	Median	Minimum	Maximum
Male	1.33	0.00	0.00	4.00
Female	0.25	0.00	0.00	3.50

Table 5.23.7 Approximately how much time in the past month have you personally spent (in hours or fractions thereof) using Google Groups in connection with your work? If you have not used the feature in the past month put in a zero. Broken out for medical and other scientific libraries

Your main subject focus is:	Mean	Median	Minimum	Maximum
Medical, Biological or Pharmaceutical	0.28	0.00	0.00	3.50
Other Scientific	0.71	0.00	0.00	4.00

Table 5.24.1 Approximately how much time in the past month have you personally spent (in hours or fractions thereof) using Google Analytics in connection with your work? If you have not used the feature in the past month put in a zero.

	Mean	Median	Minimum	Maximum
Entire sample	0.10	0.00	0.00	1.00

Table 5.24.2 Approximately how much time in the past month have you personally spent (in hours or fractions thereof) using Google Analytics in connection with your work? If you have not used the feature in the past month put in a zero. Broken out by Type of institution

Type of institution	Mean	Median	Minimum	Maximum
Academic Medical Library	0.14	0.00	0.00	1.00
Academic Scientific Library	0.14	0.00	0.00	1.00
Non-Educational Medical/Scientific Library	0.03	0.00	0.00	0.25

Table 5.24.3 Approximately how much time in the past month have you personally spent (in hours or fractions thereof) using Google Analytics in connection with your work? If you have not used the feature in the past month put in a zero. Broken out by Age range of the survey participant

Age range of the survey participant	Mean	Median	Minimum	Maximum
Under 40	0.00	0.00	0.00	0.00
40-59	0.20	0.00	0.00	1.00
60 or Over	0.00	0.00	0.00	0.00

Table 5.24.4 Approximately how much time in the past month have you personally spent (in hours or fractions thereof) using Google Analytics in connection with your work? If you have not used the feature in the past month put in a zero. Broken out by Work specialization or title of the survey participant

Work specialization or title of the survey participant	Mean	Median	Minimum	Maximum
reference or information literacy	0.00	0.00	0.00	0.00
research or subject specialist	0.20	0.00	0.00	1.00
other	0.04	0.00	0.00	0.25

Table 5.24.5 Approximately how much time in the past month have you personally spent (in hours or fractions thereof) using Google Analytics in connection with your work? If you have not used the feature in the past month put in a zero. Broken out by Compensation range of the survey participant

Compensation range of the survey participant	Mean	Median	Minimum	Maximum
Less than $55,000	0.17	0.00	0.00	1.00
$55,000+ to $70,000	0.00	0.00	0.00	0.00
More than $70,000	0.16	0.00	0.00	1.00

Table 5.24.6 Approximately how much time in the past month have you personally spent (in hours or fractions thereof) using Google Analytics in connection with your work? If you have not used the feature in the past month put in a zero. Broken out by Gender of the survey participant

Gender of the survey participant	Mean	Median	Minimum	Maximum
Male	0.33	0.00	0.00	1.00
Female	0.06	0.00	0.00	1.00

Table 5.24.7 Approximately how much time in the past month have you personally spent (in hours or fractions thereof) using Google Analytics in connection with your work? If you have not used the feature in the past month put in a zero. Broken out for medical and other scientific libraries

Your main subject focus is:	Mean	Median	Minimum	Maximum
Medical, Biological or Pharmaceutical	0.06	0.00	0.00	1.00
Other Scientific	0.21	0.00	0.00	1.00

Table 5.25.1 Approximately how much time in the past month have you personally spent (in hours or fractions thereof) using Blogger in connection with your work? If you have not used the feature in the past month put in a zero.

	Mean	Median	Minimum	Maximum
Entire sample	0.00	0.00	0.00	0.00

Table 5.26.1 Approximately how much time in the past month have you personally spent (in hours or fractions thereof) using YouTube in connection with your work? If you have not used the feature in the past month put in a zero.

	Mean	Median	Minimum	Maximum
Entire sample	3.68	1.00	0.00	30.00

Table 5.26.2 Approximately how much time in the past month have you personally spent (in hours or fractions thereof) using YouTube in connection with your work? If you have not used the feature in the past month put in a zero. Broken out by Type of institution

Type of institution	Mean	Median	Minimum	Maximum
Academic Medical Library	4.77	1.00	0.00	20.00
Academic Scientific Library	4.72	0.50	0.00	30.00
Non-Educational Medical/Scientific Library	1.79	1.50	0.00	7.00

Table 5.26.3 Approximately how much time in the past month have you personally spent (in hours or fractions thereof) using YouTube in connection with your work? If you have not used the feature in the past month put in a zero. Broken out by Age range of the survey participant

Age range of the survey participant	Mean	Median	Minimum	Maximum
Under 40	8.86	5.00	0.00	30.00
40-59	1.36	0.75	0.00	7.00
60 or Over	2.28	0.85	0.00	10.00

Table 5.26.4 Approximately how much time in the past month have you personally spent (in hours or fractions thereof) using YouTube in connection with your work? If you have not used the feature in the past month put in a zero. Broken out by Work specialization or title of the survey participant

Work specialization or title of the survey participant	Mean	Median	Minimum	Maximum
reference or information literacy	0.75	0.35	0.00	2.00
research or subject specialist	5.45	1.00	0.00	30.00
other	4.33	1.50	0.00	20.00

Table 5.26.5 Approximately how much time in the past month have you personally spent (in hours or fractions thereof) using YouTube in connection with your work? If you have not used the feature in the past month put in a zero. Broken out by Compensation range of the survey participant

Compensation range of the survey participant	Mean	Median	Minimum	Maximum
Less than $55,000	4.78	0.85	0.00	20.00
$55,000+ to $70,000	4.83	1.30	0.00	30.00
More than $70,000	1.67	0.50	0.00	6.00

Table 5.26.6 Approximately how much time in the past month have you personally spent (in hours or fractions thereof) using YouTube in connection with your work? If you have not used the feature in the past month put in a zero. Broken out by Gender of the survey participant

Gender of the survey participant	Mean	Median	Minimum	Maximum
Male	0.50	0.50	0.00	1.00
Female	4.29	1.50	0.00	30.00

Table 5.26.7 Approximately how much time in the past month have you personally spent (in hours or fractions thereof) using YouTube in connection with your work? If you have not used the feature in the past month put in a zero. Broken out for medical and other scientific libraries

Your main subject focus is:	Mean	Median	Minimum	Maximum
Medical, Biological or Pharmaceutical	2.88	1.00	0.00	20.00
Other Scientific	5.38	0.75	0.00	30.00

What other apps or features offered by Google but not listed above have you found useful and why?

Academic Medical Library

1) None
2) GoogleVoice, GoogleTalk
3) na
4) n/a
5) none
6) NA

Academic Scientific Library

1) OpenRefine
2) Gmail and chrome - best email and browser
3) none

Non-Educational Medical/Scientific Library

1) Again, assuming this is at work, I don't like to use many of the apps or features because they require a log in and I refuse to give my personal google account information to work.
2) N/A
3) None
4) Used to use the google news feature that indexed newspapers, but it disappeared a long time ago. This was extremely valuable for academic searching in political studies, sociology, current events, and other disciplines.
5) Google Docs.

Which single Google app or feature has saved you the most time or made you much more productive?

Academic Medical Library

1) Google Advanced search
2) Link from Google Scholar to our Library
3) gmail
4) Can't think of any one app or feature
5) Google Maps
6) Google Scholar
7) Chrome - it's my go to browser. I do not use internet explorer, Firefox, etc.

Academic Scientific Library

1) Drive for sure
2) Google Forms
3) Google Drive
4) Google Drive
5) Google Images
6) Scholar
7) google scholar
8) Chrome

Non-Educational Medical/Scientific Library

1) At work? The citation option for google scholar.
2) Google Scholar
3) google search
4) Gmail, Group
5) advanced search
6) Scholar
7) Google docs, forms and scholar
8) Google Scholar

Table 6.1 About what percentage of the time that you spend on medical or scientific research is done through Google Scholar or Google Books?

	Mean	Median	Minimum	Maximum
Entire sample	20.56	10.00	1.00	98.00

Table 6.2 About what percentage of the time that you spend on medical or scientific research is done through Google Scholar or Google Books? Broken out by Type of institution

Type of institution	Mean	Median	Minimum	Maximum
Academic Medical Library	7.31	7.50	1.00	12.50
Academic Scientific Library	18.63	17.50	1.00	50.00
Non-Educational Medical/Scientific Library	35.75	32.50	5.00	98.00

Table 6.3 About what percentage of the time that you spend on medical or scientific research is done through Google Scholar or Google Books? Broken out by Age range of the survey participant

Age range of the survey participant	Mean	Median	Minimum	Maximum
Under 40	33.83	20.00	5.00	98.00
40-59	20.50	10.00	3.00	50.00
60 or Over	7.42	7.50	1.00	15.00

Table 6.4 About what percentage of the time that you spend on medical or scientific research is done through Google Scholar or Google Books? Broken out by Work specialization or title of the survey participant

Work specialization or title of the survey participant	Mean	Median	Minimum	Maximum
reference or information literacy	14.50	10.00	1.00	50.00
research or subject specialist	23.77	12.50	3.00	98.00
other	20.71	10.00	5.00	50.00

Table 6.5 About what percentage of the time that you spend on medical or scientific research is done through Google Scholar or Google Books? Broken out by Compensation range of the survey participant

Compensation range of the survey participant	Mean	Median	Minimum	Maximum
Less than $55,000	12.60	10.00	5.00	30.00
$55,000+ to $70,000	29.95	16.25	1.00	98.00
More than $70,000	14.56	10.00	1.00	50.00

Table 6.6 About what percentage of the time that you spend on medical or scientific research is done through Google Scholar or Google Books? Broken out by Gender of the survey participant

Gender of the survey participant	Mean	Median	Minimum	Maximum
Male	21.50	17.50	1.00	50.00
Female	20.38	10.00	1.00	98.00

Table 6.7 About what percentage of the time that you spend on medical or scientific research is done through Google Scholar or Google Books? Broken out for medical and other scientific libraries

Your main subject focus is:	Mean	Median	Minimum	Maximum
Medical, Biological or Pharmaceutical	18.59	10.00	1.00	98.00
Other Scientific	24.50	20.00	1.00	50.00

If there was one app or feature in Google that you would like to let your peers know about which one would that be.

Academic Medical Library

1) Google Advanced search operators
2) Advanced searching--I point this out when I teach.
3) na
4) Nothing comes to mind
5) Google Scholar
6) Public Data Explorer
7) Google Drive!

Academic Scientific Library

1) GoogleDrive
2) Patent search
3) Google scholar import to Endnote
4) scholar
5) advanced settings - so that items can be transferred to citation manager
6) Chrome
7) Google Alerts

Non-Educational Medical/Scientific Library

1) Citations
2) Google Scholar and its "cited by" feature
3) Google earth
4) None
5) Scholar
6) Google Scholar
7) Google scholar

Made in the USA
Middletown, DE
05 November 2026

36552529R10130

International Survey of Postdocs in Medicine & Other Life Sciences

ISBN 978-1-57440-437-1

Contents

THE QUESTIONNAIRE

CHAPTER 1 – Introduction

1. Please give us the following contact information

    A. Name
    B. Institution
    C. Work Title
    D. Country
    E. Email Address

2. Is your institution a public or private college?

    A. Public
    B. Private

3. What is your primary subject specialization?

4. Number of years spent as a postdoc

5. Gender of survey respondent

   A. Male
   B. Female

6. Age of survey participant

   A. 25 or under
   B. 26-30
   C. 31-35
   D. 36-45
   E. Over 45

CHAPTER 2 – Superdoc positions

7. Does your institution offer permanent staff positions similar to postdocs but with greater pay and stability?

   A. Yes
   B. No
   C. Other (please specify)

8. If your institution offer such superdoc positions about what percentage of postdocs that want them attain them?

CHAPTER 3 – View of Office of Postdoc Affairs

9. Does your institution have some kind of office of postdoc affairs to offer training and guidance to postdocs on campus?

   A. Yes
   B. No
   C. Not Sure

10. How would you rate your college's office of postdoc affairs?

A. It's a joke
B. Not very useful
C. somewhat useful
D. useful
E. very useful

11. How would you rate the services provided by your university in each of the following areas?

	Very Poor	Poor	Adequate	Good	Very Good
Databases and Research Tools to Find Funding Sources					
Mentoring from those in more senior positions					
Tools and Services to Promote Research Collaboration					
Funding for Travel for Scientific Purposes					

12. If you have ever required assistance with the development of English language skills describe the helpfulness of your university in this respect.

13. How satisfied are you with the career development efforts for postdocs by your university?

A. Quite dissatisfied
B. Dissatisfied
C. Somewhat satisfied
D. Satisfied
E. Quite Satisfied

CHAPTER 4 – Compensation and Working Conditions

14. What is your current annual salary?

15. In your view, how generous is your salary compared to what you might reasonably expect to obtain elsewhere for a similar position with a similar work load?

    A. My university is not very generous at all
    B. I could probably do better elsewhere
    C. I do about as well here as elsewhere
    D. I am probably a little better off here than elsewhere
    E. I am much better off here than elsewhere

16. How satisfied are you with the provisions for personal housing for you at your university?

    A. Very dissatisfied
    B. Dissatisfied
    C. Somewhat Satisfied
    D. Satisfied
    E. Very Satisfied

17. About what percentage of your current compensation is dependent upon funding external to your current institution?

18. How satisfied are you with the quality of the information technology provided by your university or research institute?

    A. Very dissatisfied
    B. Dissatisfied
    C. Somewhat satisfied
    D. Satisfied
    E. Very Satisfied

19. About how much do you estimate that it costs your university to send you to symposia, conferences, and other scientific meetings in your field in the past year. Include payment of conference fees, travel expenses, lodging and other expenses paid or reimbursed by your university.

20. Has your university ever extended to you any form or guaranteed income or "grace period" between grants when you receive either salary or stipend, or benefits (such as health insurance or office space) while you are in the process of applying for grants? If so how long have you received such support and what support did you receive?

CHAPTER 5 – Visa and Similar Issues

21. If you are not a citizen of the country in which you are working as a postdoc or equivalent, how satisfied are you with your visa/working permit situation in your host country?

   A. It's quite problematic
   B. It's occasionally problematic
   C. It's OK and not something I think about

CHAPTER 6 – Perception of Conditions for Postdocs in Various Countries

22. In general, how good are working conditions for postdocs in each of the following areas or countries

	Very Bad	Bad	Passable	Good	Very Good
USA					
Canada					
UK					
Ireland					
Australia					
New Zealand					

23. In general, how good are the prospects for obtaining permanent positions after serving as a postdoc in each of the following areas or countries

	Very Bad	Bad	Passable	Good	Very Good
USA					
Canada					
UK or Ireland					
Australia/New Zealand					

CHAPTER 7 – Searching for Work

24. How did you make the contact to get your current position? Through an ad? Career Fair. Scientific websites? At meetings? Through faculty mentors?

25. Which websites, if any, have you found useful in alerting you to postdoc and other scientific job prospects?

26. Which phrase captures what you believe is most likely to happen to you career-wise in three years?

A. I will likely have a tenure track job with a higher education institution.
B. I will likely remain a postdoc or its near equivalent in the institution that I currently work for.
C. I will likely remain a postdoc or its near equivalent for a new institution
D. I will likely have or be looking for a job outside of academia
E. I have or will get a position similar to postdocs sometimes referred to as superdocs with better pay and stability
F. Other (please specify)

CHAPTER 8 – The Power Structure and the Postdoc

27. Have you ever been sexually harassed by a principal investigator or other authority figure with potential power over you in any of your postdoc positions?

A. Yes
B. No

28. Rate the fairness and transparently of procedures and processes in place to help you combat abusive behavior by faculty with power over you.

    A. There are no such procedures and we are all very vulnerable
    B. Procedures are weak and many postdocs put up with more than they should
    C. Procedures seem adequate to discourage most abuse
    D. A strong system and culture is in place to prevent abuse of postdocs by those with more power

CHAPTER 9 – Teaching

29. Have you done any of the following in your current position?

    A. Taught classes as part of my employment contract
    B. Taught classes as an adjunct for extra compensation
    C. Tutored students for extra compensation

30. In which medical and life science fields do you anticipate the best prospects for research funding over the next five years?

31. How do you feel that the election of Donald Trump as President of the United States might affect your future career?

CHAPTER 10 – Advice for the Future

32. What advice can you offer to your peers about managing as a postdoc?

33. Which higher education institutions do you believe have exemplary postdoc working condition and programs and what do admire about them?

University Affiliations of the Participants

Australian National University
Brown Medical School
Brown University
Columbia University
Columbia University Medical Center
Drexel University
Duke-NUS Medical School
Emory University
Georgia Institute of Technology
Griffith University
Monash University
Pennsylvania State University
Rutgers Robert Wood Johnson Medical School
Rutgers University
St. Louis University
The University of Birmingham
The University of Western Australia
University College Dublin
University of Birmingham
University of California Riverside
University of Connecticut
University of Idaho
University of Leeds
University of Nottingham
University of South Florida
University of Utah
University of Western Australia
Yale School of Medicine
Yale University

Characteristics of the Sample

Country

	#
USA	52
UK	19
Other	15
Total	86

Is your institution a public or private college?

	#
Public	57
Private	29
Total	86

	#
Immunology	6
Neuroscience/Psychology	13
Cell/Molecular Biology	28
Healthcare Delivery	8
Chemistry	7
Other	24
Total	86

Number of years spent as a postdoc

	#
Less than 1 year	20
1.01 - 2.1 years	20
2.1 - 4.8 years	22
More than 4.8 years	24
Total	86

Gender of survey respondent

	#
Male	32
Female	54
Total	86

Age of survey participant

	#
30 or under	29
31-35	37
36 and over	20
Total	86

SUMMARY OF MAIN FINDINGS

Views of the Availability of Permanent Staff Positions Similar to Postdocs but with Greater Pay and Stability

We asked: Does your institution offer permanent staff positions similar to postdocs but with greater pay and stability?

22.09% of all postdocs surveyed said that their institution offered "superdoc" positions, permanent staff positions similar to postdocs but with greater pay and stability. Males and females reported with nearly the same frequency that "superdoc" positions were available. Respondents from US institutions reported the greatest availability of "superdoc" positions; 26.92% noted that "superdoc" positions were available from their institutions. 21.05% of UK respondents also reported the availability of "superdoc" positions but just 6.67% of respondents outside of the US and UK indicated that "superdoc" positions were available from their institutions.

The availability of "superdoc" positions at private colleges was twice that of public colleges, with 37.93% of respondents at private institutions indicating the availability of "superdoc" positions, compared to just 14.04% of public institution respondents. Neuroscience/Psychology, Chemistry and 'Other' offered the most opportunity for "superdoc" positions of any specialization surveyed, with 38.46%, 28.57% and 25.00% of respondents in each of these respective specializations reporting the availability of "superdoc" positions. Immunology postdocs, on the other hand, indicated that no "superdoc" positions whatsoever were available at their institutions.

Interestingly, the share of respondents who said their institution offered "superdoc" positions decreased as the number of years as a postdoc increased. 30.00% of respondents having completed less than 1.01 years as a postdoc said their institution offered "superdoc" positions, while only 4.17% of respondents who had spent more than 4.8 years as a postdoc reported the availability of "superdoc" positions.

Views of the Attainability of Superdoc Positions

We asked: If your institution offer such superdoc positions about what percentage of postdocs that want them attain them?

Although availability of "superdoc" positions outside of the US and UK was low, attainability was much higher in areas outside of the US and UK. Respondents outside of the US and UK said that 100% of postdocs seeking "superdoc" positions were able to attain them. Conversely, US and UK respondents reported that only 31.38% and 25.33%, respectively, of postdocs seeking "superdoc" positions were able to attain them. Private colleges were more than twice as likely as their public counterparts to offer "superdoc" positions, however "superdoc" positions were much more attainable at public institutions. 49.20% of those seeking "superdoc" positions at public universities attained such a position, compared to just 13.14% of those seeking "superdoc" positions at private universities.

Cell/Molecular Biology and Neuroscience/Psychology "superdoc" positions were the most attainable among those specializations surveyed; 41.38% of those seeking "superdoc" positions in Cell/Molecular Biology were able to attain such a position and 40.00% of those seeking "superdoc" positions in Neuroscience/Psychology were also able to attain such a position. However, just 27.50% and 19.50% of those seeking "superdoc" positions in Chemistry and 'Other', respectively, were able to attain such positions. Additionally, "superdoc" positions, when available, were far more attainable for senior postdocs, females, and those aged over 30.

Views of the Availability of a Postdocs Affairs Office Offering Training and Guidance

We asked: Does your institution have some kind of office of postdoc affairs to offer training and guidance to postdocs on campus?

More than two-thirds of postdocs said that their institution had some kind of postdocs affairs office. Such offices were most widely available in the UK, 84.21%, and were slightly more common at public colleges, 71.93%, than private, 62.07%. Postdocs specializing in Neuroscience/Psychology reported that affairs offices were readily available while those specializing in Healthcare Delivery said that only half their institutions had such an office. Respondents who had spent between 2.1 and 4.8 years as a postdoc stated that affairs offices were almost universally available, with 95.45% of intuitions having such an office, while all other postdocs were much more likely to say their institution did not have such an office or that they were not sure of the availability of such an office. Females and postdocs over 30 were also far more likely than their counterparts to report that their institution had an affairs office.

Views of the Quality of the Postdocs Affairs Office

We asked: How would you rate your college's office of postdoc affairs?

Almost a third, 30.77%, of postdocs in the USA reported that their college's postdoc affairs office was 'a joke' or not very useful, compared to 21.05% of those in the UK and none of those in other areas. Although postdocs at public and private colleges found their postdocs affairs offices almost equally useful, respondents from private colleges were twice as likely to rate their institution's offices at one of the two extremes, 10.34% stating that such offices were 'a joke' and an additional 10.34% calling them very useful. Postdocs across all specializations found their college's postdocs affairs offices at least somewhat useful, although 29.29% of those specializing in Cell/Molecular Biology and Chemistry reported that these offices were 'a joke' or not very useful. Females and postdocs over 30 also reported greater satisfaction than their counterparts with postdoc affairs offices.

Views of the Quality of University Services Provided to Postdocs

We asked: How would you rate the services provided by your university in each of the following areas: Databases and Research Tools to Find Funding Sources, Mentoring from those in more Senior Positions, Tools and Services to Promote Research Collaboration, and Funding for Travel for Scientific Purposes?

Postdocs in all countries and specializations were, as a whole, satisfied by their university's databases and research tools for finding funding sources, with 75.58% of all respondents rating these services as at least adequate, although males, respondents in the USA, and those specializing in Healthcare Delivery were more likely to rate such services as very poor and less likely to rate them as very good.

Respondents who had spent 2.1 years or more as a postdoc were far more likely than their less senior peers to be dissatisfied with mentoring services at their university. Only 59.09% of those having spent between 2.1 and 4.8 years as a postdoc and 54.17% of those having spent 4.8 years or more as a postdoc expressed satisfaction with mentoring services, compared to 75.00% of those having spent less than 2.1 years as a postdoc. Other than years as a postdoc, no other characteristic appeared to very strongly influence satisfaction with mentoring services.

Postdocs at private colleges, specializing in Immunology, or having spent less than 1.01 years as a postdoc were more likely than their peers to express satisfaction with tools and services to promote research collaboration. Postdocs specializing in Healthcare Delivery expressed a very low level of satisfaction with such tools and services, with only 37.50% of respondents specializing in Healthcare Delivery rating these services as at least adequate.

Compared to their peers, respondents in the USA, at private colleges, and those specializing in Neuroscience/ Psychology, Cell/Molecular Biology and Healthcare Delivery were less satisfied with funding for travel for scientific purposes. Postdocs specializing in Healthcare Delivery expressed the greatest dissatisfaction, with only 12.50% of respondents rating these services as at least adequate.

Satisfaction with Career Development Efforts for Postdocs

We asked: How satisfied are you with the career development efforts for postdocs by your university?

Postdocs specializing in Neuroscience/Psychology or Chemisty, aged 30 or under, or having spent between 1.01 and 4.8 years as a postdoc were most satisfied by their university's career development efforts. High levels of dissatisfaction were found among postdocs specializing in Immunology and Cell/Molecular Biology as well as those who had spent 4.8 years or more as a post doc. 66.67%, 46.43%, and 54.17% of respondents in each of these respective categories rated their college's career development efforts as less than adequate.

Views of the Helpfulness of the University in Assisting with the Development of English Language Skills

We asked the open-ended question: If you have ever required assistance with the development of English language skills describe the helpfulness of your university in this respect.

Nearly 80% of respondents have never required assistance with the development of English language skills. Of those postdocs who had required such assistance, more than two-thirds said that their university had been helpful in the development of these skills.

Current Annual Salaries of Postdocs

We asked: What is your current annual salary?

The mean salary for all postdocs surveyed was $53,107 and ranged from $18,000 to $329,001. Postdocs in the USA earned the least on average, $45,860, and had the smallest salary variation. However, postdocs in the UK had the lowest median salary, $36,750, suggesting that the mean UK salary is artificially high due to a very high outlier salary of $329,001. Postdocs outside of the USA and UK earned the most on average, $72,543, but also had a very low minimum salary of $18,000. Median salaries for males and females were roughly equal, as were those for public and private colleges. Median salaries also did not vary widely across specializations, with Immunology postdocs earning the most at $48,750 and Cell/Molecular Biology and Chemistry postdocs earning the least at $45,000. There appears to be a strong positive relationship between salary and age and a weak positive relationship between salary and years spent as a postdoc.

Views of Current Salary Compared to Salary for Similar Positions Elsewhere

We asked: In your view how generous is your salary compared to what you might reasonably expect to obtain elsewhere for a similar position with a similar work load?

Just over half of postdocs thought that their current salary was at least as good or better than what they would expect to be paid for a similar position elsewhere. 59.99% of postdocs outside of the USA and UK were satisfied with their current salaries, slightly higher than the 53.84% in the USA but much greater than 36.85% in the UK. Those at public institutions were slightly more content with their current salary compared to those at private institutions. Those specializing in Immunology, Healthcare Delivery and Chemistry reported relatively low salary satisfaction, while all other specializations reported about average satisfaction. Salary dissatisfaction tended to increase with years spent as a postdoc, while respondents aged 36 and up reported far greater satisfaction than their younger counterparts, with 65.00% of believing that their current salary was as good or better than what they could earn elsewhere. Males and females expressed roughly equal salary satisfaction.

Satisfaction with Personal Housing Provided by the University

We asked: How satisfied are you with the provisions for personal housing for you at your university?

20.93% of all respondents did not provide an answer to this question. Of those who did respond, a slightly greater share, 43.03%, expressed dissatisfaction with provisions for personal housing at their university. Over a third of respondents in the UK and Other areas did not respond to this question. However, even considering the low response rate in other countries, respondents in the USA still expressed far greater dissatisfaction than their counterparts, with 57.69% indicating that they were dissatisfied or very dissatisfied with their housing provisions. Postdocs from public universities expressed roughly equal satisfaction and dissatisfaction with their housing, while those from private universities were very dissatisfied; 41.38% of postdocs from private universities indicated that they were very dissatisfied with their university's personal housing provisions. 37.50% of men were very dissatisfied with their housing, compared to just 14.81% of women.

Postdoc Dependence on Funding External to Current Institution

We asked: About what percentage of your current compensation is dependent upon funding external to your current institution?

The average postdoc earned 70.53% of their compensation from funding external to their current university. The median postdoc was fully reliant on external funding. Those in the USA were, on average, far less reliant on external funding than those outside the USA. The Neuroscience/Psychology, Chemistry, and Cell/Molecular Biology specializations were the least dependent on external funding. Women depended on external funding for 77.11% of their compensation, compared to 59.77% for men. Age and type of institution (i.e., public or private) had virtually no impact on reliance on external funding.

Satisfaction with Information Technology Provided by the University or Research Institute

We asked: How satisfied are you with the quality of the information technology provided by your university or research institute?

A vast majority, 72.09%, of postdocs were at least somewhat satisfied with the quality of their institution's information technology. Satisfaction did not vary widely across countries, type of institution, age, or gender. Respondents who had spent more than 4.8 years as a postdoc expressed a high degree of dissatisfaction compared to their peers. The bulk of those specializing in Cell/Molecular Biology and Other were much more satisfied with their institution's information technology than their peers.

Estimated Cost to University of Sending Postdocs to Symposia, Conferences, and Other Scientific Meetings Over the Past Year

We asked: About how much do you estimate that it costs your university to send you to symposia, conferences, and other scientific meetings in your field in the past year. Include payment of conference fees, travel expenses, lodging and other expenses paid or reimbursed by your university. ($ US)

Last year universities in the UK spent an estimated $936.69 per person sending postdocs to symposia, conferences and other scientific meetings, roughly half what was spent in the USA and in Other countries. Median dollars spent per postdoc increased with age and were greatest for the Immunology and Neuroscience/Psychology specializations. Males and private universities had greater mean dollars spent per postdoc than their counterparts, however median dollars were the same across these groups, suggesting that mean estimates were artificially high due to one or more high-end outliers.

Provision of University Guaranteed Income or "Grace Period" Between Grants

We asked the open-ended question: Has your university ever extended to you any form or guaranteed income or "grace period" between grants when you receive either salary or stipend, or benefits (such as health insurance or office space) while you are in the process of applying for grants? If so how long have you received such support and what support did you receive?

90% of postdocs had never been extended any form of guaranteed income or "grace period" by their university. Half of the remaining respondents received guaranteed income between grants for one and a half to 6 months. One respondent was guaranteed 100% of his/her salary for 2 years and another respondent was paid for one year off a startup grant.

Satisfaction with Visa/Working Permit Situation in Host County for Non-Citizens

We asked: If you are not a citizen of the country in which you are working as a postdoc or equivalent, how satisfied are you with your visa/working permit situation in your host country?

Of those who provided a response to this question, nearly two-thirds indicated that their visa/working permit situation was at least occasionally problematic. Postdocs in the USA reporting having much greater trouble with their visa/working permit than their counterparts, however it is important to note that response rates to this question outside of the USA were very low. 83.33% of postdocs from private universities who responded to this question had at least occasional problems with their visa/working permit, far greater than the 53.85% of public university postdocs who reported issues. Women were slightly more satisfied than men with their visa/working permit situation.

View of Quality of Working Conditions for Postdocs in Various Countries

We asked: In general, how good are working conditions for postdocs in USA, Canada, UK, Ireland, Australia, and New Zealand?

Of all the countries mentioned in the survey, respondents had the least favourable impression of postdoc working conditions in the USA, with 26.67% of those who responded to this question rating USA working conditions as bad or very bad. 11.54% of postdocs working in the USA rated working conditions there as bad or very bad. 15.14% of those who responded to this question considered postdoc working conditions in Canada to be bad, however only 1.92% of respondents in the USA thought Canada working conditions to be bad. Respondents viewed UK working conditions most favourably, with 97.57% of those who provided a response to this question describing UK working conditions as passable or better. No postdocs working in the UK considered working conditions there to be bad.

View of Attainability of Permanent Positions After Serving as a Postdoc in Various Countries

We asked: In general, how good are the prospects for obtaining permanent positions after serving as a postdoc in USA, Canada, UK or Ireland, and Australia/New Zealand?

Respondents felt they had the best prospects of obtaining permanent positions after serving as postdocs in the USA or Canada. 13.96% of all respondents (including those working in other countries) thought the prospects were good or very good for obtaining a permanent position in the USA and 11.63% of respondents thought so for Canada. Conversely, only 5.82% of respondents thought they had a good or very good chance of obtaining a permanent position in the UK or Ireland. 8.14% thought their chances were good or very good in Australia/New Zealand.

38.45% of USA respondents thought the prospects for obtaining a permanent position in the USA were good or very good, but only about a fifth of USA respondents thought the prospects were good or very good in each of the other countries that they were asked about. 31.57% of UK respondents thought postdocs had a good or very good chance of obtaining a permanent positon in the US, but only 21.05% thought the prospects were good or very good in the UK. Men and women thought they had comparable chances of obtaining permanent positions in Australia/New Zealand but a higher proportion of men than women rated their chances as good or very good in the USA, Canada, and the UK or Ireland.

Method of First Contact to Obtain Current Position

We asked the open-ended question: How did you make the contact to get your current position? Through an ad? Career Fair. Scientific websites? At meetings? Through faculty mentors?

Reaching out to a faculty mentor was the most common method of finding a postdoc position, with 35.29% of respondents finding their current position this way. The next highest share, 30.88%, saw their current position on a website or ad. Other frequently cited methods of contact were a direct contact, talking to a friend, colleague, or other networking, and at a conference or meeting.

Useful Websites for Finding Postdoc and Other Scientific Job Prospects

We asked the open-ended question: Which websites, if any, have you found useful in alerting you to postdoc and other scientific job prospects?

22.64% of respondents listed Nature Jobs as a useful website for finding postdoc and other scientific job prospects, making it the most frequently used website among respondents. The second most common website was jobs.ac.uk, mentioned by 16.98% of respondents. Other frequently mentioned websites were ResearchGate, LinkedIn and Indeed.

Anticipated Career Prospects in Three Years

We asked the closed and open-ended question: Which phrase captures what you believe is most likely to happen to you career-wise in three years?

Responses to this question were split fairly evenly between four possible alternatives: roughly a quarter of respondents expected to have a tenure track job with a higher education institution in three-years, a quarter expected to have a post doc position at their current institution or at a new institution, or have a superdoc position, a quarter expected to be looking for a job outside of academia, and the remaining quarter provided no response or had some 'Other' expectation. Respondents in the USA and UK were much more confident about staying in academia and gaining a tenure track job than those in other countries. 28.85% of postdocs in the USA and 21.05% in the UK expected to have a tenure track job in three years, compared to 13.33% in other countries. Similarly, 46.67% of postdocs in countries outside of the USA and UK expected to be looking for a job outside of academia, compared to just 25.00% in the USA and 21.05% in the UK. Only 15.00% of respondents aged 36 and over expected to leave academia in the next three years, compared to over 30% of respondents under 36.

History of Sexual Harassment by a Principal Investigator or Other Authority Figure

We asked: Have you ever been sexually harassed by a principal investigator or other authority figure with potential power over you in any of your postdoc positions?

Only 3.49% of respondents indicated that they had been sexually harassed by a principal investigator or other authority figure in any of their postdoc positons. The proportion of postdocs in the USA reporting sexual harassment was in line with the overall average at 3.85%, while the UK rate was higher at 5.26%. Respondents in other countries reported no history of sexual harassment. Reported sexual harassment rates were extremely high for the Healthcare Delivery and Chemistry specializations, 12.50% and 14.29% respectively.

Additionally, men reported no history of sexual harassment while 5.56% of women indicated that they had been sexually harassed by an authority figure in a current or previous postdoc position.

View of Fairness and Transparency of Procedures and Processes for Combating Abusive Behaviour by Faculty with Power Over Postdocs

We asked: Rate the fairness and transparently of procedures and processes in place to help you combat abusive behaviour by faculty with power over you.

Nearly a third of respondents reported that procedures to combat abusive behaviour were inadequate. Results suggest that the most fair and transparent procedures are in place in other countries outside of the USA and UK while the USA has the weakest procedures. There was a clear negative relationship between years spent as a postdoc and impressions of procedures for combating abuse behaviour. Only 10.00% of those who had spent less than 1.01 years as a postdoc felt that procedures for combating abuse behaviour were inadequate, compared to 41.67% of those who had been a postdoc for more than 4.8 years. Women had less faith in procedures for combating abuse than men, with only 46.29% of women believing that current procedures were adequate to discourage abuse compared to 65.63% of men.

History of Teaching Classes as Part of Employment Contract, Teaching Classes as an Adjunct for Extra Compensation, or Tutoring Students for Extra Compensation

We asked: Have you done any of the following in your current position?

16.28% of postdocs had taught classes as part of their employment contract, 9.30% had taught classes as an adjunct for extra compensation and 2.33% had tutored students for extra compensation. No postdocs in the USA had taught classes as part of their employment contract, however postdocs in the USA were the only ones who had tutored students for extra compensation. Postdoc teaching arrangements appear to be largely dictated by university type. Postdocs at public universities were much more likely than their private college counterparts. to have taught classes as part of their employment contract. Conversely, postdocs at private universities were much more likely than their public university counterparts to have taught classes as an adjunct. All specializations with the exception of Healthcare Delivery were more likely to have taught classes as part of an employment contract than as an adjunct. Postdocs with more than 4.8 years of experience were much more likely to have taught classes as part of their employment contract than their less experienced counterparts. A higher proportion of women had taught adjunct classes but only men had tutored students.

Expectations of Medical and Life Science Fields with the Best Research Funding Prospects Over the Next Five Years

We asked the open-ended question: In which medical and life science fields do you anticipate the best prospects for research funding over the next five years?

Nearly half of respondents mentioned cancer as a field with good funding prospects over the next five years. Postdocs also felt optimistic about funding prospects for neuroscience, immunology, genetics, genomics, cell/molecular biology and bioinformatics.

Views of the Effect of Donald Trump as President of the United States on Future Careers for Postdocs

We asked the open-ended question: How do you feel that the election of Donald Trump as President of the United States might affect your future career?

Impressions of the election of Donald Trump as President of the United States were, on the whole, very pessimistic. Almost all respondents expected that a Donald Trump presidency would either have a negative impact or no impact on future postdoc careers. However numerous respondents believed that the impact to postdocs outside of the US would be minimal. Several respondents indicated that the election results would prevent them from seeking work in the US and others expressed concern about their visa status and funding cuts.

Advice to Peers for Managing as a Postdoc

We asked the open-ended question: What advice can you offer to your peers about managing as a postdoc?

Advice for managing as a postdoc included choosing a mentor wisely, establishing good working communication and networking. Postdocs also advised peers to think critically, work hard, persevere against adversity or discouragement, take advantage of all potential opportunities, and gain as much as possible from the experience. Many postdocs also advised against becoming a postdoc in the first place.

Views About Higher Education Institutions with Exemplary Postdoc Working Conditions and Programs

We asked the open-ended question: Which higher education institutions do you believe have exemplary postdoc working condition and programs and what do admire about them?

More than half of respondents did not mention a specific higher education institution that they believed had exemplary working conditions; in fact, many expressed skepticisms that such an institution exists. Poor response and skepticism were particularly high among postgrads with more than 4.8 years of experience. Of the respondents who did cite a specific university, those viewed as having exemplary working conditions included University of Utah, NYU, Stanford and University College London.

Table 1.1 Does your institution offer permanent staff positions similar to postdocs but with greater pay and stability?

	No Answer	Yes	No	Unsure
Entire sample	3.49%	22.09%	60.47%	13.95%

Table 1.2 Does your institution offer permanent staff positions similar to postdocs but with greater pay and stability? Broken out by Country

Country	No Answer	Yes	No	Unsure
USA	1.92%	26.92%	57.69%	13.46%
UK	5.26%	21.05%	68.42%	5.26%
Other	6.67%	6.67%	60.00%	26.67%

Table 1.3 Does your institution offer permanent staff positions similar to postdocs but with greater pay and stability? Broken out for public and private higher education institutions

Is your institution a public or private college?	No Answer	Yes	No	Unsure
Public	5.26%	14.04%	64.91%	15.79%
Private	0.00%	37.93%	51.72%	10.34%

Table 1.4 Does your institution offer permanent staff positions similar to postdocs but with greater pay and stability? Broken out by Specialization

Specialization	No Answer	Yes	No	Unsure
Immunology	0.00%	0.00%	100.00%	0.00%
Neuroscience/Psychology	0.00%	38.46%	46.15%	15.38%
Cell/Molecular Biology	3.57%	17.86%	67.86%	10.71%
Healthcare Delivery	12.50%	12.50%	50.00%	25.00%
Chemistry	0.00%	28.57%	57.14%	14.29%
Other	4.17%	25.00%	54.17%	16.67%

Table 1.5 Does your institution offer permanent staff positions similar to postdocs but with greater pay and stability? Broken out by Number of years spent as a postdoc

Number of years spent as a postdoc	No Answer	Yes	No	Unsure
Less than 1.01	5.00%	30.00%	45.00%	20.00%
1.01 - 2.1	5.00%	30.00%	50.00%	15.00%
2.1 - 4.8	0.00%	27.27%	59.09%	13.64%
More than 4.8	4.17%	4.17%	83.33%	8.33%

Table 1.6 Does your institution offer permanent staff positions similar to postdocs but with greater pay and stability? Broken out by Gender of survey respondent

Gender of survey respondent	No Answer	Yes	No	Unsure
Male	0.00%	21.88%	62.50%	15.63%
Female	5.56%	22.22%	59.26%	12.96%

Table 1.7 Does your institution offer permanent staff positions similar to postdocs but with greater pay and stability? Broken out by Age of survey participant

Age of survey participant	No Answer	Yes	No	Unsure
30 or under	3.45%	27.59%	55.17%	13.79%
31-35	5.41%	27.03%	54.05%	13.51%
36 and over	0.00%	5.00%	80.00%	15.00%

Table 2.1 If your institution offer such superdoc positions about what percentage of postdocs that want them attain them?

	Mean	Median	Minimum	Maximum
Entire sample	34.35	10.00	1.00	100.00

Table 2.2 If your institution offer such superdoc positions about what percentage of postdocs that want them attain them? Broken out by Country

Country	Mean	Median	Minimum	Maximum
USA	31.38	10.00	1.00	100.00
UK	25.33	5.00	1.00	70.00
Other	100.00	100.00	100.00	100.00

Table 2.3 If your institution offer such superdoc positions about what percentage of postdocs that want them attain them? Broken out for public and private higher education institutions

Is your institution a public or private college?	Mean	Median	Minimum	Maximum
Public	49.20	50.00	2.00	100.00
Private	13.14	10.00	1.00	50.00

Table 2.4 If your institution offer such superdoc positions about what percentage of postdocs that want them attain them? Broken out by Specialization

Specialization	Mean	Median	Minimum	Maximum
Neuroscience/Psychology	40.00	10.00	10.00	100.00
Cell/Molecular Biology	41.38	50.00	1.00	100.00
Chemistry	27.50	27.50	5.00	50.00
Other	19.50	3.50	1.00	70.00

Table 2.5 If your institution offer such superdoc positions about what percentage of postdocs that want them attain them? Broken out by Number of years spent as a postdoc

Number of years spent as a postdoc	Mean	Median	Minimum	Maximum
Less than 1.01	17.50	7.50	5.00	50.00
1.01 - 2.1	27.33	6.00	1.00	100.00
2.1 - 4.8	36.00	50.00	10.00	60.00
More than 4.8	85.00	85.00	70.00	100.00

Table 2.6 If your institution offer such superdoc positions about what percentage of postdocs that want them attain them? Broken out by Gender of survey respondent

Gender of survey respondent	Mean	Median	Minimum	Maximum
Male	28.40	10.00	1.00	100.00
Female	42.86	50.00	5.00	100.00

Table 2.7 If your institution offer such superdoc positions about what percentage of postdocs that want them attain them? Broken out by Age of survey participant

Age of survey participant	Mean	Median	Minimum	Maximum
30 or under	14.20	5.00	1.00	50.00
31-35	42.75	50.00	1.00	100.00

Table 3.1 Does your institution have some kind of office of postdoc affairs to offer training and guidance to postdocs on campus?

	No Answer	Yes	No	Not Sure
Entire sample	5.81%	68.60%	15.12%	10.47%

Table 3.2 Does your institution have some kind of office of postdoc affairs to offer training and guidance to postdocs on campus? Broken out by Country

Country	No Answer	Yes	No	Not Sure
USA	3.85%	69.23%	13.46%	13.46%
UK	10.53%	84.21%	5.26%	0.00%
Other	6.67%	46.67%	33.33%	13.33%

Table 3.3 Does your institution have some kind of office of postdoc affairs to offer training and guidance to postdocs on campus? Broken out for public and private higher education institutions

Is your institution a public or private college?	No Answer	Yes	No	Not Sure
Public	5.26%	71.93%	14.04%	8.77%
Private	6.90%	62.07%	17.24%	13.79%

Table 3.4 Does your institution have some kind of office of postdoc affairs to offer training and guidance to postdocs on campus? Broken out by Specialization

Specialization	No Answer	Yes	No	Not Sure
Immunology	0.00%	66.67%	33.33%	0.00%
Neuroscience/Psychology	7.69%	84.62%	7.69%	0.00%
Cell/Molecular Biology	3.57%	64.29%	14.29%	17.86%
Healthcare Delivery	25.00%	50.00%	12.50%	12.50%
Chemistry	0.00%	71.43%	28.57%	0.00%
Other	4.17%	70.83%	12.50%	12.50%

Table 3.5 Does your institution have some kind of office of postdoc affairs to offer training and guidance to postdocs on campus? Broken out by Number of years spent as a postdoc

Number of years spent as a postdoc	No Answer	Yes	No	Not Sure
Less than 1.01	10.00%	65.00%	10.00%	15.00%
1.01 - 2.1	10.00%	55.00%	25.00%	10.00%
2.1 - 4.8	0.00%	95.45%	0.00%	4.55%
More than 4.8	4.17%	58.33%	25.00%	12.50%

Table 3.6 Does your institution have some kind of office of postdoc affairs to offer training and guidance to postdocs on campus? Broken out by Gender of survey respondent

Gender of survey respondent	No Answer	Yes	No	Not Sure
Male	3.13%	56.25%	25.00%	15.63%
Female	7.41%	75.93%	9.26%	7.41%

Table 3.7 Does your institution have some kind of office of postdoc affairs to offer training and guidance to postdocs on campus? Broken out by Age of survey participant

Age of survey participant	No Answer	Yes	No	Not Sure
30 or under	13.79%	55.17%	20.69%	10.34%
31-35	2.70%	75.68%	13.51%	8.11%
36 and over	0.00%	75.00%	10.00%	15.00%

Table 4.1 How would you rate your college's office of postdoc affairs?

	No Answer	It's a joke	Not very useful	somewhat useful	useful	very useful
Entire sample	18.60%	6.98%	16.28%	27.91%	24.42%	5.81%

Table 4.2 How would you rate your college's office of postdoc affairs? Broken out by Country

Country	No Answer	It's a joke	Not very useful	somewhat useful	useful	very useful
USA	11.54%	9.62%	21.15%	28.85%	23.08%	5.77%
UK	10.53%	5.26%	15.79%	36.84%	31.58%	0.00%
Other	53.33%	0.00%	0.00%	13.33%	20.00%	13.33%

Table 4.3 How would you rate your college's office of postdoc affairs? Broken out for public and private higher education institutions

Is your institution a public or private college?	No Answer	It's a joke	Not very useful	somewhat useful	useful	very useful
Public	19.30%	5.26%	17.54%	29.82%	24.56%	3.51%
Private	17.24%	10.34%	13.79%	24.14%	24.14%	10.34%

Table 4.4 How would you rate your college's office of postdoc affairs? Broken out by Specialization

Specialization	No Answer	It's a joke	Not very useful	somewhat useful	useful	very useful
Immunology	33.33%	0.00%	16.67%	16.67%	16.67%	16.67%
Neuroscience/Psychology	15.38%	0.00%	15.38%	23.08%	30.77%	15.38%
Cell/Molecular Biology	10.71%	14.29%	25.00%	32.14%	17.86%	0.00%
Healthcare Delivery	50.00%	0.00%	12.50%	12.50%	25.00%	0.00%
Chemistry	14.29%	14.29%	0.00%	14.29%	42.86%	14.29%
Other	16.67%	4.17%	12.50%	37.50%	25.00%	4.17%

Table 4.5 How would you rate your college's office of postdoc affairs? Broken out by Number of years spent as a postdoc

Number of years spent as a postdoc	No Answer	It's a joke	Not very useful	somewhat useful	useful	very useful
Less than 1.01	10.00%	5.00%	15.00%	30.00%	35.00%	5.00%
1.01 - 2.1	30.00%	15.00%	10.00%	20.00%	25.00%	0.00%
2.1 - 4.8	0.00%	4.55%	27.27%	36.36%	18.18%	13.64%
More than 4.8	33.33%	4.17%	12.50%	25.00%	20.83%	4.17%

Table 4.6 How would you rate your college's office of postdoc affairs? Broken out by Gender of survey respondent

Gender of survey respondent	No Answer	It's a joke	Not very useful	somewhat useful	useful	very useful
Male	18.75%	12.50%	21.88%	21.88%	21.88%	3.13%
Female	18.52%	3.70%	12.96%	31.48%	25.93%	7.41%

Table 4.7 How would you rate your college's office of postdoc affairs? Broken out by Age of survey participant

Age of survey participant	No Answer	It's a joke	Not very useful	somewhat useful	useful	very useful
30 or under	27.59%	13.79%	10.34%	20.69%	17.24%	10.34%
31-35	10.81%	2.70%	24.32%	35.14%	24.32%	2.70%
36 and over	20.00%	5.00%	10.00%	25.00%	35.00%	5.00%

Table 5 How would you rate the services provided by your university in each of the following areas?

Table 5.1.1 How would you rate the services provided by your university in Databases and Research Tools to Find Funding Sources?

	No Answer	Very Poor	Poor	Adequate	Good	Very Good
Entire sample	5.81%	4.65%	13.95%	33.72%	25.58%	16.28%

Table 5.1.2 How would you rate the services provided by your university in Databases and Research Tools to Find Funding Sources? Broken out by Country

Country	No Answer	Very Poor	Poor	Adequate	Good	Very Good
USA	3.85%	5.77%	17.31%	30.77%	28.85%	13.46%
UK	10.53%	0.00%	10.53%	36.84%	21.05%	21.05%
Other	6.67%	6.67%	6.67%	40.00%	20.00%	20.00%

Table 5.1.3 How would you rate the services provided by your university in Databases and Research Tools to Find Funding Sources? Broken out for public and private higher education institutions

Is your institution a public or private college?	No Answer	Very Poor	Poor	Adequate	Good	Very Good
Public	5.26%	3.51%	14.04%	38.60%	21.05%	17.54%
Private	6.90%	6.90%	13.79%	24.14%	34.48%	13.79%

Table 5.1.4 How would you rate the services provided by your university in Databases and Research Tools to Find Funding Sources? Broken out by Specialization

Specialization	No Answer	Very Poor	Poor	Adequate	Good	Very Good
Immunology	0.00%	0.00%	0.00%	50.00%	33.33%	16.67%
Neuroscience/Psychology	7.69%	7.69%	7.69%	30.77%	30.77%	15.38%
Cell/Molecular Biology	3.57%	3.57%	10.71%	39.29%	25.00%	17.86%
Healthcare Delivery	25.00%	12.50%	12.50%	25.00%	12.50%	12.50%
Chemistry	0.00%	0.00%	42.86%	42.86%	14.29%	0.00%
Other	4.17%	4.17%	16.67%	25.00%	29.17%	20.83%

Table 5.1.5 How would you rate the services provided by your university in Databases and Research Tools to Find Funding Sources? Broken out by Number of years spent as a postdoc

Number of years spent as a postdoc	No Answer	Very Poor	Poor	Adequate	Good	Very Good
Less than 1.01	10.00%	0.00%	5.00%	25.00%	35.00%	25.00%
1.01 - 2.1	10.00%	5.00%	15.00%	35.00%	30.00%	5.00%
2.1 - 4.8	0.00%	4.55%	27.27%	31.82%	13.64%	22.73%
More than 4.8	4.17%	8.33%	8.33%	41.67%	25.00%	12.50%

Table 5.1.6 How would you rate the services provided by your university in Databases and Research Tools to Find Funding Sources? Broken out by Gender of survey respondent

Gender of survey respondent	No Answer	Very Poor	Poor	Adequate	Good	Very Good
Male	3.13%	12.50%	18.75%	28.13%	21.88%	15.63%
Female	7.41%	0.00%	11.11%	37.04%	27.78%	16.67%

Table 5.1.7 How would you rate the services provided by your university in Databases and Research Tools to Find Funding Sources? Broken out by Age of survey participant

Age of survey participant	No Answer	Very Poor	Poor	Adequate	Good	Very Good
30 or under	13.79%	0.00%	10.34%	31.03%	31.03%	13.79%
31-35	2.70%	2.70%	18.92%	37.84%	18.92%	18.92%
36 and over	0.00%	15.00%	10.00%	30.00%	30.00%	15.00%

Table 5.2.1 How would you rate the services provided by your university in Mentoring from those in more senior positions?

	No Answer	Very Poor	Poor	Adequate	Good	Very Good
Entire sample	6.98%	9.30%	18.60%	22.09%	30.23%	12.79%

Table 5.2.2 How would you rate the services provided by your university in Mentoring from those in more senior positions? Broken out by Country

Country	No Answer	Very Poor	Poor	Adequate	Good	Very Good
USA	5.77%	7.69%	23.08%	17.31%	34.62%	11.54%
UK	10.53%	10.53%	15.79%	26.32%	15.79%	21.05%
Other	6.67%	13.33%	6.67%	33.33%	33.33%	6.67%

Table 5.2.3 How would you rate the services provided by your university in Mentoring from those in more senior positions? Broken out for public and private higher education institutions

Is your institution a public or private college?	No Answer	Very Poor	Poor	Adequate	Good	Very Good
Public	5.26%	10.53%	17.54%	24.56%	28.07%	14.04%
Private	10.34%	6.90%	20.69%	17.24%	34.48%	10.34%

Table 5.2.4 How would you rate the services provided by your university in Mentoring from those in more senior positions? Broken out by Specialization

Specialization	No Answer	Very Poor	Poor	Adequate	Good	Very Good
Immunology	0.00%	16.67%	33.33%	50.00%	0.00%	0.00%
Neuroscience/Psychology	7.69%	7.69%	7.69%	23.08%	38.46%	15.38%
Cell/Molecular Biology	3.57%	3.57%	25.00%	21.43%	32.14%	14.29%
Healthcare Delivery	25.00%	12.50%	0.00%	25.00%	37.50%	0.00%
Chemistry	0.00%	14.29%	14.29%	14.29%	42.86%	14.29%
Other	8.33%	12.50%	20.83%	16.67%	25.00%	16.67%

Table 5.2.5 How would you rate the services provided by your university in Mentoring from those in more senior positions? Broken out by Number of years spent as a postdoc

Number of years spent as a postdoc	No Answer	Very Poor	Poor	Adequate	Good	Very Good
Less than 1.01	10.00%	0.00%	15.00%	5.00%	45.00%	25.00%
1.01 - 2.1	10.00%	5.00%	10.00%	35.00%	30.00%	10.00%
2.1 - 4.8	4.55%	9.09%	27.27%	18.18%	27.27%	13.64%
More than 4.8	4.17%	20.83%	20.83%	29.17%	20.83%	4.17%

Table 5.2.6 How would you rate the services provided by your university in Mentoring from those in more senior positions? Broken out by Gender of survey respondent

Gender of survey respondent	No Answer	Very Poor	Poor	Adequate	Good	Very Good
Male	3.13%	12.50%	18.75%	25.00%	25.00%	15.63%
Female	9.26%	7.41%	18.52%	20.37%	33.33%	11.11%

Table 5.2.7 How would you rate the services provided by your university in Mentoring from those in more senior positions? Broken out by Age of survey participant

Age of survey participant	No Answer	Very Poor	Poor	Adequate	Good	Very Good
30 or under	13.79%	10.34%	6.90%	24.14%	27.59%	17.24%
31-35	5.41%	5.41%	32.43%	18.92%	29.73%	8.11%
36 and over	0.00%	15.00%	10.00%	25.00%	35.00%	15.00%

Table 5.3.1 How would you rate the services provided by your university in Tools and Services to Promote Research Collaboration?

	No Answer	Very Poor	Poor	Adequate	Good	Very Good
Entire sample	6.98%	8.14%	16.28%	34.88%	22.09%	11.63%

Table 5.3.2 How would you rate the services provided by your university in Tools and Services to Promote Research Collaboration? Broken out by Country

Country	No Answer	Very Poor	Poor	Adequate	Good	Very Good
USA	5.77%	11.54%	13.46%	28.85%	26.92%	13.46%
UK	10.53%	0.00%	21.05%	57.89%	0.00%	10.53%
Other	6.67%	6.67%	20.00%	26.67%	33.33%	6.67%

Table 5.3.3 How would you rate the services provided by your university in Tools and Services to Promote Research Collaboration? Broken out for public and private higher education institutions

Is your institution a public or private college?	No Answer	Very Poor	Poor	Adequate	Good	Very Good
Public	5.26%	3.51%	17.54%	38.60%	24.56%	10.53%
Private	10.34%	17.24%	13.79%	27.59%	17.24%	13.79%

Table 5.3.4 How would you rate the services provided by your university in Tools and Services to Promote Research Collaboration? Broken out by Specialization

Specialization	No Answer	Very Poor	Poor	Adequate	Good	Very Good
Immunology	0.00%	16.67%	0.00%	33.33%	33.33%	16.67%
Neuroscience/Psychology	7.69%	0.00%	23.08%	38.46%	23.08%	7.69%
Cell/Molecular Biology	3.57%	10.71%	17.86%	28.57%	21.43%	17.86%
Healthcare Delivery	25.00%	12.50%	25.00%	25.00%	12.50%	0.00%
Chemistry	0.00%	0.00%	28.57%	57.14%	14.29%	0.00%
Other	8.33%	8.33%	8.33%	37.50%	25.00%	12.50%

Table 5.3.5 How would you rate the services provided by your university in Tools and Services to Promote Research Collaboration? Broken out by Number of years spent as a postdoc

Number of years spent as a postdoc	No Answer	Very Poor	Poor	Adequate	Good	Very Good
Less than 1.01	10.00%	5.00%	5.00%	15.00%	30.00%	35.00%
1.01 - 2.1	10.00%	5.00%	20.00%	30.00%	30.00%	5.00%
2.1 - 4.8	4.55%	9.09%	22.73%	40.91%	18.18%	4.55%
More than 4.8	4.17%	12.50%	16.67%	50.00%	12.50%	4.17%

Table 5.3.6 How would you rate the services provided by your university in Tools and Services to Promote Research Collaboration? Broken out by Gender of survey respondent

Gender of survey respondent	No Answer	Very Poor	Poor	Adequate	Good	Very Good
Male	3.13%	12.50%	15.63%	34.38%	18.75%	15.63%
Female	9.26%	5.56%	16.67%	35.19%	24.07%	9.26%

Table 5.3.7 How would you rate the services provided by your university in Tools and Services to Promote Research Collaboration? Broken out by Age of survey participant

Age of survey participant	No Answer	Very Poor	Poor	Adequate	Good	Very Good
30 or under	13.79%	0.00%	13.79%	24.14%	31.03%	17.24%
31-35	5.41%	8.11%	21.62%	35.14%	21.62%	8.11%
36 and over	0.00%	20.00%	10.00%	50.00%	10.00%	10.00%

Table 5.4.1 How would you rate the services provided by your university in Funding for Travel for Scientific Purposes?

	No Answer	Very Poor	Poor	Adequate	Good	Very Good
Entire sample	8.14%	11.63%	17.44%	33.72%	17.44%	11.63%

Table 5.4.2 How would you rate the services provided by your university in Funding for Travel for Scientific Purposes? Broken out by Country

Country	No Answer	Very Poor	Poor	Adequate	Good	Very Good
USA	5.77%	11.54%	25.00%	32.69%	15.38%	9.62%
UK	10.53%	10.53%	10.53%	31.58%	26.32%	10.53%
Other	13.33%	13.33%	0.00%	40.00%	13.33%	20.00%

Table 5.4.3 How would you rate the services provided by your university in Funding for Travel for Scientific Purposes? Broken out for public and private higher education institutions

Is your institution a public or private college?	No Answer	Very Poor	Poor	Adequate	Good	Very Good
Public	7.02%	12.28%	14.04%	36.84%	19.30%	10.53%
Private	10.34%	10.34%	24.14%	27.59%	13.79%	13.79%

Table 5.4.4 How would you rate the services provided by your university in Funding for Travel for Scientific Purposes? Broken out by Specialization

Specialization	No Answer	Very Poor	Poor	Adequate	Good	Very Good
Immunology	0.00%	0.00%	16.67%	83.33%	0.00%	0.00%
Neuroscience/Psychology	7.69%	15.38%	23.08%	23.08%	7.69%	23.08%
Cell/Molecular Biology	3.57%	10.71%	25.00%	35.71%	17.86%	7.14%
Healthcare Delivery	37.50%	25.00%	25.00%	0.00%	0.00%	12.50%
Chemistry	0.00%	0.00%	14.29%	42.86%	28.57%	14.29%
Other	8.33%	12.50%	4.17%	33.33%	29.17%	12.50%

Table 5.4.5 How would you rate the services provided by your university in Funding for Travel for Scientific Purposes? Broken out by Number of years spent as a postdoc

Number of years spent as a postdoc	No Answer	Very Poor	Poor	Adequate	Good	Very Good
Less than 1.01	10.00%	5.00%	15.00%	25.00%	25.00%	20.00%
1.01 - 2.1	10.00%	20.00%	10.00%	40.00%	5.00%	15.00%
2.1 - 4.8	4.55%	9.09%	27.27%	31.82%	18.18%	9.09%
More than 4.8	8.33%	12.50%	16.67%	37.50%	20.83%	4.17%

Table 5.4.6 How would you rate the services provided by your university in Funding for Travel for Scientific Purposes? Broken out by Gender of survey respondent

Gender of survey respondent	No Answer	Very Poor	Poor	Adequate	Good	Very Good
Male	3.13%	15.63%	15.63%	40.63%	12.50%	12.50%
Female	11.11%	9.26%	18.52%	29.63%	20.37%	11.11%

Table 5.4.7 How would you rate the services provided by your university in Funding for Travel for Scientific Purposes? Broken out by Age of survey participant

Age of survey participant	No Answer	Very Poor	Poor	Adequate	Good	Very Good
30 or under	13.79%	13.79%	0.00%	34.48%	20.69%	17.24%
31-35	5.41%	10.81%	29.73%	32.43%	13.51%	8.11%
36 and over	5.00%	10.00%	20.00%	35.00%	20.00%	10.00%

Table 6.1 How satisfied are you with the career development efforts for postdocs by your university?

	No Answer	Quite Dissatisfied	Dissatisfied	Somewhat Satisfied	Satisfied	Quite Satisfied
Entire sample	5.81%	15.12%	19.77%	24.42%	26.74%	8.14%

Table 6.2 How satisfied are you with the career development efforts for postdocs by your university? Broken out by Country

Country	No Answer	Quite Dissatisfied	Dissatisfied	Somewhat Satisfied	Satisfied	Quite Satisfied
USA	3.85%	13.46%	23.08%	30.77%	23.08%	5.77%
UK	10.53%	15.79%	15.79%	10.53%	36.84%	10.53%
Other	6.67%	20.00%	13.33%	20.00%	26.67%	13.33%

Table 6.3 How satisfied are you with the career development efforts for postdocs by your university? Broken out for public and private higher education institutions

Is your institution a public or private college?	No Answer	Quite Dissatisfied	Dissatisfied	Somewhat Satisfied	Satisfied	Quite Satisfied
Public	5.26%	14.04%	22.81%	28.07%	24.56%	5.26%
Private	6.90%	17.24%	13.79%	17.24%	31.03%	13.79%

Table 6.4 How satisfied are you with the career development efforts for postdocs by your university? Broken out by Specialization

Specialization	No Answer	Quite Dissatisfied	Dissatisfied	Somewhat Satisfied	Satisfied	Quite Satisfied
Immunology	0.00%	16.67%	50.00%	16.67%	0.00%	16.67%
Neuroscience/Psychology	7.69%	0.00%	7.69%	30.77%	38.46%	15.38%
Cell/Molecular Biology	3.57%	14.29%	32.14%	17.86%	21.43%	10.71%
Healthcare Delivery	25.00%	25.00%	12.50%	25.00%	12.50%	0.00%
Chemistry	0.00%	28.57%	0.00%	28.57%	42.86%	0.00%
Other	4.17%	16.67%	12.50%	29.17%	33.33%	4.17%

Table 6.5 How satisfied are you with the career development efforts for postdocs by your university? Broken out by Number of years spent as a postdoc

Number of years spent as a postdoc	No Answer	Quite Dissatisfied	Dissatisfied	Somewhat Satisfied	Satisfied	Quite Satisfied
Less than 1.01	10.00%	15.00%	20.00%	15.00%	30.00%	10.00%
1.01 - 2.1	10.00%	10.00%	10.00%	40.00%	25.00%	5.00%
2.1 - 4.8	0.00%	9.09%	18.18%	31.82%	27.27%	13.64%
More than 4.8	4.17%	25.00%	29.17%	12.50%	25.00%	4.17%

Table 6.6 How satisfied are you with the career development efforts for postdocs by your university? Broken out by Gender of survey respondent

Gender of survey respondent	No Answer	Quite Dissatisfied	Dissatisfied	Somewhat Satisfied	Satisfied	Quite Satisfied
Male	3.13%	18.75%	21.88%	25.00%	21.88%	9.38%
Female	7.41%	12.96%	18.52%	24.07%	29.63%	7.41%

Table 6.7 How satisfied are you with the career development efforts for postdocs by your university? Broken out by Age of survey participant

Age of survey participant	No Answer	Quite Dissatisfied	Dissatisfied	Somewhat Satisfied	Satisfied	Quite Satisfied
30 or under	13.79%	13.79%	6.90%	20.69%	31.03%	13.79%
31-35	2.70%	16.22%	27.03%	29.73%	18.92%	5.41%
36 and over	0.00%	15.00%	25.00%	20.00%	35.00%	5.00%

If you have ever required assistance with the development of English language skills describe the helpfulness of your university in this respect.

Less than 1.01

1) I haven't
2) Provided ESL short courses.
3) NA
4) No
5) I have never required it.
6) no
7) NA

1.01 - 2.1

1) no
2) very helpful
3) No
4) no idea
5) N/A

2.1 - 4.8

1) N/A
2) very helpful
3) NO
4) no help at all
5) very helpful
6) n/a
7) N/A
8) not relevant
9) Good
10) n/a
11) NA
12) No
13) no

More than 4.8

1) no
2) N/A
3) NA
4) No
5) No assistance offered.
6) No

7) n/a
8) NA

Table 7.1 How satisfied are you with the career development efforts for postdocs by your university?

	No Answer	Quite Dissatisfied	Dissatisfied	Somewhat Satisfied	Satisfied	Quite Satisfied
Entire sample	5.81%	15.12%	19.77%	24.42%	26.74%	8.14%

Table 7.2 How satisfied are you with the career development efforts for postdocs by your university? Broken out by Country

Country	No Answer	Quite Dissatisfied	Dissatisfied	Somewhat Satisfied	Satisfied	Quite Satisfied
USA	3.85%	13.46%	23.08%	30.77%	23.08%	5.77%
UK	10.53%	15.79%	15.79%	10.53%	36.84%	10.53%
Other	6.67%	20.00%	13.33%	20.00%	26.67%	13.33%

Table 7.3 How satisfied are you with the career development efforts for postdocs by your university? Broken out for public and private higher education institutions

Is your institution a public or private college?	No Answer	Quite Dissatisfied	Dissatisfied	Somewhat Datisfied	Satisfied	Quite Satisfied
Public	5.26%	14.04%	22.81%	28.07%	24.56%	5.26%
Private	6.90%	17.24%	13.79%	17.24%	31.03%	13.79%

Table 7.4 How satisfied are you with the career development efforts for postdocs by your university? Broken out by Specialization

Specialization	No Answer	Quite Dissatisfied	Dissatisfied	Somewhat Satisfied	Satisfied	Quite Satisfied
Immunology	0.00%	16.67%	50.00%	16.67%	0.00%	16.67%
Neuroscience/Psychology	7.69%	0.00%	7.69%	30.77%	38.46%	15.38%
Cell/Molecular Biology	3.57%	14.29%	32.14%	17.86%	21.43%	10.71%
Healthcare Delivery	25.00%	25.00%	12.50%	25.00%	12.50%	0.00%
Chemistry	0.00%	28.57%	0.00%	28.57%	42.86%	0.00%
Other	4.17%	16.67%	12.50%	29.17%	33.33%	4.17%

Table 7.5 How satisfied are you with the career development efforts for postdocs by your university? Broken out by Number of years spent as a postdoc

Number of years spent as a postdoc	No Answer	Quite Dissatisfied	Dissatisfied	Somewhat Satisfied	Satisfied	Quite Satisfied
Less than 1.01	10.00%	15.00%	20.00%	15.00%	30.00%	10.00%
1.01 - 2.1	10.00%	10.00%	10.00%	40.00%	25.00%	5.00%
2.1 - 4.8	0.00%	9.09%	18.18%	31.82%	27.27%	13.64%
More than 4.8	4.17%	25.00%	29.17%	12.50%	25.00%	4.17%

Table 7.6 How satisfied are you with the career development efforts for postdocs by your university? Broken out by Gender of survey respondent

Gender of survey respondent	No Answer	Quite Dissatisfied	Dissatisfied	Somewhat Satisfied	Satisfied	Quite Satisfied
Male	3.13%	18.75%	21.88%	25.00%	21.88%	9.38%
Female	7.41%	12.96%	18.52%	24.07%	29.63%	7.41%

Table 7.7 How satisfied are you with the career development efforts for postdocs by your university? Broken out by Age of survey participant

Age of survey participant	No Answer	Quite Dissatisfied	Dissatisfied	Somewhat Satisfied	Satisfied	Quite Satisfied
30 or under	13.79%	13.79%	6.90%	20.69%	31.03%	13.79%
31-35	2.70%	16.22%	27.03%	29.73%	18.92%	5.41%
36 and over	0.00%	15.00%	25.00%	20.00%	35.00%	5.00%

Table 8.1 What is your current annual salary? ($ US)

	Mean	Median	Minimum	Maximum
Entire sample	53107.03	46000.00	18000.00	329001.25

Table 8.2 What is your current annual salary? Broken out by Country

Country	Mean	Median	Minimum	Maximum
USA	45860.09	46500.00	30000.00	55000.00
UK	57244.17	36750.00	31000.00	329001.25
Other	72543.25	77570.25	18000.00	120000.00

Table 8.3 What is your current annual salary? Broken out for public and private higher education institutions

Is your institution a public or private college?	Mean	Median	Minimum	Maximum
Public	55696.44	46125.00	18000.00	329001.25
Private	48135.36	45000.00	37000.00	92000.00

Table 8.4 What is your current annual salary? Broken out by Specialization

Specialization	Mean	Median	Minimum	Maximum
Immunology	53478.38	48750.00	37800.00	77570.25
Neuroscience/Psychology	52087.09	47000.00	32958.00	105000.00
Cell/Molecular Biology	47190.86	45000.00	30000.00	92000.00
Healthcare Delivery	47000.00	47000.00	31000.00	60000.00
Chemistry	49142.86	45000.00	35000.00	84000.00
Other	64432.28	46000.00	18000.00	329001.25

Table 8.5 What is your current annual salary? Broken out by Number of years spent as a postdoc

Number of years spent as a postdoc	Mean	Median	Minimum	Maximum
Less than 1.01	59030.33	43346.00	18000.00	329001.25
1.01 - 2.1	47312.50	47000.00	30000.00	60000.00
2.1 - 4.8	45741.45	45000.00	31000.00	80000.00
More than 4.8	59374.56	49950.00	32000.00	120000.00

Table 8.6 What is your current annual salary? Broken out by Gender of survey respondent

Gender of survey respondent	Mean	Median	Minimum	Maximum
Male	60202.19	45000.00	18000.00	329001.25
Female	48430.67	47000.00	31000.00	105000.00

Table 8.7 What is your current annual salary? Broken out by Age of survey participant

Age of survey participant	Mean	Median	Minimum	Maximum
30 or under	41494.98	43000.00	18000.00	60000.00
31-35	58625.42	46625.00	30000.00	329001.25
36 and over	59112.94	50400.00	42000.00	120000.00

Table 9.1 In your view how generous is your salary compared to what you might reasonably expect to obtain elsewhere for a similar position with a similar work load?

	No Answer	My university is not very generous at all	I could probably do better elsewhere	I do about as well here as elsewhere	I am probably a little better off here than elsewhere	I am much better off here than elsewhere
Entire sample	11.63%	13.95%	23.26%	27.91%	16.28%	6.98%

Table 9.2 In your view how generous is your salary compared to what you might reasonably expect to obtain elsewhere for a similar position with a similar work load? Broken out by Country

Country	No Answer	My university is not very generous at all	I could probably do better elsewhere	I do about as well here as elsewhere	I am probably a little better off here than elsewhere	I am much better off here than elsewhere
USA	11.54%	17.31%	17.31%	32.69%	13.46%	7.69%
UK	15.79%	10.53%	36.84%	26.32%	10.53%	0.00%
Other	6.67%	6.67%	26.67%	13.33%	33.33%	13.33%

Table 9.3 In your view how generous is your salary compared to what you might reasonably expect to obtain elsewhere for a similar position with a similar work load? Broken out for public and private higher education institutions

Is your institution a public or private college?	No Answer	My university is not very generous at all	I could probably do better elsewhere	I do about as well here as elsewhere	I am probably a little better off here than elsewhere	I am much better off here than elsewhere
Public	12.28%	8.77%	26.32%	28.07%	15.79%	8.77%
Private	10.34%	24.14%	17.24%	27.59%	17.24%	3.45%

Table 9.4 In your view how generous is your salary compared to what you might reasonably expect to obtain elsewhere for a similar position with a similar work load? Broken out by Specialization

Specialization	No Answer	My university is not very generous at all	I could probably do better elsewhere	I do about as well here as elsewhere	I am probably a little better off here than elsewhere	I am much better off here than elsewhere
Immunology	0.00%	33.33%	33.33%	16.67%	16.67%	0.00%
Neuroscience/Psychology	15.38%	15.38%	15.38%	23.08%	30.77%	0.00%
Cell/Molecular Biology	7.14%	17.86%	17.86%	39.29%	14.29%	3.57%
Healthcare Delivery	25.00%	12.50%	25.00%	25.00%	0.00%	12.50%
Chemistry	0.00%	0.00%	57.14%	42.86%	0.00%	0.00%
Other	16.67%	8.33%	20.83%	16.67%	20.83%	16.67%

Table 9.5 In your view how generous is your salary compared to what you might reasonably expect to obtain elsewhere for a similar position with a similar work load? Broken out by Number of years spent as a postdoc

Number of years spent as a postdoc	No Answer	My university is not very generous at all	I could probably do better elsewhere	I do about as well here as elsewhere	I am probably a little better off here than elsewhere	I am much better off here than elsewhere
Less than 1.01	20.00%	5.00%	15.00%	35.00%	15.00%	10.00%
1.01 - 2.1	20.00%	15.00%	25.00%	15.00%	15.00%	10.00%
2.1 - 4.8	4.55%	22.73%	13.64%	31.82%	22.73%	4.55%
More than 4.8	4.17%	12.50%	37.50%	29.17%	12.50%	4.17%

Table 9.6 In your view how generous is your salary compared to what you might reasonably expect to obtain elsewhere for a similar position with a similar work load? Broken out by Gender of survey respondent

Gender of survey respondent	No Answer	My university is not very generous at all	I could probably do better elsewhere	I do about as well here as elsewhere	I am probably a little better off here than elsewhere	I am much better off here than elsewhere
Male	9.38%	15.63%	25.00%	28.13%	9.38%	12.50%
Female	12.96%	12.96%	22.22%	27.78%	20.37%	3.70%

Table 9.7 In your view how generous is your salary compared to what you might reasonably expect to obtain elsewhere for a similar position with a similar work load? Broken out by Age of survey participant

Age of survey participant	No Answer	My university is not very generous at all	I could probably do better elsewhere	I do about as well here as elsewhere	I am probably a little better off here than elsewhere	I am much better off here than elsewhere
30 or under	17.24%	13.79%	20.69%	27.59%	10.34%	10.34%
31-35	8.11%	18.92%	27.03%	21.62%	21.62%	2.70%
36 and over	10.00%	5.00%	20.00%	40.00%	15.00%	10.00%

Table 10.1 How satisfied are you with the provisions for personal housing for you at your university?

	No Answer	Very dissatisfied	Dissatisfied	Somewhat Satisfied	Satisfied	Very Satisfied
Entire sample	20.93%	23.26%	19.77%	20.93%	13.95%	1.16%

Table 10.2 How satisfied are you with the provisions for personal housing for you at your university? Broken out by Country

Country	No Answer	Very dissatisfied	Dissatisfied	Somewhat Satisfied	Satisfied	Very Satisfied
USA	11.54%	30.77%	26.92%	17.31%	13.46%	0.00%
UK	36.84%	10.53%	5.26%	31.58%	10.53%	5.26%
Other	33.33%	13.33%	13.33%	20.00%	20.00%	0.00%

Table 10.3 How satisfied are you with the provisions for personal housing for you at your university? Broken out for public and private higher education institutions

Is your institution a public or private college?	No Answer	Very dissatisfied	Dissatisfied	Somewhat Satisfied	Satisfied	Very Satisfied
Public	26.32%	14.04%	21.05%	22.81%	14.04%	1.75%
Private	10.34%	41.38%	17.24%	17.24%	13.79%	0.00%

Table 10.4 How satisfied are you with the provisions for personal housing for you at your university? Broken out by Specialization

Specialization	No Answer	Very dissatisfied	Dissatisfied	Somewhat Satisfied	Satisfied	Very Satisfied
Immunology	16.67%	33.33%	16.67%	16.67%	16.67%	0.00%
Neuroscience/Psychology	30.77%	23.08%	7.69%	15.38%	15.38%	7.69%
Cell/Molecular Biology	7.14%	39.29%	21.43%	25.00%	7.14%	0.00%
Healthcare Delivery	37.50%	25.00%	0.00%	25.00%	12.50%	0.00%
Chemistry	14.29%	14.29%	28.57%	28.57%	14.29%	0.00%
Other	29.17%	4.17%	29.17%	16.67%	20.83%	0.00%

Table 10.5 How satisfied are you with the provisions for personal housing for you at your university? Broken out by Number of years spent as a postdoc

Number of years spent as a postdoc	No Answer	Very dissatisfied	Dissatisfied	Somewhat Satisfied	Satisfied	Very Satisfied
Less than 1.01	20.00%	10.00%	20.00%	20.00%	30.00%	0.00%
1.01 - 2.1	20.00%	25.00%	15.00%	30.00%	10.00%	0.00%
2.1 - 4.8	4.55%	36.36%	22.73%	18.18%	13.64%	4.55%
More than 4.8	37.50%	20.83%	20.83%	16.67%	4.17%	0.00%

Table 10.6 How satisfied are you with the provisions for personal housing for you at your university? Broken out by Gender of survey respondent

Gender of survey respondent	No Answer	Very dissatisfied	Dissatisfied	Somewhat Satisfied	Satisfied	Very Satisfied
Male	12.50%	37.50%	21.88%	9.38%	18.75%	0.00%
Female	25.93%	14.81%	18.52%	27.78%	11.11%	1.85%

Table 10.7 How satisfied are you with the provisions for personal housing for you at your university? Broken out by Age of survey participant

Age of survey participant	No Answer	Very dissatisfied	Dissatisfied	Somewhat Satisfied	Satisfied	Very Satisfied
30 or under	17.24%	10.34%	17.24%	34.48%	17.24%	3.45%
31-35	24.32%	35.14%	21.62%	5.41%	13.51%	0.00%
36 and over	20.00%	20.00%	20.00%	30.00%	10.00%	0.00%

Table 11.1 About what percentage of your current compensation is dependent upon funding external to your current institution?

	Mean	Median	Minimum	Maximum
Entire sample	70.53	100.00	0.00	100.00

Table 11.2 About what percentage of your current compensation is dependent upon funding external to your current institution? Broken out by Country

Country	Mean	Median	Minimum	Maximum
USA	60.97	90.00	0.00	100.00
UK	90.00	100.00	40.00	100.00
Other	80.58	100.00	0.00	100.00

Table 11.3 About what percentage of your current compensation is dependent upon funding external to your current institution? Broken out for public and private higher education institutions

Is your institution a public or private college?	Mean	Median	Minimum	Maximum
Public	70.28	100.00	0.00	100.00
Private	71.05	98.00	0.00	100.00

Table 11.4 About what percentage of your current compensation is dependent upon funding external to your current institution? Broken out by Specialization

Specialization	Mean	Median	Minimum	Maximum
Immunology	78.00	90.00	50.00	100.00
Neuroscience/Psychology	56.70	83.50	0.00	100.00
Cell/Molecular Biology	66.89	96.50	0.00	100.00
Healthcare Delivery	76.00	100.00	0.00	100.00
Chemistry	60.00	100.00	0.00	100.00
Other	83.33	100.00	0.00	100.00

Table 11.5 About what percentage of your current compensation is dependent upon funding external to your current institution? Broken out by Number of years spent as a postdoc

Number of years spent as a postdoc	Mean	Median	Minimum	Maximum
Less than 1.01	72.27	100.00	0.00	100.00
1.01 - 2.1	56.69	67.00	0.00	100.00
2.1 - 4.8	65.82	100.00	0.00	100.00
More than 4.8	84.71	100.00	0.00	100.00

Table 11.6 About what percentage of your current compensation is dependent upon funding external to your current institution? Broken out by Gender of survey respondent

Gender of survey respondent	Mean	Median	Minimum	Maximum
Male	59.77	82.50	0.00	100.00
Female	77.11	100.00	0.00	100.00

Table 11.7 About what percentage of your current compensation is dependent upon funding external to your current institution? Broken out by Age of survey participant

Age of survey participant	Mean	Median	Minimum	Maximum
30 or under	67.86	100.00	0.00	100.00
31-35	72.57	100.00	0.00	100.00
36 and over	71.21	100.00	0.00	100.00

Table 12.1 How satisfied are you with the quality of the information technology provided by your university or research institute?

	No Answer	Very dissatisfied	Dissatisfied	Somewhat Satisfied	Satisfied	Very Satisfied
Entire sample	11.63%	4.65%	11.63%	22.09%	43.02%	6.98%

Table 12.2 How satisfied are you with the quality of the information technology provided by your university or research institute? Broken out by Country

Country	No Answer	Very dissatisfied	Dissatisfied	Somewhat Satisfied	Satisfied	Very Satisfied
USA	11.54%	7.69%	11.54%	21.15%	38.46%	9.62%
UK	15.79%	0.00%	5.26%	26.32%	52.63%	0.00%
Other	6.67%	0.00%	20.00%	20.00%	46.67%	6.67%

Table 12.3 How satisfied are you with the quality of the information technology provided by your university or research institute? Broken out for public and private higher education institutions

Is your institution a public or private college?	No Answer	Very dissatisfied	Dissatisfied	Somewhat Satisfied	Satisfied	Very Satisfied
Public	12.28%	5.26%	12.28%	17.54%	47.37%	5.26%
Private	10.34%	3.45%	10.34%	31.03%	34.48%	10.34%

Table 12.4 How satisfied are you with the quality of the information technology provided by your university or research institute? Broken out by Specialization

Specialization	No Answer	Very dissatisfied	Dissatisfied	Somewhat Satisfied	Satisfied	Very Satisfied
Immunology	0.00%	0.00%	33.33%	33.33%	33.33%	0.00%
Neuroscience/Psychology	15.38%	15.38%	15.38%	7.69%	30.77%	15.38%
Cell/Molecular Biology	7.14%	7.14%	3.57%	25.00%	50.00%	7.14%
Healthcare Delivery	25.00%	0.00%	12.50%	25.00%	25.00%	12.50%
Chemistry	0.00%	0.00%	42.86%	14.29%	42.86%	0.00%
Other	16.67%	0.00%	4.17%	25.00%	50.00%	4.17%

Table 12.5 How satisfied are you with the quality of the information technology provided by your university or research institute? Broken out by Number of years spent as a postdoc

Number of years spent as a postdoc	No Answer	Very dissatisfied	Dissatisfied	Somewhat Satisfied	Satisfied	Very Satisfied
Less than 1.01	20.00%	0.00%	5.00%	10.00%	55.00%	10.00%
1.01 - 2.1	20.00%	15.00%	10.00%	20.00%	25.00%	10.00%
2.1 - 4.8	4.55%	0.00%	4.55%	36.36%	45.45%	9.09%
More than 4.8	4.17%	4.17%	25.00%	20.83%	45.83%	0.00%

Table 12.6 How satisfied are you with the quality of the information technology provided by your university or research institute? Broken out by Gender of survey respondent

Gender of survey respondent	No Answer	Very dissatisfied	Dissatisfied	Somewhat Satisfied	Satisfied	Very Satisfied
Male	9.38%	9.38%	9.38%	25.00%	37.50%	9.38%
Female	12.96%	1.85%	12.96%	20.37%	46.30%	5.56%

Table 12.7 How satisfied are you with the quality of the information technology provided by your university or research institute? Broken out by Age of survey participant

Age of survey participant	No Answer	Very dissatisfied	Dissatisfied	Somewhat Satisfied	Satisfied	Very Satisfied
30 or under	17.24%	3.45%	10.34%	20.69%	41.38%	6.90%
31-35	8.11%	5.41%	10.81%	24.32%	45.95%	5.41%
36 and over	10.00%	5.00%	15.00%	20.00%	40.00%	10.00%

Table 13.1 About how much do you estimate that it costs your university to send you to symposia, conferences, and other scientific meetings in your field in the past year. Include payment of conference fees, travel expenses, lodging and other expenses paid or reimbursed by your university. ($ US)

	Mean	Median	Minimum	Maximum
Entire sample	1762.12	1000.00	0.00	20000.00

Table 13.2 About how much do you estimate that it costs your university to send you to symposia, conferences, and other scientific meetings in your field in the past year. Include payment of conference fees, travel expenses, lodging and other expenses paid or reimbursed by your university. Broken out by Country

Country	Mean	Median	Minimum	Maximum
USA	2022.22	1000.00	0.00	20000.00
UK	936.69	252.00	0.00	5000.00
Other	1886.36	1500.00	0.00	5000.00

Table 13.3 About how much do you estimate that it costs your university to send you to symposia, conferences, and other scientific meetings in your field in the past year. Include payment of conference fees, travel expenses, lodging and other expenses paid or reimbursed by your university. Broken out for public and private higher education institutions

Is your institution a public or private college?	Mean	Median	Minimum	Maximum
Public	1536.59	1000.00	0.00	10000.00
Private	2180.95	1000.00	0.00	20000.00

Table 13.4 About how much do you estimate that it costs your university to send you to symposia, conferences, and other scientific meetings in your field in the past year. Include payment of conference fees, travel expenses, lodging and other expenses paid or reimbursed by your university. Broken out by Specialization

Specialization	Mean	Median	Minimum	Maximum
Immunology	1833.33	1500.00	0.00	5000.00
Neuroscience/Psychology	2500.00	1500.00	0.00	10000.00
Cell/Molecular Biology	1259.52	1000.00	0.00	3000.00
Healthcare Delivery	4560.00	1000.00	0.00	20000.00
Chemistry	575.00	0.00	0.00	1875.00
Other	1506.80	600.00	0.00	6000.00

Table 13.5 About how much do you estimate that it costs your university to send you to symposia, conferences, and other scientific meetings in your field in the past year. Include payment of conference fees, travel expenses, lodging and other expenses paid or reimbursed by your university. Broken out by Number of years spent as a postdoc

Number of years spent as a postdoc	Mean	Median	Minimum	Maximum
Less than 1.01	1330.56	1000.00	0.00	3000.00
1.01 - 2.1	3676.92	1800.00	0.00	20000.00
2.1 - 4.8	1039.47	1000.00	0.00	3000.00
More than 4.8	1379.05	1000.00	0.00	5000.00

Table 13.6 About how much do you estimate that it costs your university to send you to symposia, conferences, and other scientific meetings in your field in the past year. Include payment of conference fees, travel expenses, lodging and other expenses paid or reimbursed by your university. Broken out by Gender of survey respondent

Gender of survey respondent	Mean	Median	Minimum	Maximum
Male	2514.29	1000.00	0.00	20000.00
Female	1357.10	1000.00	0.00	6000.00

Table 13.7 About how much do you estimate that it costs your university to send you to symposia, conferences, and other scientific meetings in your field in the past year. Include payment of conference fees, travel expenses, lodging and other expenses paid or reimbursed by your university. Broken out by Age of survey participant

Age of survey participant	Mean	Median	Minimum	Maximum
30 or under	1025.00	0.00	0.00	6000.00
31-35	2170.00	1000.00	0.00	20000.00
36 and over	2000.13	1370.00	0.00	10000.00

Has your university ever extended to you any form or guaranteed income or "grace period" between grants when you receive either salary or stipend, or benefits (such as health insurance or office space) while you are in the process of applying for grants? If so how long have you received such support and what support did you receive?

Less than 1.01 Years Spent as a Postdoc

1) not yet
2) No
3) No.
4) NA
5) No
6) no
7) No
8) not sure
9) No

1.01 - 2.1

1) N/a, federal NIH T32 postdoc continued funding
2) NA
3) no
4) No, there is no 'grace period'.
5) 100 percent of my salary was guaranteed for 2 years. After those two years, my salary is completely dependent upon funding availability from either my own grants or those of my PI
6) No
7) No.
8) No
9) No
10) not applicable
11) Paid for 1 year off my advisor's startup grant
12) No

2.1 - 4.8

1) No
2) N/A
3) no
4) N/A
5) No
6) No
7) yes, for two months, this was between finishing my PhD and starting my post doc

8) no
9) No
10) N/A
11) No
12) not at all.
13) No
14) payment is stable
15) No
16) No
17) no
18) no
19) No
20) no

More than 4.8

1) no
2) no
3) WT VIP Bridging Scheme - personal fellowship application to money held within the University to bridge for 6 months between 2 grants on the basis I was going for an external personal fellowship application. Support included salary only for the duration of the extended period (3 months in the end).
4) N/A
5) N/A
6) Yes - Full salary on temporary contract for 1 month and a half in between one grant finishing and another starting
7) No
8) No
9) no
10) No
11) No
12) No
13) No
14) No
15) No
16) n/a
17) No
18) n/a
19) no
20) NA

Table 14.1 If you are not a citizen of the country in which you are working as a postdoc or equivalent, how satisfied are you with your visa/working permit situation in your host country?

	No Answer	It's quite problematic	It's occasionally problematic	It's OK and not something I think about
Entire sample	55.81%	8.14%	19.77%	16.28%

Table 14.2 If you are not a citizen of the country in which you are working as a postdoc or equivalent, how satisfied are you with your visa/working permit situation in your host country? Broken out by Country

Country	No Answer	It's quite problematic	It's occasionally problematic	It's OK and not something I think about
USA	46.15%	11.54%	26.92%	15.38%
UK	73.68%	0.00%	10.53%	15.79%
Other	66.67%	6.67%	6.67%	20.00%

Table 14.3 If you are not a citizen of the country in which you are working as a postdoc or equivalent, how satisfied are you with your visa/working permit situation in your host country? Broken out for public and private higher education institutions

Is your institution a public or private college?	No Answer	It's quite problematic	It's occasionally problematic	It's OK and not something I think about
Public	54.39%	7.02%	17.54%	21.05%
Private	58.62%	10.34%	24.14%	6.90%

Table 14.4 If you are not a citizen of the country in which you are working as a postdoc or equivalent, how satisfied are you with your visa/working permit situation in your host country? Broken out by Specialization

Specialization	No Answer	It's quite problematic	It's occasionally problematic	It's OK and not something I think about
Immunology	33.33%	16.67%	0.00%	50.00%
Neuroscience/Psychology	92.31%	7.69%	0.00%	0.00%
Cell/Molecular Biology	28.57%	14.29%	32.14%	25.00%
Healthcare Delivery	75.00%	12.50%	12.50%	0.00%
Chemistry	42.86%	0.00%	28.57%	28.57%
Other	70.83%	0.00%	20.83%	8.33%

Table 14.5 If you are not a citizen of the country in which you are working as a postdoc or equivalent, how satisfied are you with your visa/working permit situation in your host country? Broken out by Number of years spent as a postdoc

Number of years spent as a postdoc	No Answer	It's quite problematic	It's occasionally problematic	It's OK and not something I think about
Less than 1.01	55.00%	5.00%	15.00%	25.00%
1.01 - 2.1	65.00%	10.00%	20.00%	5.00%
2.1 - 4.8	40.91%	9.09%	36.36%	13.64%
More than 4.8	62.50%	8.33%	8.33%	20.83%

Table 14.6 If you are not a citizen of the country in which you are working as a postdoc or equivalent, how satisfied are you with your visa/working permit situation in your host country? Broken out by Gender of survey respondent

Gender of survey respondent	No Answer	It's quite problematic	It's occasionally problematic	It's OK and not something I think about
Male	28.13%	15.63%	31.25%	25.00%
Female	72.22%	3.70%	12.96%	11.11%

Table 14.7 If you are not a citizen of the country in which you are working as a postdoc or equivalent, how satisfied are you with your visa/working permit situation in your host country? Broken out by Age of survey participant

Age of survey participant	No Answer	It's quite problematic	It's occasionally problematic	It's OK and not something I think about
30 or under	72.41%	0.00%	17.24%	10.34%
31-35	43.24%	8.11%	24.32%	24.32%
36 and over	55.00%	20.00%	15.00%	10.00%

Table 15 In general, how good are working conditions for postdocs in each of the following areas or countries

Table 15.1.1 In general, how good are working conditions for postdocs in the USA?

	No Answer	Very Bad	Bad	Passable	Good	Very Good
Entire sample	30.23%	6.98%	11.63%	24.42%	19.77%	6.98%

Table 15.1.2 In general, how good are working conditions for postdocs in the USA? Broken out by Country

Country	No Answer	Very Bad	Bad	Passable	Good	Very Good
USA	15.38%	5.77%	5.77%	32.69%	32.69%	7.69%
UK	57.89%	0.00%	21.05%	15.79%	0.00%	5.26%
Other	46.67%	20.00%	20.00%	6.67%	0.00%	6.67%

Table 15.1.3 In general, how good are working conditions for postdocs in the USA? Broken out for public and private higher education institutions

Is your institution a public or private college?	No Answer	Very Bad	Bad	Passable	Good	Very Good
Public	33.33%	5.26%	14.04%	21.05%	19.30%	7.02%
Private	24.14%	10.34%	6.90%	31.03%	20.69%	6.90%

Table 15.1.4 In general, how good are working conditions for postdocs in the USA? Broken out by Specialization

Specialization	No Answer	Very Bad	Bad	Passable	Good	Very Good
Immunology	16.67%	16.67%	33.33%	16.67%	16.67%	0.00%
Neuroscience/Psychology	46.15%	0.00%	15.38%	23.08%	7.69%	7.69%
Cell/Molecular Biology	14.29%	7.14%	10.71%	28.57%	32.14%	7.14%
Healthcare Delivery	37.50%	12.50%	12.50%	12.50%	12.50%	12.50%
Chemistry	14.29%	28.57%	0.00%	42.86%	14.29%	0.00%
Other	45.83%	0.00%	8.33%	20.83%	16.67%	8.33%

Table 15.1.5 In general, how good are working conditions for postdocs in the USA? Broken out by Number of years spent as a postdoc

Number of years spent as a postdoc	No Answer	Very Bad	Bad	Passable	Good	Very Good
Less than 1.01	35.00%	0.00%	5.00%	25.00%	20.00%	15.00%
1.01 - 2.1	30.00%	5.00%	5.00%	30.00%	25.00%	5.00%
2.1 - 4.8	13.64%	0.00%	18.18%	31.82%	31.82%	4.55%
More than 4.8	41.67%	20.83%	16.67%	12.50%	4.17%	4.17%

Table 15.1.6 In general, how good are working conditions for postdocs in the USA? Broken out by Gender of survey respondent

Gender of survey respondent	No Answer	Very Bad	Bad	Passable	Good	Very Good
Male	25.00%	6.25%	9.38%	18.75%	28.13%	12.50%
Female	33.33%	7.41%	12.96%	27.78%	14.81%	3.70%

Table 15.1.7 In general, how good are working conditions for postdocs in the USA? Broken out by Age of survey participant

Age of survey participant	No Answer	Very Bad	Bad	Passable	Good	Very Good
30 or under	31.03%	3.45%	13.79%	27.59%	17.24%	6.90%
31-35	24.32%	5.41%	13.51%	24.32%	27.03%	5.41%
36 and over	40.00%	15.00%	5.00%	20.00%	10.00%	10.00%

Table 15.2.1 In general, how good are working conditions for postdocs in Canada?

	No Answer	Very Bad	Bad	Passable	Good	Very Good
Entire sample	61.63%	0.00%	5.81%	12.79%	11.63%	8.14%

Table 15.2.2 In general, how good are working conditions for postdocs in Canada? Broken out by Country

Country	No Answer	Very Bad	Bad	Passable	Good	Very Good
USA	65.38%	0.00%	1.92%	9.62%	13.46%	9.62%
UK	63.16%	0.00%	10.53%	15.79%	5.26%	5.26%
Other	46.67%	0.00%	13.33%	20.00%	13.33%	6.67%

Table 15.2.3 In general, how good are working conditions for postdocs in Canada? Broken out for public and private higher education institutions

Is your institution a public or private college?	No Answer	Very Bad	Bad	Passable	Good	Very Good
Public	59.65%	0.00%	8.77%	14.04%	8.77%	8.77%
Private	65.52%	0.00%	0.00%	10.34%	17.24%	6.90%

Table 15.2.4 In general, how good are working conditions for postdocs in Canada? Broken out by Specialization

Specialization	No Answer	Very Bad	Bad	Passable	Good	Very Good
Immunology	33.33%	0.00%	0.00%	33.33%	16.67%	16.67%
Neuroscience/Psychology	84.62%	0.00%	0.00%	7.69%	7.69%	0.00%
Cell/Molecular Biology	60.71%	0.00%	0.00%	3.57%	17.86%	17.86%
Healthcare Delivery	62.50%	0.00%	12.50%	12.50%	12.50%	0.00%
Chemistry	42.86%	0.00%	28.57%	14.29%	14.29%	0.00%
Other	62.50%	0.00%	8.33%	20.83%	4.17%	4.17%

Table 15.2.5 In general, how good are working conditions for postdocs in Canada? Broken out by Number of years spent as a postdoc

Number of years spent as a postdoc	No Answer	Very Bad	Bad	Passable	Good	Very Good
Less than 1.01	60.00%	0.00%	0.00%	15.00%	15.00%	10.00%
1.01 - 2.1	80.00%	0.00%	10.00%	5.00%	5.00%	0.00%
2.1 - 4.8	54.55%	0.00%	0.00%	13.64%	22.73%	9.09%
More than 4.8	54.17%	0.00%	12.50%	16.67%	4.17%	12.50%

Table 15.2.6 In general, how good are working conditions for postdocs in Canada? Broken out by Gender of survey respondent

Gender of survey respondent	No Answer	Very Bad	Bad	Passable	Good	Very Good
Male	62.50%	0.00%	3.13%	9.38%	12.50%	12.50%
Female	61.11%	0.00%	7.41%	14.81%	11.11%	5.56%

Table 15.2.7 In general, how good are working conditions for postdocs in Canada? Broken out by Age of survey participant

Age of survey participant	No Answer	Very Bad	Bad	Passable	Good	Very Good
30 or under	51.72%	0.00%	6.90%	13.79%	20.69%	6.90%
31-35	64.86%	0.00%	8.11%	13.51%	5.41%	8.11%
36 and over	70.00%	0.00%	0.00%	10.00%	10.00%	10.00%

Table 15.3.1 In general, how good are working conditions for postdocs in the UK?

	No Answer	Very Bad	Bad	Passable	Good	Very Good
Entire sample	52.33%	0.00%	1.16%	17.44%	23.26%	5.81%

Table 15.3.2 In general, how good are working conditions for postdocs in the UK? Broken out by Country

Country	No Answer	Very Bad	Bad	Passable	Good	Very Good
USA	61.54%	0.00%	0.00%	15.38%	17.31%	5.77%
UK	31.58%	0.00%	0.00%	26.32%	36.84%	5.26%
Other	46.67%	0.00%	6.67%	13.33%	26.67%	6.67%

Table 15.3.3 In general, how good are working conditions for postdocs in the UK? Broken out for public and private higher education institutions

Is your institution a public or private college?	No Answer	Very Bad	Bad	Passable	Good	Very Good
Public	49.12%	0.00%	1.75%	17.54%	28.07%	3.51%
Private	58.62%	0.00%	0.00%	17.24%	13.79%	10.34%

Table 15.3.4 In general, how good are working conditions for postdocs in the UK? Broken out by Specialization

Specialization	No Answer	Very Bad	Bad	Passable	Good	Very Good
Immunology	33.33%	0.00%	0.00%	16.67%	50.00%	0.00%
Neuroscience/Psychology	84.62%	0.00%	0.00%	7.69%	0.00%	7.69%
Cell/Molecular Biology	53.57%	0.00%	0.00%	10.71%	28.57%	7.14%
Healthcare Delivery	62.50%	0.00%	12.50%	12.50%	12.50%	0.00%
Chemistry	28.57%	0.00%	0.00%	28.57%	42.86%	0.00%
Other	41.67%	0.00%	0.00%	29.17%	20.83%	8.33%

Table 15.3.5 In general, how good are working conditions for postdocs in the UK? Broken out by Number of years spent as a postdoc

Number of years spent as a postdoc	No Answer	Very Bad	Bad	Passable	Good	Very Good
Less than 1.01	50.00%	0.00%	0.00%	15.00%	15.00%	20.00%
1.01 - 2.1	75.00%	0.00%	5.00%	10.00%	10.00%	0.00%
2.1 - 4.8	50.00%	0.00%	0.00%	18.18%	27.27%	4.55%
More than 4.8	37.50%	0.00%	0.00%	25.00%	37.50%	0.00%

Table 15.3.6 In general, how good are working conditions for postdocs in the UK? Broken out by Gender of survey respondent

Gender of survey respondent	No Answer	Very Bad	Bad	Passable	Good	Very Good
Male	56.25%	0.00%	0.00%	9.38%	25.00%	9.38%
Female	50.00%	0.00%	1.85%	22.22%	22.22%	3.70%

Table 15.3.7 In general, how good are working conditions for postdocs in the UK? Broken out by Age of survey participant

Age of survey participant	No Answer	Very Bad	Bad	Passable	Good	Very Good
30 or under	44.83%	0.00%	3.45%	13.79%	27.59%	10.34%
31-35	54.05%	0.00%	0.00%	24.32%	16.22%	5.41%
36 and over	60.00%	0.00%	0.00%	10.00%	30.00%	0.00%

Table 15.4.1 In general, how good are working conditions for postdocs in Ireland?

	No Answer	Very Bad	Bad	Passable	Good	Very Good
Entire sample	61.63%	0.00%	1.16%	19.77%	15.12%	2.33%

Table 15.4.2 In general, how good are working conditions for postdocs in Ireland? Broken out by Country

Country	No Answer	Very Bad	Bad	Passable	Good	Very Good
USA	63.46%	0.00%	0.00%	21.15%	13.46%	1.92%
UK	68.42%	0.00%	0.00%	15.79%	15.79%	0.00%
Other	46.67%	0.00%	6.67%	20.00%	20.00%	6.67%

Table 15.4.3 In general, how good are working conditions for postdocs in Ireland? Broken out for public and private higher education institutions

Is your institution a public or private college?	No Answer	Very Bad	Bad	Passable	Good	Very Good
Public	59.65%	0.00%	1.75%	17.54%	19.30%	1.75%
Private	65.52%	0.00%	0.00%	24.14%	6.90%	3.45%

Table 15.4.4 In general, how good are working conditions for postdocs in Ireland? Broken out by Specialization

Specialization	No Answer	Very Bad	Bad	Passable	Good	Very Good
Immunology	33.33%	0.00%	0.00%	50.00%	16.67%	0.00%
Neuroscience/Psychology	84.62%	0.00%	0.00%	7.69%	7.69%	0.00%
Cell/Molecular Biology	60.71%	0.00%	0.00%	10.71%	25.00%	3.57%
Healthcare Delivery	62.50%	0.00%	12.50%	25.00%	0.00%	0.00%
Chemistry	28.57%	0.00%	0.00%	42.86%	28.57%	0.00%
Other	66.67%	0.00%	0.00%	20.83%	8.33%	4.17%

Table 15.4.5 In general, how good are working conditions for postdocs in Ireland? Broken out by Number of years spent as a postdoc

Number of years spent as a postdoc	No Answer	Very Bad	Bad	Passable	Good	Very Good
Less than 1.01	60.00%	0.00%	0.00%	15.00%	20.00%	5.00%
1.01 - 2.1	80.00%	0.00%	5.00%	10.00%	5.00%	0.00%
2.1 - 4.8	50.00%	0.00%	0.00%	27.27%	18.18%	4.55%
More than 4.8	58.33%	0.00%	0.00%	25.00%	16.67%	0.00%

Table 15.4.6 In general, how good are working conditions for postdocs in Ireland? Broken out by Gender of survey respondent

Gender of survey respondent	No Answer	Very Bad	Bad	Passable	Good	Very Good
Male	62.50%	0.00%	0.00%	15.63%	15.63%	6.25%
Female	61.11%	0.00%	1.85%	22.22%	14.81%	0.00%

Table 15.4.7 In general, how good are working conditions for postdocs in Ireland? Broken out by Age of survey participant

Age of survey participant	No Answer	Very Bad	Bad	Passable	Good	Very Good
30 or under	51.72%	0.00%	3.45%	17.24%	24.14%	3.45%
31-35	64.86%	0.00%	0.00%	18.92%	13.51%	2.70%
36 and over	70.00%	0.00%	0.00%	25.00%	5.00%	0.00%

Table 15.5.1 In general, how good are working conditions for postdocs in Australia?

	No Answer	Very Bad	Bad	Passable	Good	Very Good
Entire sample	56.98%	0.00%	3.49%	16.28%	16.28%	6.98%

Table 15.5.2 In general, how good are working conditions for postdocs in Australia? Broken out by Country

Country	No Answer	Very Bad	Bad	Passable	Good	Very Good
USA	61.54%	0.00%	0.00%	15.38%	15.38%	7.69%
UK	68.42%	0.00%	5.26%	10.53%	10.53%	5.26%
Other	26.67%	0.00%	13.33%	26.67%	26.67%	6.67%

Table 15.5.3 In general, how good are working conditions for postdocs in Australia? Broken out for public and private higher education institutions

Is your institution a public or private college?	No Answer	Very Bad	Bad	Passable	Good	Very Good
Public	54.39%	0.00%	5.26%	15.79%	17.54%	7.02%
Private	62.07%	0.00%	0.00%	17.24%	13.79%	6.90%

Table 15.5.4 In general, how good are working conditions for postdocs in Australia? Broken out by Specialization

Specialization	No Answer	Very Bad	Bad	Passable	Good	Very Good
Immunology	16.67%	0.00%	0.00%	33.33%	33.33%	16.67%
Neuroscience/Psychology	84.62%	0.00%	0.00%	7.69%	7.69%	0.00%
Cell/Molecular Biology	57.14%	0.00%	0.00%	3.57%	25.00%	14.29%
Healthcare Delivery	62.50%	0.00%	12.50%	25.00%	0.00%	0.00%
Chemistry	28.57%	0.00%	0.00%	42.86%	28.57%	0.00%
Other	58.33%	0.00%	8.33%	20.83%	8.33%	4.17%

Table 15.5.5 In general, how good are working conditions for postdocs in Australia? Broken out by Number of years spent as a postdoc

Number of years spent as a postdoc	No Answer	Very Bad	Bad	Passable	Good	Very Good
Less than 1.01	55.00%	0.00%	0.00%	15.00%	20.00%	10.00%
1.01 - 2.1	80.00%	0.00%	5.00%	10.00%	5.00%	0.00%
2.1 - 4.8	50.00%	0.00%	0.00%	13.64%	31.82%	4.55%
More than 4.8	45.83%	0.00%	8.33%	25.00%	8.33%	12.50%

Table 15.5.6 In general, how good are working conditions for postdocs in Australia? Broken out by Gender of survey respondent

Gender of survey respondent	No Answer	Very Bad	Bad	Passable	Good	Very Good
Male	53.13%	0.00%	3.13%	15.63%	18.75%	9.38%
Female	59.26%	0.00%	3.70%	16.67%	14.81%	5.56%

Table 15.5.7 In general, how good are working conditions for postdocs in Australia? Broken out by Age of survey participant

Age of survey participant	No Answer	Very Bad	Bad	Passable	Good	Very Good
30 or under	51.72%	0.00%	3.45%	13.79%	27.59%	3.45%
31-35	59.46%	0.00%	2.70%	16.22%	13.51%	8.11%
36 and over	60.00%	0.00%	5.00%	20.00%	5.00%	10.00%

Table 15.6.1 In general, how good are working conditions for postdocs in New Zealand?

	No Answer	Very Bad	Bad	Passable	Good	Very Good
Entire sample	61.63%	0.00%	2.33%	13.95%	16.28%	5.81%

Table 15.6.2 In general, how good are working conditions for postdocs in New Zealand? Broken out by Country

Country	No Answer	Very Bad	Bad	Passable	Good	Very Good
USA	63.46%	0.00%	0.00%	15.38%	15.38%	5.77%
UK	68.42%	0.00%	5.26%	10.53%	10.53%	5.26%
Other	46.67%	0.00%	6.67%	13.33%	26.67%	6.67%

Table 15.6.3 In general, how good are working conditions for postdocs in New Zealand? Broken out for public and private higher education institutions

Is your institution a public or private college?	No Answer	Very Bad	Bad	Passable	Good	Very Good
Public	59.65%	0.00%	3.51%	12.28%	17.54%	7.02%
Private	65.52%	0.00%	0.00%	17.24%	13.79%	3.45%

Table 15.6.4 In general, how good are working conditions for postdocs in New Zealand? Broken out by Specialization

Specialization	No Answer	Very Bad	Bad	Passable	Good	Very Good
Immunology	33.33%	0.00%	0.00%	16.67%	33.33%	16.67%
Neuroscience/Psychology	84.62%	0.00%	0.00%	7.69%	7.69%	0.00%
Cell/Molecular Biology	60.71%	0.00%	0.00%	3.57%	25.00%	10.71%
Healthcare Delivery	62.50%	0.00%	12.50%	25.00%	0.00%	0.00%
Chemistry	28.57%	0.00%	0.00%	42.86%	28.57%	0.00%
Other	66.67%	0.00%	4.17%	16.67%	8.33%	4.17%

Table 15.6.5 In general, how good are working conditions for postdocs in New Zealand? Broken out by Number of years spent as a postdoc

Number of years spent as a postdoc	No Answer	Very Bad	Bad	Passable	Good	Very Good
Less than 1.01	60.00%	0.00%	0.00%	15.00%	20.00%	5.00%
1.01 - 2.1	80.00%	0.00%	5.00%	10.00%	5.00%	0.00%
2.1 - 4.8	50.00%	0.00%	0.00%	13.64%	31.82%	4.55%
More than 4.8	58.33%	0.00%	4.17%	16.67%	8.33%	12.50%

Table 15.6.6 In general, how good are working conditions for postdocs in New Zealand? Broken out by Gender of survey respondent

Gender of survey respondent	No Answer	Very Bad	Bad	Passable	Good	Very Good
Male	62.50%	0.00%	0.00%	9.38%	18.75%	9.38%
Female	61.11%	0.00%	3.70%	16.67%	14.81%	3.70%

Table 15.6.7 In general, how good are working conditions for postdocs in New Zealand? Broken out by Age of survey participant

Age of survey participant	No Answer	Very Bad	Bad	Passable	Good	Very Good
30 or under	51.72%	0.00%	3.45%	13.79%	27.59%	3.45%
31-35	64.86%	0.00%	2.70%	13.51%	13.51%	5.41%
36 and over	70.00%	0.00%	0.00%	15.00%	5.00%	10.00%

Table 16 In general, how good are the prospects for obtaining permanent positions after serving as a postdoc in each of the following areas or countries?

Table 16.1.1 In general, how good are the prospects for obtaining permanent positions after serving as a postdoc in USA?

	No Answer	Very Bad	Bad	Passable	Good	Very Good
Entire sample	30.23%	10.47%	24.42%	20.93%	10.47%	3.49%

Table 16.1.2 In general, how good are the prospects for obtaining permanent positions after serving as a postdoc in USA? Broken out by Country

Country	No Answer	Very Bad	Bad	Passable	Good	Very Good
USA	15.38%	13.46%	32.69%	21.15%	15.38%	1.92%
UK	52.63%	10.53%	5.26%	21.05%	5.26%	5.26%
Other	53.33%	0.00%	20.00%	20.00%	0.00%	6.67%

Table 16.1.3 In general, how good are the prospects for obtaining permanent positions after serving as a postdoc in USA? Broken out for public and private higher education institutions

Is your institution a public or private college?	No Answer	Very Bad	Bad	Passable	Good	Very Good
Public	31.58%	10.53%	19.30%	26.32%	8.77%	3.51%
Private	27.59%	10.34%	34.48%	10.34%	13.79%	3.45%

Table 16.1.4 In general, how good are the prospects for obtaining permanent positions after serving as a postdoc in USA? Broken out by Specialization

Specialization	No Answer	Very Bad	Bad	Passable	Good	Very Good
Immunology	16.67%	16.67%	50.00%	16.67%	0.00%	0.00%
Neuroscience/Psychology	46.15%	7.69%	23.08%	15.38%	7.69%	0.00%
Cell/Molecular Biology	17.86%	14.29%	32.14%	25.00%	10.71%	0.00%
Healthcare Delivery	37.50%	0.00%	12.50%	25.00%	12.50%	12.50%
Chemistry	0.00%	14.29%	14.29%	42.86%	14.29%	14.29%
Other	45.83%	8.33%	16.67%	12.50%	12.50%	4.17%

Table 16.1.5 In general, how good are the prospects for obtaining permanent positions after serving as a postdoc in USA? Broken out by Number of years spent as a postdoc

Number of years spent as a postdoc	No Answer	Very Bad	Bad	Passable	Good	Very Good
Less than 1.01	30.00%	5.00%	35.00%	10.00%	10.00%	10.00%
1.01 - 2.1	30.00%	5.00%	20.00%	25.00%	20.00%	0.00%
2.1 - 4.8	13.64%	13.64%	22.73%	31.82%	13.64%	4.55%
More than 4.8	45.83%	16.67%	20.83%	16.67%	0.00%	0.00%

Table 16.1.6 In general, how good are the prospects for obtaining permanent positions after serving as a postdoc in USA? Broken out by Gender of survey respondent

Gender of survey respondent	No Answer	Very Bad	Bad	Passable	Good	Very Good
Male	28.13%	6.25%	25.00%	25.00%	9.38%	6.25%
Female	31.48%	12.96%	24.07%	18.52%	11.11%	1.85%

Table 16.1.7 In general, how good are the prospects for obtaining permanent positions after serving as a postdoc in USA? Broken out by Age of survey participant

Age of survey participant	No Answer	Very Bad	Bad	Passable	Good	Very Good
30 or under	27.59%	10.34%	20.69%	17.24%	17.24%	6.90%
31-35	24.32%	8.11%	32.43%	27.03%	8.11%	0.00%
36 and over	45.00%	15.00%	15.00%	15.00%	5.00%	5.00%

Table 16.2.1 In general, how good are the prospects for obtaining permanent positions after serving as a postdoc in Canada?

	No Answer	Very Bad	Bad	Passable	Good	Very Good
Entire sample	60.47%	3.49%	12.79%	11.63%	8.14%	3.49%

Table 16.2.2 In general, how good are the prospects for obtaining permanent positions after serving as a postdoc in Canada? Broken out by Country

Country	No Answer	Very Bad	Bad	Passable	Good	Very Good
USA	61.54%	1.92%	13.46%	11.54%	9.62%	1.92%
UK	63.16%	10.53%	10.53%	0.00%	10.53%	5.26%
Other	53.33%	0.00%	13.33%	26.67%	0.00%	6.67%

Table 16.2.3 In general, how good are the prospects for obtaining permanent positions after serving as a postdoc in Canada? Broken out for public and private higher education institutions

Is your institution a public or private college?	No Answer	Very Bad	Bad	Passable	Good	Very Good
Public	57.89%	5.26%	12.28%	14.04%	7.02%	3.51%
Private	65.52%	0.00%	13.79%	6.90%	10.34%	3.45%

Table 16.2.4 In general, how good are the prospects for obtaining permanent positions after serving as a postdoc in Canada? Broken out by Specialization

Specialization	No Answer	Very Bad	Bad	Passable	Good	Very Good
Immunology	33.33%	0.00%	16.67%	50.00%	0.00%	0.00%
Neuroscience/Psychology	84.62%	0.00%	7.69%	7.69%	0.00%	0.00%
Cell/Molecular Biology	60.71%	3.57%	7.14%	7.14%	17.86%	3.57%
Healthcare Delivery	62.50%	0.00%	12.50%	0.00%	12.50%	12.50%
Chemistry	28.57%	0.00%	14.29%	42.86%	14.29%	0.00%
Other	62.50%	8.33%	20.83%	4.17%	0.00%	4.17%

Table 16.2.5 In general, how good are the prospects for obtaining permanent positions after serving as a postdoc in Canada? Broken out by Number of years spent as a postdoc

Number of years spent as a postdoc	No Answer	Very Bad	Bad	Passable	Good	Very Good
Less than 1.01	55.00%	5.00%	20.00%	10.00%	5.00%	5.00%
1.01 - 2.1	80.00%	0.00%	10.00%	10.00%	0.00%	0.00%
2.1 - 4.8	50.00%	4.55%	4.55%	13.64%	22.73%	4.55%
More than 4.8	58.33%	4.17%	16.67%	12.50%	4.17%	4.17%

Table 16.2.6 In general, how good are the prospects for obtaining permanent positions after serving as a postdoc in Canada? Broken out by Gender of survey respondent

Gender of survey respondent	No Answer	Very Bad	Bad	Passable	Good	Very Good
Male	65.63%	3.13%	3.13%	12.50%	9.38%	6.25%
Female	57.41%	3.70%	18.52%	11.11%	7.41%	1.85%

Table 16.2.7 In general, how good are the prospects for obtaining permanent positions after serving as a postdoc in Canada? Broken out by Age of survey participant

Age of survey participant	No Answer	Very Bad	Bad	Passable	Good	Very Good
30 or under	51.72%	6.90%	10.34%	17.24%	10.34%	3.45%
31-35	59.46%	2.70%	13.51%	13.51%	8.11%	2.70%
36 and over	75.00%	0.00%	15.00%	0.00%	5.00%	5.00%

Table 16.3.1 In general, how good are the prospects for obtaining permanent positions after serving as a postdoc in the UK or Ireland?

	No Answer	Very Bad	Bad	Passable	Good	Very Good
Entire sample	50.00%	3.49%	24.42%	16.28%	3.49%	2.33%

Table 16.3.2 In general, how good are the prospects for obtaining permanent positions after serving as a postdoc in the UK or Ireland? Broken out by Country

Country	No Answer	Very Bad	Bad	Passable	Good	Very Good
USA	61.54%	1.92%	17.31%	15.38%	3.85%	0.00%
UK	21.05%	10.53%	47.37%	10.53%	5.26%	5.26%
Other	46.67%	0.00%	20.00%	26.67%	0.00%	6.67%

Table 16.3.3 In general, how good are the prospects for obtaining permanent positions after serving as a postdoc in the UK or Ireland? Broken out for public and private higher education institutions

Is your institution a public or private college?	No Answer	Very Bad	Bad	Passable	Good	Very Good
Public	45.61%	5.26%	26.32%	17.54%	1.75%	3.51%
Private	58.62%	0.00%	20.69%	13.79%	6.90%	0.00%

Table 16.3.4 In general, how good are the prospects for obtaining permanent positions after serving as a postdoc in the UK or Ireland? Broken out by Specialization

Specialization	No Answer	Very Bad	Bad	Passable	Good	Very Good
Immunology	33.33%	0.00%	33.33%	33.33%	0.00%	0.00%
Neuroscience/Psychology	76.92%	0.00%	15.38%	7.69%	0.00%	0.00%
Cell/Molecular Biology	53.57%	3.57%	21.43%	17.86%	3.57%	0.00%
Healthcare Delivery	62.50%	0.00%	25.00%	0.00%	12.50%	0.00%
Chemistry	14.29%	0.00%	28.57%	42.86%	0.00%	14.29%
Other	41.67%	8.33%	29.17%	12.50%	4.17%	4.17%

Table 16.3.5 In general, how good are the prospects for obtaining permanent positions after serving as a postdoc in the UK or Ireland? Broken out by Number of years spent as a postdoc

Number of years spent as a postdoc	No Answer	Very Bad	Bad	Passable	Good	Very Good
Less than 1.01	45.00%	5.00%	20.00%	10.00%	10.00%	10.00%
1.01 - 2.1	75.00%	0.00%	20.00%	5.00%	0.00%	0.00%
2.1 - 4.8	45.45%	4.55%	22.73%	22.73%	4.55%	0.00%
More than 4.8	37.50%	4.17%	33.33%	25.00%	0.00%	0.00%

Table 16.3.6 In general, how good are the prospects for obtaining permanent positions after serving as a postdoc in the UK or Ireland? Broken out by Gender of survey respondent

Gender of survey respondent	No Answer	Very Bad	Bad	Passable	Good	Very Good
Male	56.25%	3.13%	15.63%	15.63%	6.25%	3.13%
Female	46.30%	3.70%	29.63%	16.67%	1.85%	1.85%

Table 16.3.7 In general, how good are the prospects for obtaining permanent positions after serving as a postdoc in the UK or Ireland? Broken out by Age of survey participant

Age of survey participant	No Answer	Very Bad	Bad	Passable	Good	Very Good
30 or under	37.93%	6.90%	27.59%	17.24%	3.45%	6.90%
31-35	54.05%	2.70%	24.32%	16.22%	2.70%	0.00%
36 and over	60.00%	0.00%	20.00%	15.00%	5.00%	0.00%

Table 16.4.1 In general, how good are the prospects for obtaining permanent positions after serving as a postdoc in Australia/New Zealand?

	No Answer	Very Bad	Bad	Passable	Good	Very Good
Entire sample	56.98%	8.14%	12.79%	13.95%	5.81%	2.33%

Table 16.4.2 In general, how good are the prospects for obtaining permanent positions after serving as a postdoc in Australia/New Zealand? Broken out by Country

Country	No Answer	Very Bad	Bad	Passable	Good	Very Good
USA	61.54%	1.92%	11.54%	17.31%	5.77%	1.92%
UK	68.42%	10.53%	5.26%	5.26%	10.53%	0.00%
Other	26.67%	26.67%	26.67%	13.33%	0.00%	6.67%

Table 16.4.3 In general, how good are the prospects for obtaining permanent positions after serving as a postdoc in Australia/New Zealand? Broken out for public and private higher education institutions

Is your institution a public or private college?	No Answer	Very Bad	Bad	Passable	Good	Very Good
Public	54.39%	10.53%	12.28%	14.04%	5.26%	3.51%
Private	62.07%	3.45%	13.79%	13.79%	6.90%	0.00%

Table 16.4.4 In general, how good are the prospects for obtaining permanent positions after serving as a postdoc in Australia/New Zealand? Broken out by Specialization

Specialization	No Answer	Very Bad	Bad	Passable	Good	Very Good
Immunology	16.67%	0.00%	33.33%	33.33%	0.00%	16.67%
Neuroscience/Psychology	84.62%	0.00%	7.69%	7.69%	0.00%	0.00%
Cell/Molecular Biology	57.14%	7.14%	7.14%	14.29%	14.29%	0.00%
Healthcare Delivery	62.50%	0.00%	12.50%	25.00%	0.00%	0.00%
Chemistry	28.57%	14.29%	14.29%	28.57%	14.29%	0.00%
Other	58.33%	16.67%	16.67%	4.17%	0.00%	4.17%

Table 16.4.5 In general, how good are the prospects for obtaining permanent positions after serving as a postdoc in Australia/New Zealand? Broken out by Number of years spent as a postdoc

Number of years spent as a postdoc	No Answer	Very Bad	Bad	Passable	Good	Very Good
Less than 1.01	55.00%	5.00%	15.00%	15.00%	5.00%	5.00%
1.01 - 2.1	80.00%	0.00%	10.00%	10.00%	0.00%	0.00%
2.1 - 4.8	50.00%	4.55%	9.09%	22.73%	13.64%	0.00%
More than 4.8	45.83%	20.83%	16.67%	8.33%	4.17%	4.17%

Table 16.4.6 In general, how good are the prospects for obtaining permanent positions after serving as a postdoc in Australia/New Zealand? Broken out by Gender of survey respondent

Gender of survey respondent	No Answer	Very Bad	Bad	Passable	Good	Very Good
Male	53.13%	12.50%	12.50%	15.63%	3.13%	3.13%
Female	59.26%	5.56%	12.96%	12.96%	7.41%	1.85%

Table 16.4.7 In general, how good are the prospects for obtaining permanent positions after serving as a postdoc in Australia/New Zealand? Broken out by Age of survey participant

Age of survey participant	No Answer	Very Bad	Bad	Passable	Good	Very Good
30 or under	51.72%	6.90%	10.34%	20.69%	6.90%	3.45%
31-35	59.46%	5.41%	16.22%	10.81%	8.11%	0.00%
36 and over	60.00%	15.00%	10.00%	10.00%	0.00%	5.00%

How did you make the contact to get your current position? Through an ad? Career Fair. Scientific websites? At meetings? Through faculty mentors?

Less than 1.01 Years as a Postdoc

1) Science jobs.com
2) A conference
3) Scientific websites.
4) Faculty mentors
5) Through faculty mentors
6) Ad online
7) Through an ad and then recommendation through a faculty member
8) Mentors
9) Faculty Mentors and personal emails
10) Through faculty mentor
11) Through an advert
12) Faculty mentor
13) Ad on websites.

1.01 - 2.1

1) Online search
2) colleague
3) faculty member
4) Through publicly listed job advertisements.
5) Faculty Mentor
6) Through a faculty mentor at my PhD institution.
7) Directly contacted through email.
8) Direct contact
9) Meetings and faculty mentors, I did research with my mentors and applied for postdoc with them
10) manual search
11) Faculty mentors
12) Emailed advisor directly
13) E-mail blast during my final year of my PhD

2.1 - 4.8

1) Through an ad and attendance at a national meeting.
2) Through an advert
3) I contacted directly the PI.
4) Through an ad
5) Through faculty mentors
6) I send e-mails directly
7) An ad and personal contacts.
8) Through my PhD supervisor

9) through faculty mentors
10) Faculty mentor
11) Through a job advert on a jobs.ac.uk. I attended an interview and a different job was subsequently made for my specific skill set.
12) On advice from faculty to member, I reached out to my current supervisor by e-mail.
13) through faculty mentor
14) Faculty mentor
15) networking
16) Through a friend
17) ad
18) through faculty I knew
19) Scientific websites
20) Ad

More than 4.8

1) Ad
2) nil
3) Faculty Mentors - ambition of my own to pursue the fellowship route.
4) Talking to a fellow post doc who mentioned her PI was looking for someone with my skillset
5) Internally
6) Ad / Committee contact
7) Current grant I was a 'named' researcher in the grant
8) Redeployment program of the University and my former PI who prompted me for the job when we could not get any funding for her to keep me in her group.
9) At Conference
10) Through faculty mentors
11) Faculty
12) Personal communication
13) Through an ad
14) Word of mouth
15) Meeting
16) Direct contact based on institute's web page.
17) I was asked to return to an old position
18) Advertising
19) Conference
20) Through my PhD supervisor
21) Faculty mentor
22) At a conference

Which websites, if any, have you found useful in alerting you to postdoc and other scientific job prospects?

Less than 1.01

1) Indeed
2) Nature jobs, university web pages
3) Naturejobs
4) NA
5) jobvector.com jobs.ac.uk
6) The Node (for developmental Cell/Molecular Biology)
7) sciencecarreers.com
8) job.ac.uk
9) none
10) Tair jobs, ASPB career, HigherEd jobs

1.01 - 2.1

1) science careers , indeed
2) Research gate,
3) no
4) ANU jobs website.
5) ResearchGate, LinkedIn, AcademicKeys
6) Linkedin, Nature Careers, Science Magazine, Indeed.com
7) APS website for postdocs, higheredjobs.com
8) naturejobs
9) None
10) The Chronicle of Higher Education

2.1 - 4.8

1) Neuronline, highered
2) LinkedIn, irishjobs.ie
3) Academic keys, researchgate
4) Nature jobs, science jobs, Indeed
5) evoldir, sicb jobs
6) jobs.ac.uk times higher education
7) jobs.ac.uk
8) jobs.ac.uk and university jobs websites
9) Linkedin
10) n/a. networking
11) NA
12) N/A
13) nature jobs
14) nature jobs

15) Nature

More than 4.8

1) university
2) nil
3) Researchgate LinkedIn
4) bham.ac.uk, jobs.ac.uk
5) N/A
6) LinkedIn, Researchgate, Nature Jobs, academia.edu, jobs.ac.uk
7) Seek, Nature Jobs
8) AAAS, Nature, APS etc.
9) none
10) jobs.ac.uk
11) GenomeWeb
12) Researchgate
13) None
14) Research gate. Linked in.
15) n/a
16) CCP4 bulletin board Nature Jobs
17) jobs.ac.uk
18) findapostdoc.com

Table 17.1 Which phrase captures what you believe is most likely to happen to you career-wise in three years?

	No Answer	Other	I will likely have a tenure track job with a higher education institution.	I will likely remain a postdoc or its near equivalent in the institution that I currently work for.	I will likely remain a postdoc or its near equivalent for a new institution	I will likely have or be looking for a job outside of academia	I have or will get a position similar to postdocs sometimes referred to as superdocs with better pay and stability
Entire sample	15.12%	8.14%	24.42%	11.63%	8.14%	27.91%	4.65%

Table 17.2 Which phrase captures what you believe is most likely to happen to you career-wise in three years? Broken out by Country

Country	No Answer	Other	I will likely have a tenure track job with a higher education institution.	I will likely remain a postdoc or its near equivalent in the institution that I currently work for.	I will likely remain a postdoc or its near equivalent for a new institution	I will likely have or be looking for a job outside of academia	I have or will get a position similar to postdocs sometimes referred to as superdocs with better pay and stability
USA	13.46%	7.69%	28.85%	11.54%	7.69%	25.00%	5.77%
UK	15.79%	10.53%	21.05%	21.05%	5.26%	21.05%	5.26%
Other	20.00%	6.67%	13.33%	0.00%	13.33%	46.67%	0.00%

Table 17.3 Which phrase captures what you believe is most likely to happen to you career-wise in three years? Broken out for public and private higher education institutions

Is your institution a public or private college?	No Answer	Other	I will likely have a tenure track job with a higher education institution.	I will likely remain a postdoc or its near equivalent in the institution that I currently work for.	I will likely remain a postdoc or its near equivalent for a new institution	I will likely have or be looking for a job outside of academia	I have or will get a position similar to postdocs sometimes referred to as superdocs with better pay and stability
Public	14.04%	10.53%	21.05%	10.53%	10.53%	28.07%	5.26%
Private	17.24%	3.45%	31.03%	13.79%	3.45%	27.59%	3.45%

Table 17.4 Which phrase captures what you believe is most likely to happen to you career-wise in three years? Broken out by Specialization

Specialization	No Answer	Other	I will likely have a tenure track job with a higher education institution.	I will likely remain a postdoc or its near equivalent in the institution that I currently work for.	I will likely remain a postdoc or its near equivalent for a new institution	I will likely have or be looking for a job outside of academia	I have or will get a position similar to postdocs sometimes referred to as superdocs with better pay and stability
Immunology	0.00%	0.00%	16.67%	0.00%	16.67%	66.67%	0.00%
Neuroscience/ Psychology	30.77%	0.00%	23.08%	23.08 %	0.00%	23.08%	0.00%
Cell/Molecular Biology	7.14%	17.86%	21.43%	14.29 %	7.14%	25.00%	7.14%
Healthcare Delivery	25.00%	12.50%	50.00%	0.00%	12.50%	0.00%	0.00%
Chemistry	0.00%	0.00%	28.57%	0.00%	14.29%	57.14%	0.00%
Other	20.83%	4.17%	20.83%	12.50 %	8.33%	25.00%	8.33%

Table 17.5 Which phrase captures what you believe is most likely to happen to you career-wise in three years? Broken out by Number of years spent as a postdoc

Number of years spent as a postdoc	No Answer	Other	I will likely have a tenure track job with a higher education institution.	I will likely remain a postdoc or its near equivalent in the institution that I currently work for.	I will likely remain a postdoc or its near equivalent for a new institution	I will likely have or be looking for a job outside of academia	I have or will get a position similar to postdocs sometimes referred to as superdocs with better pay and stability
Less than 1.01	25.00%	5.00%	20.00%	15.00%	10.00%	25.00%	0.00%
1.01 - 2.1	25.00%	5.00%	35.00%	10.00%	5.00%	20.00%	0.00%
2.1 - 4.8	9.09%	4.55%	36.36%	9.09%	9.09%	22.73%	9.09%
More than 4.8	4.17%	16.67%	8.33%	12.50%	8.33%	41.67%	8.33%

Table 17.6 Which phrase captures what you believe is most likely to happen to you career-wise in three years? Broken out by Gender of survey respondent

Gender of survey respondent	No Answer	Other	I will likely have a tenure track job with a higher education institution.	I will likely remain a postdoc or its near equivalent in the institution that I currently work for.	I will likely remain a postdoc or its near equivalent for a new institution	I will likely have or be looking for a job outside of academia	I have or will get a position similar to postdocs sometimes referred to as superdocs with better pay and stability
Male	9.38%	6.25%	34.38%	9.38%	12.50%	25.00%	3.13%
Female	18.52%	9.26%	18.52%	12.96%	5.56%	29.63%	5.56%

Table 17.7 Which phrase captures what you believe is most likely to happen to you career-wise in three years? Broken out by Age of survey participant

Age of survey participant	No Answer	Other	I will likely have a tenure track job with a higher education institution.	I will likely remain a postdoc or its near equivalent in the institution that I currently work for.	I will likely remain a postdoc or its near equivalent for a new institution	I will likely have or be looking for a job outside of academia	I have or will get a position similar to postdocs sometimes referred to as superdocs with better pay and stability
30 or under	20.69%	3.45%	24.14%	10.34%	10.34%	31.03%	0.00%
31-35	10.81%	8.11%	27.03%	13.51%	5.41%	32.43%	2.70%
36 and over	15.00%	15.00%	20.00%	10.00%	10.00%	15.00%	15.00%

Which phrase captures what you believe is most likely to happen to you career-wise in three years? Other answers.

Less than 1.01 Years as a Postdoc (no responses in the "Other" Category)

1.01 - 2.1

1) Applying for 5 year senior fellowship, which will subsequently be under written for as a tenure track position at the level of UK senior lecturer/reader
2) I will likely apply for teaching faculty positions
3) Not sure what i want yet
4) not sure

2.1 - 4.8

1) At the moment, I am not sure, it can be any of the previous options. It depends on soon to be submitted publications and Brexit.
2) Don't know yet, will try for tenure track for sure

More than 4.8

1) Probably retire

Table 18.1 Have you ever been sexually harassed by a principal investigator or other authority figure with potential power over you in any of your postdoc positions?

	No Answer	Yes	No
Entire sample	15.12%	3.49%	81.40%

Table 18.2 Have you ever been sexually harassed by a principal investigator or other authority figure with potential power over you in any of your postdoc positions? Broken out by Country

Country	No Answer	Yes	No
USA	13.46%	3.85%	82.69%
UK	15.79%	5.26%	78.95%
Other	20.00%	0.00%	80.00%

Table 18.3 Have you ever been sexually harassed by a principal investigator or other authority figure with potential power over you in any of your postdoc positions? Broken out for public and private higher education institutions

Is your institution a public or private college?	No Answer	Yes	No
Public	14.04%	3.51%	82.46%
Private	17.24%	3.45%	79.31%

Table 18.4 Have you ever been sexually harassed by a principal investigator or other authority figure with potential power over you in any of your postdoc positions? Broken out by Specialization

Specialization	No Answer	Yes	No
Immunology	0.00%	0.00%	100.00%
Neuroscience/Psychology	30.77%	0.00%	69.23%
Cell/Molecular Biology	7.14%	0.00%	92.86%
Healthcare Delivery	25.00%	12.50%	62.50%
Chemistry	0.00%	14.29%	85.71%
Other	20.83%	4.17%	75.00%

Table 18.5 Have you ever been sexually harassed by a principal investigator or other authority figure with potential power over you in any of your postdoc positions? Broken out by Number of years spent as a postdoc

Number of years spent as a postdoc	No Answer	Yes	No
Less than 1.01	25.00%	0.00%	75.00%
1.01 - 2.1	25.00%	5.00%	70.00%
2.1 - 4.8	9.09%	4.55%	86.36%
More than 4.8	4.17%	4.17%	91.67%

Table 18.6 Have you ever been sexually harassed by a principal investigator or other authority figure with potential power over you in any of your postdoc positions? Broken out by Gender of survey respondent

Gender of survey respondent	No Answer	Yes	No
Male	9.38%	0.00%	90.63%
Female	18.52%	5.56%	75.93%

Table 18.7 Have you ever been sexually harassed by a principal investigator or other authority figure with potential power over you in any of your postdoc positions? Broken out by Age of survey participant

Age of survey participant	No Answer	Yes	No
30 or under	20.69%	6.90%	72.41%
31-35	10.81%	0.00%	89.19%
36 and over	15.00%	5.00%	80.00%

Table 19.1 Rate the fairness and transparently of procedures and processes in place to help you combat abusive behavior by faculty with power over you.

	No Answer	There are no such procedures and we are all very vulnerable	Procedures are weak and many postdocs put up with more than they should	Procedures seem adequate to discourage most abuse	A strong system and culture is in place to prevent abuse of postdocs by those with more power
Entire sample	17.44%	8.14%	20.93%	31.40%	22.09%

Table 19.2 Rate the fairness and transparently of procedures and processes in place to help you combat abusive behavior by faculty with power over you. Broken out by Country

Country	No Answer	There are no such procedures and we are all very vulnerable	Procedures are weak and many postdocs put up with more than they should	Procedures seem adequate to discourage most abuse	A strong system and culture is in place to prevent abuse of postdocs by those with more power
USA	17.31%	7.69%	25.00%	26.92%	23.08%
UK	15.79%	10.53%	15.79%	36.84%	21.05%
Other	20.00%	6.67%	13.33%	40.00%	20.00%

Table 19.3 Rate the fairness and transparently of procedures and processes in place to help you combat abusive behavior by faculty with power over you. Broken out for public and private higher education institutions

Is your institution a public or private college?	No Answer	There are no such procedures and we are all very vulnerable	Procedures are weak and many postdocs put up with more than they should	Procedures seem adequate to discourage most abuse	A strong system and culture is in place to prevent abuse of postdocs by those with more power
Public	15.79%	7.02%	21.05%	36.84%	19.30%
Private	20.69%	10.34%	20.69%	20.69%	27.59%

Table 19.4 Rate the fairness and transparently of procedures and processes in place to help you combat abusive behavior by faculty with power over you. Broken out by Specialization

Specialization	No Answer	There are no such procedures and we are all very vulnerable	Procedures are weak and many postdocs put up with more than they should	Procedures seem adequate to discourage most abuse	A strong system and culture is in place to prevent abuse of postdocs by those with more power
Immunology	16.67%	16.67%	16.67%	33.33%	16.67%
Neuroscience/Psychology	30.77%	7.69%	30.77%	30.77%	0.00%
Cell/Molecular Biology	10.71%	0.00%	28.57%	28.57%	32.14%
Healthcare Delivery	25.00%	12.50%	12.50%	37.50%	12.50%
Chemistry	0.00%	28.57%	14.29%	28.57%	28.57%
Other	20.83%	8.33%	12.50%	33.33%	25.00%

Table 19.5 Rate the fairness and transparently of procedures and processes in place to help you combat abusive behavior by faculty with power over you. Broken out by Number of years spent as a postdoc

Number of years spent as a postdoc	No Answer	There are no such procedures and we are all very vulnerable	Procedures are weak and many postdocs put up with more than they should	Procedures seem adequate to discourage most abuse	A strong system and culture is in place to prevent abuse of postdocs by those with more power
Less than 1.01	35.00%	0.00%	10.00%	20.00%	35.00%
1.01 - 2.1	25.00%	10.00%	15.00%	35.00%	15.00%
2.1 - 4.8	9.09%	4.55%	31.82%	31.82%	22.73%
More than 4.8	4.17%	16.67%	25.00%	37.50%	16.67%

Table 19.6 Rate the fairness and transparently of procedures and processes in place to help you combat abusive behavior by faculty with power over you. Broken out by Gender of survey respondent

Gender of survey respondent	No Answer	There are no such procedures and we are all very vulnerable	Procedures are weak and many postdocs put up with more than they should	Procedures seem adequate to discourage most abuse	A strong system and culture is in place to prevent abuse of postdocs by those with more power
Male	12.50%	9.38%	12.50%	31.25%	34.38%
Female	20.37%	7.41%	25.93%	31.48%	14.81%

Table 19.7 Rate the fairness and transparently of procedures and processes in place to help you combat abusive behavior by faculty with power over you. Broken out by Age of survey participant

Age of survey participant	No Answer	There are no such procedures and we are all very vulnerable	Procedures are weak and many postdocs put up with more than they should	Procedures seem adequate to discourage most abuse	A strong system and culture is in place to prevent abuse of postdocs by those with more power
30 or under	20.69%	6.90%	17.24%	34.48%	20.69%
31-35	16.22%	8.11%	24.32%	27.03%	24.32%
36 and over	15.00%	10.00%	20.00%	35.00%	20.00%

Table 20.1 Have you done any of the following in your current position?

	No Answer	Taught classes as part of my employment contract	Taught classes as an adjunct for extra compensation	Tutored students for extra compensation
Entire sample	72.09%	16.28%	9.30%	2.33%

Table 20.2 Have you done any of the following in your current position? Broken out by Country

Country	No Answer	Taught classes as part of my employment contract	Taught classes as an adjunct for extra compensation	Tutored students for extra compensation
USA	84.62%	0.00%	11.54%	3.85%
UK	57.89%	36.84%	5.26%	0.00%
Other	46.67%	46.67%	6.67%	0.00%

Table 20.3 Have you done any of the following in your current position? Broken out for public and private higher education institutions

Is your institution a public or private college?	No Answer	Taught classes as part of my employment contract	Taught classes as an adjunct for extra compensation	Tutored students for extra compensation
Public	70.18%	22.81%	5.26%	1.75%
Private	75.86%	3.45%	17.24%	3.45%

Table 20.4 Have you done any of the following in your current position? Broken out by Specialization

Specialization	No Answer	Taught classes as part of my employment contract	Taught classes as an adjunct for extra compensation	Tutored students for extra compensation
Immunology	50.00%	33.33%	16.67%	0.00%
Neuroscience/Psychology	69.23%	23.08%	7.69%	0.00%
Cell/Molecular Biology	82.14%	7.14%	7.14%	3.57%
Healthcare Delivery	75.00%	0.00%	25.00%	0.00%
Chemistry	85.71%	14.29%	0.00%	0.00%
Other	62.50%	25.00%	8.33%	4.17%

Table 20.5 Have you done any of the following in your current position? Broken out by Number of years spent as a postdoc

Number of years spent as a postdoc	No Answer	Taught classes as part of my employment contract	Taught classes as an adjunct for extra compensation	Tutored students for extra compensation
Less than 1.01	90.00%	5.00%	5.00%	0.00%
1.01 - 2.1	80.00%	0.00%	15.00%	5.00%
2.1 - 4.8	81.82%	9.09%	9.09%	0.00%
More than 4.8	41.67%	45.83%	8.33%	4.17%

Table 20.6 Have you done any of the following in your current position? Broken out by Gender of survey respondent

Gender of survey respondent	No Answer	Taught classes as part of my employment contract	Taught classes as an adjunct for extra compensation	Tutored students for extra compensation
Male	75.00%	15.63%	3.13%	6.25%
Female	70.37%	16.67%	12.96%	0.00%

Table 20.7 Have you done any of the following in your current position? Broken out by Age of survey participant

Age of survey participant	No Answer	Taught classes as part of my employment contract	Taught classes as an adjunct for extra compensation	Tutored students for extra compensation
30 or under	79.31%	10.34%	10.34%	0.00%
31-35	70.27%	16.22%	10.81%	2.70%
36 and over	65.00%	25.00%	5.00%	5.00%

In which medical and life science fields do you anticipate the best prospects for research funding over the next five years?

Less than 1.01 Years as a Postdoc

1) Immunology
2) cancer
3) Cancer research.
4) Cancer, hepatitis, and neurodegeneration.
5) Neuroscience, cancer, precision medicine/genetics/data medical sciences
6) Ageing-related issues: Alzheimer's, heart diseases, medical devices, antimicrobial resistance, cancer research
7) Genomics and neuroCell/Molecular Biology
8) Patient centered outcomes and quality of life research.
9) Genetics
10) Cancer research
11) Infection and MicroCell/Molecular Biology
12) disease modeling, biomarkers,
13) Systems Cell/Molecular Biology, mathematical modeling, bioinformatics

1.01 - 2.1

1) personal medicine
2) Genomics, cancer control and prevention
3) Cell/Molecular Biology
4) Dementia and ageing
5) Biomedical Engineering and orthopaedic surgery
6) Anything neurology
7) Med. Chem., Mol. Biol./Biotech, Organometallics/Inorganic.
8) Cancer
9) Epigenetics, neuroscience
10) genomics and structural Cell/Molecular Biology
11) Neuroscience
12) Very uncertain with the new political climate in the USA.

2.1 - 4.8

1) For me? Possibly psychiatry over more basic neuroscience funding.
2) Immunology - personalised therapies
3) cancer research
4) Cancer immunology
5) Cancer Cell/Molecular Biology
6) Neuroscience   Immunology
7) Genomics
8) Antimicrobial resistance, ageing, cancer

9) Cancer, alzheimer's, diabetes
10) Cancer research
11) bio-mimicking systems, molecular Cell/Molecular Biology
12) Nanomedicine
13) cancer
14) Human medicine
15) Cell Cell/Molecular Biology
16) Alzheimer's and Cancer
17) Cardiology
18) aging, cancer

More than 4.8

1) Cancer immunology
2) none
3) Translational Medicine in the fields of Chronic Inflammation, Ageing and Obesity.
4) translational/clinical science
5) vaccine development
6) Cancer Research
7) In Australia, biomedical research in general will be better funded over any other field of science. I particularly find this applied science focus centered on medicine a sad state of affairs. I think we need to shift focus toward sustainability centered research more than we already do.
8) Gene editing
9) none
10) antimicrobial resistance, global food security cancer research
11) Bioinformatics
12) Cancer, clinical,
13) Bioinformatics
14) Plant Cell/Molecular Biology. Genetics.
15) Don't know
16) Immunology Cancer
17) Mental Health and Demenita
18) Cancer
19) Cancer, cardiovasular

How do you feel that the election of Donald Trump as President of the United States might affect your future career?

Less than 1.01

1) Scary.
2) Sure it will, I am an immigrant in USA, less support for science, not visa for me...
3) No.
4) Horribly. His supporters are generally anti-science, heavily pro-religious fundamentalists. I anticipate accelerated exodus of top scientists and medical professionals out of the US. I am already looking for positions in private sectors in Canada and Europe.
5) I feel pessimistic about the economy, NIH funding (and as a result, institutional hiring practices), and ant-scientific and academic sentiment. This makes me worry about access/utilization of embryonic stem cells for research purposes as well. I feel I am less likely to achieve an academic faculty position than I would have been with a different president.
6) It rules out America as a place where I would like to work in the next 4 years, but my aim was to return to Europe anyways (Brexit affects my decision more than Trump being elected).
7) I am worried about a negative impact on NSF and NIH funding
8) Not much
9) I think scientific funding in the United States will be hit hard while Donald Trump is in office and while he is receiving advice from uneducated, science-fearing people in the government.
10) I feel he will negatively affect my future and career.
11) Funding shortages
12) It has removed any inclination to work in the United States
13) Certain sections of government that were once options (EPA) are probably not viable in the future. I think that policies may be put in place that increase the toxic load of the environment while simultaneously rejecting the need of scientists, such as myself, who are there to analyze that load and access safety, mitigation and exposure data. In regards to pharmaceutical, medical and clinically related careers I am unclear as to how his policies will affect these because I'm now sure how the government oversight of these industries occurs, and to what extent different policies effect careers in these industries.

1.01 - 2.1

1) may be
2) Doubt it influences it at all
3) dirty people elected
4) bad

5) No effect whatsoever.
6) decreased availability of graduate students and undergraduates due to lower enrollment of international students.
7) It will negatively affect my career. Grant funding is at an all-time low. Due to the national debt that will be accumulated under him, the odds of grand funding increasing at unlikely.
8) Minimally.
9) Uncertain, unsafe, worried
10) I am devastated. I am concerned that there will be funding cuts to an already poor funding environment. I worry that it will make it more difficult for me to get funding for my research and I worry that there will be serious impacts on education, which will also greatly impact my career and the careers of so many others.
11) no idea
12) Very afraid of having cutouts for science and more problems for obtaining a visa.
13) Unknown, probably bad
14) I am worried about funding for sexual and reproductive health research (my subject matter).

2.1 - 4.8

1) I'm afraid of hiring freezes in government jobs leading to an overflow of (over-)qualified candidates for academic jobs, making it difficult for me to compete. I worry that the economy will take a major downturn and all potential jobs might be difficult to come by. I worry that if I don't find a long-term job this year, chances may be much more slim in the next few years.
2) It rules out working in the US for me - not something I was very strongly considering, but something that I might otherwise have done.
3) I am afraid of funding.
4) I am a H1B visa holder!
5) their might have a budget cut or problem in Visa
6) Not much
7) I am terrified... I worry about anyone in fields relating to Trumps views surrounding climate change, the EPA etc.
8) I'm very concerned both with Trump and Brexit that funding opportunities will diminish
9) no idea
10) Eliminate any possibility of an academic career
11) N/A
12) As a Canadian citizen, my current (US-based) work visa is contingent on NAFTA, which he has said he would repeal. This may cause short-term issues. Longer term, I expect there to be fewer funding opportunities, increasing the likelihood of my returning to Canada.
13) Only for the best (-: Hilary would have been a total disaster
14) Reduce research foundings for academia

15) not sure
16) I'm not sure at this moment.
17) Negatively
18) not at all
19) Yes
20) Yes, I do

More than 4.8

1) It is going to be tough to get funding. Postdoc might loose their job
2) gone worst
3) Based in the UK I don't think this will have a direct effect on UK or EU science funding.
4) Not too much directly, Brexit may have more of an impact if funding becomes more difficult to obtain from European sources
5) I feel it is extremely detrimental to the government funding NIH research programs. It was already low since our invasion of the Middle East. It does not look like it will get any better under the new regime.
6) Unless he starts a world war unlikely to have any impact on my career in the UK
7) Not sure, being in the UK, I feel that Brexit is already affecting me more. I never not intended to move to work in the USA, even before his election.
8) Impossible for me to say with any accuracy. My research career is already on its last legs owing to the low level of investment into research in Australia. Given the historical influence of the American economy on the world as a whole, I don't foresee a great benefit from Trump's election on the state of research here in Australia. Though it obviously remains to be seen, I don't think such a clearly close minded individual could have a positive effect on anything.
9) I do not know
10) few jobs to no jobs
11) I now have no desire to move to the USA (I was previously considering this). Climate change will become more central in my research
12) Negatively
13) Bad for the US bad may not impact other countries
14) Less collaborative funding
15) Neutral
16) Not at all.
17) Not at all. This isn't USA.
18) Unsure
19) n/a
20) As a Muslim, it might make travelling therefore collaboration difficult
21) Badly!

What advice can you offer to your peers about managing as a postdoc?

Less than 1.01

1) have clear this is what you want, in doubt, change paths
2) Choose mentor wisely.
3) Being a post-doc is a gift, it's a rare opportunity to play around without being the head of a lab. When life and science try to get you down- remember that. Job prospects aren't always great in academia so enjoy it while you can!
4) Please talk with your postdoc not only about research but also career development.
5) Try to develop contacts with professors in the department (a little bit like your committee as a graduate student), as it is very easy to become isolated
6) Work very hard.
7) Keep up with your work and try to make a schedule of future and ongoing experiments.
8) Focus on getting usable results and continue to grow your professional network, you never know when a contact may come in handy
9) It's banged into our heads as graduate students, but networking is really key. But networking doesn't have to be "talking to strangers" it's socializing with people you work with, talking to everyone you are introduced to or bump into. And don't sweat if every contact doesn't pan out, you are still integrating yourself into a society, and the more people that know your name, the better.
10) Work hard, but think critically. Step out of your technical comfort zone and learn as much as you can from a field potentially useful but completely different from your own.

1.01 - 2.1

1) Publish, write grants, say no to anything that doesn't pertain to program of research, start preparing job search materials a year ahead of when you plan to apply
2) complicated
3) never give or take any excuse
4) Don't let criticism and knock-backs get to you. Do your best and hope it all works out.
5) Be clear with yourself and your PI about your expectations
6) Don't do it.
7) If your advisor is a dud, while it is incredibly unpleasant, move on. Better to take the pain right away than suffer through it for years.
8) Enjoy the time with low bureaucracy issues and high independence
9) Protect your time and remain committed to your own personal career development.
10) be independent
11) Always think about what's best for your career but don't forget to treat your fellow postdocs and students fairly and well

2.1 - 4.8

1) Do what works for you and be open and communicative with your boss about your time you can devote to research and career development. Find an appropriate mentor for your desired career path, who may not be your PI.
2) I'd suggest working hard, but within work hours as much as possible. Try not to take your work home with you as much as possible, take your time off without guilt. Try and plan your projects and work with one eye on the future, what will this gain for you in terms of your next move?
3) Give them advice on their career, help them to go through the next step.
4) Stay there and try hard as that's what you can do.
5) Treat it as a 9 to 5 (or at least 9-6) when you can for your own sanity if you can especially if you have additional research-related commitments outside of your postdoctoral lab.
6) Be prepared to give up most of your life! It does come with perks - such as the conferences and travel. However, I tended to wonder where I would be if I had invested this much energy in a job outside of academia
7) don't become one
8) Only take a postdoc position in a famous lab, do as much career building and networking for careers outside of academia as possible, and leave as soon as possible.
9) Use any available time to expand your skill set.
10) find the right professor NOT the right lab
11) Be motivated and responsible.
12) Research
13) read, be interested in what you do

More than 4.8

1) leave this field
2) Find yourself a good mentor at the position you would aspire to be - and use them to gain the knowledge required to get to that position. Make sure that they are not immediately linked with your research lab, so the advice can be impartial. Ensure that you surround yourself with a multitude of mentors, both scientific, career based and personal to allow you to succeed. These can be internal to your institute or external individuals and peers met at conferences.
3) try to stick to one particular line of research so that your track record is coherent
4) GET OUT!
5) Take advantage of opportunities when they arise, and make the most of any training available at your institution for career development
6) Do not do more than 2 post-docs. Always think one step ahead about your career plans. Network as much as you can, collaborate with many labs. it is about who you know as much, if not more than, who you are.
7) Publish well early on and get on Fellowship track. Alternatively, look for alternative innovation opportunities in funding that are starting to take form now. Non-standard sources of funding that attempt to link industry directly to academia.

8) be patient and continue what you are doing with full enthusiasm and your day will come.
9) don't do it
10) If something appeals to you, apply for it and don't worry if you don't tick all the boxes. Take advantage of all possible opportunities and get yourself known to academic staff beyond your immediate research group. Make sure you have some down time.
11) Find a supervisor that cares about your career progress not just the science that you're doing for them.
12) Always have options
13) Look for mentor.
14) Move away from academia unless you are incredibly committed.
15) Keep the big picture in mind. Develop transferrable skills in addition to those required by a postdoc to ease the transition out of research.
16) Make sure you gain something for everything you do. You are not there to boost your PI's career
17) Take advantage of all the training courses your institute offers in anything even slightly interesting/useful. It's not a 9-5 job, expect to put extra hours in but don't be forced into doing this regularly unless you're willing.

Which higher education institutions do you believe have exemplary postdoc working condition and programs and what do admire about them?

Less than 1.01

1) Sloan Kettering cancer center, Rockefeller University
2) Don't know a lot about post-doc conditions at other institutions. I think most of working conditions have to do with support systems for people of a certain age- I'm a single mom and I bet any country with better healthcare and childcare than the US would be better than the US. Institution doesn't really matter for that.
3) I prefer the English system in general to the German one (where I did my PhD) because more focus is laid on promoting PostDocs, e.g. by regular performance review meetings with your line manager and offering extra courses.
4) University of California (Davis, Berkeley): strong post doc union that negotiates for good benefits and community
5) University of Utah. I admire their emphasis in academics.
6) None
7) not sure
8) In terms of pay, the UC system has the highest for postdocs, but in terms of resources for career development this particular school seems very limited.

1.01 - 2.1

1) Not sure I have enough information to answer. In general, R1 institutions have the research resources necessary to support early career research training
2) IST austria
3) I don't really know, it seems pretty harsh everywhere.
4) Stanford -- very active postdoctoral association and social network
5) None.
6) Don't know. I very much appreciate the benefits, retirement/vacation/health, at my institution.
7) NYU School of Medicine- great postdoc affairs office
8) Possibly Princeton and Stanford because they treat their postdocs as true employees rather than temporary contractors

2.1 - 4.8

1) I'm not aware of any to be honest
2) Washington University, Class of work, better environment, better facility
3) I have been quite impressed with the University of Utah.
4) I don't know, I'm not sure there are many.
5) Rockefeller. They offer a substantial location bonus to account for the increased cost of living, and offer nice, affordable housing for postdocs.

6) Canadian universities probably and German ones. Here in the USA the taxes on our minute salary are ridiculous.
7) N/A
8) don't know
9) Stanford University, Harvard University
10) NYU, UCL, Columbia

More than 4.8

1) UPenn
2) I don't know almost all postdoc is horrible never appreciated and it is depressing everywhere
3) Unknown - each institute has its faults. The bigger the budgets for training, the bigger the pressures are for success.
4) There is such a thing?
5) I do not know any....
6) don't know
7) Not sure
8) No institute I worked with offered help programs for postdocs to secure a better position (including Max-Planck-Institute, EMBL Heidelberg, VCCRI Sydney).
9) No idea
10) This is a research question that you should investigate. You shouldn't be expecting individual (very busy) researchers to have done such research for you. This survey is poor quality - some very unclear questions, some irrelevant, some ambitious, and I'm kind of sorry I started answering it. I am not interested in the results, because I think you will have a lot of missing or inaccurate data which will reduce the quality of the results.
11) None that I know of.
12) Don't know of any

Made in United States
North Haven, CT
04 November 2026

21727460R00076